Tate Guide to
Modern Art Terms

29ᵀᴴ July 2017

Dear Karen,
Happy Birthday,
Enjoy!

Love A°
xxx

Tate Guide to Modern Art Terms

Simon Wilson
and Jessica Lack

Tate Publishing

First published 2016 by order of the Tate Trustees
by Tate Publishing, a division of Tate Enterprises Ltd,
Millbank, London SW1P 4RG
www.tate.org.uk/publishing

A catalogue record for this book is available from the British Library
ISBN 978 1 84976 399 8

Distributed in the United States and Canada by ABRAMS, New York
Library of Congress Control Number: 2015953123

Designed by Turnbull Grey
Cover graphics by Alan Kitching
Reproduction by DL Imaging Ltd, London
Printed and bound in Great Britain by TJ International, Padstow

Measurements of artworks are given in centimetres, height before width

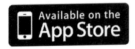

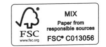

Introduction

Human beings are natural labellers – it is how we make sense of the world. This glossary is an attempt to bring together and define the meaning of some of the best known but also some of the more obscure of the myriad labels that have been given to the often confusingly varied phenomena of what we call modern art. It also includes definitions of materials and techniques.

In defining terms we have tried to track them back to source. A basic example, and a historical starting point for this glossary, is the origin of Impressionism in the title of Claude Monet's painting *Impression, Sunrise*, exhibited to general derision at what subsequently became known as the *First Impressionist Exhibition* in Paris in 1874.

In this second edition we've added over 150 new terms, such as the Calligraphic School of Art, a major movement in abstraction in the Middle East, based on traditional Arabic calligraphy. Additions such as this reflect the way globalisation has reshaped the cultural landscape over the past decade. Art fairs, biennales and social media have provided a platform for artists across the world and introduced us to many modern art movements, groups and techniques hitherto little known outside their native countries. These artists pioneered new art forms and ideas, often in the wake of decolonisation, war and revolution, and their radical visions are provoking a re-writing of the history of art, and setting an ambitious agenda for the contemporary art world today.

For those definitions relating to materials and techniques we have been fortunate to be able to call on the expertise of the Conservation Department at Tate. Additional terms have been written by Tate's Curatorial, Research, Publishing and Media departments. Between us we hope to have provided a reliable guide through the complex terminologies that surround modern and contemporary art.

Simon Wilson and Jessica Lack

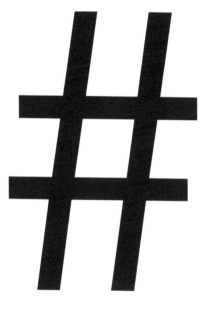

43 Group A modern art movement formed in Colombo, Ceylon (now Sri Lanka) in 1943 by a group of young, pro-independence painters who were committed to promoting a Sri Lankan form of modernism. Many of the members associated with the group, like Harry Peiris and Justin Deraniyagala, were well travelled, had studied in Europe and were frustrated by the reactionary approach to modern art back in Colombo. There was no common stylistic technique that connected the artists of the 43 Group, except a commitment to free expression and an appreciation of Post-Impressionism and Expressionism. Salon-style meetings were held at the house of Lionel Wendt, a photographer and patron of the arts. In 1955 the group exhibited at the Venice Biennale, where it was championed as a radical example of modern Asian art. The group disbanded in the mid-1960s as the political climate worsened in Sri Lanka and many members emigrated. Artists associated with the 43 Group include George Keyt, Ivan Peries, Harry Pieris, Richard Gabriel, Aubrey Collette, L.T.P. Manjusri, W.J.G. Beling, George Claessen and their patron, the photographer Lionel Wendt.

85 New Wave Coined by the curator and critic Gao Minglu, 85 New Wave defined a nationwide avant-garde movement that emerged in China in the mid-1980s. During the Cultural Revolution of the 1960s and 1970s, China had been forced to renounce much of its traditional culture and heritage as part of Mao's purge of the educated class. When the Cultural Revolution ended in the mid-1970s, there were few galleries, museums or educational establishments left to support artistic practice. 85 New Wave emerged in the mid-1980s as an explosive answer to this repression. Between 1985 and 1989, some seventy-nine arts organisations across the country were founded: putting on exhibitions, staging conferences and writing manifestos. It was also a time of radical politics, with the student democratic movement spearheading a more open society, although this was to end in a brutal suppression after the demonstrations in Tiananmen Square. Many Chinese artists of the 85 New Wave, such as the Xiamen Dada group in Fujian and the rational painting movement in Northern China, were inspired by innovations in art happening in Europe and America.

798 Art Zone An artistic community based in an old industrial area of north-east Beijing. It began in the early 2000s when young Chinese artists, looking for cheap studio space outside the direct influence of the government, moved into a largely abandoned military electronics complex, known as Factory 798, on the fringes of Beijing. This vast Bauhaus-style warehouse had been built by the East Germans in the 1950s and still retains Maoist slogans on its walls. The area became known for radical contemporary art and in 2004 the first Dashanzi International Art Festival was held, placing the area on the international art map. In recent years the district has attracted huge national and international investment, and today Factory 798 is home to some fifty commercial art galleries as well as the not-for-profit Ullens Center for Contemporary Art. The inevitable gentrification has caused rents to rise pushing out artists and grass roots initiatives. Today Dashanzi Art District is used as an example of Beijing's cosmopolitan status by the Chinese government.

a

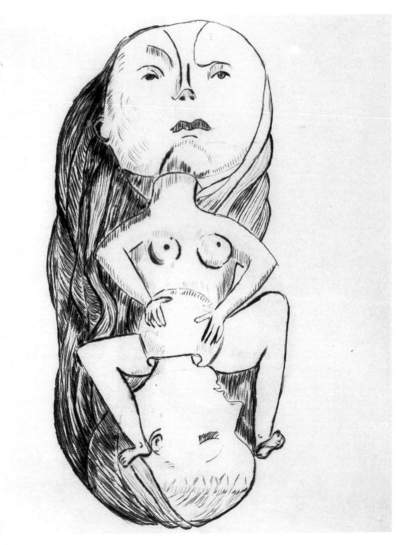

abject art

Louise Bourgeois
Birth 1994
Drypoint on paper
23.6 × 18.2
Tate. Purchased 1994

AAA see <u>American Abstract Artists</u>

Abbaye de Creteil In 1906 a group of French writers, artists and composers established the Abbaye de Creteil at a villa in Creteil south-east of Paris. The movement included the painters Albert Gleizes, Charles Berthold-Mahn and Jacques d'Otemar, the poets Charles Vildrac, Georges Duhamel, René Arcos, Alexandre Mercereau, Jules Romains and Henri-Martin Barzun, the composer Albert Doyen and the printer Lucien Linard. The group was partly inspired by the French Renaissance writer François Rabelais, who had written about a self-supporting commune in a monastery called the Abbaye de Thelema that had championed group labour and intellectual self-improvement. The Abbaye de Creteil community only lasted until February 1908, yet in its brief existence it supported the work of Roger Allard, later to become a proponent of <u>Cubism</u> and the works of the leading French poet Pierre-Jean Jouve.

abject art The abject is a complex psychological, philosophical and linguistic concept developed by Julia Kristeva in her 1980 book *Powers of Horror*. She was partly influenced by the earlier ideas of the French writer, thinker and dissident <u>Surrealist</u> Georges Bataille. It can be said, very simply, that the abject consists of those elements, particularly of the body, that transgress and threaten our sense of cleanliness and propriety. Kristeva herself commented: 'refuse and corpses show me what I permanently thrust aside in order to live.' In practice the abject covers all the bodily functions, or aspects of the body, that are deemed impure or inappropriate for public display or discussion. The abject has a strong <u>feminist</u> context, in that female bodily functions in particular are 'abjected' by a patriarchal social order. In the 1980s and 1990s many artists became aware of this theory and reflected it in their work. In 1993 the Whitney Museum, New York, staged an exhibition titled *Abject Art: Repulsion and Desire in American Art*, which gave the term a wider currency in art. Cindy Sherman is seen as a key contributor to the abject in art, as well as many others including Louise Bourgeois, Helen Chadwick, Paul McCarthy, Gilbert & George, Robert Gober, Carolee Schneemann, Kiki Smith and Jake and Dinos Chapman. (See also <u>body art</u>)

abstract art The word 'abstract', strictly speaking, means to separate or withdraw something from something else. In that sense it applies to art in which the artist has started with some visible object and abstracted elements from it to arrive at a simplified or schematised <u>form</u>. The term is also applied to art using forms that have no source at all in external reality. These forms are often, but not necessarily, geometric. Some artists of this tendency have preferred terms such as <u>Concrete art</u> or <u>non-objective art</u>, but in practice the word 'abstract' is used across the board and the distinction between the terms is not always obvious. A cluster of theoretical ideas lies behind abstract art: the idea of art for art's sake – that art should be purely about the creation of beautiful effects; the idea that art can or should be like music – that just as music is patterns of sound, art's effects should be created by pure patterns of form, colour and line; the idea, derived from the ancient Greek philosopher Plato, that the highest form of <u>beauty</u> lies not in the forms of the real world, but in geometry; the idea that abstract art, to the extent that it does not represent the material world, can be seen to represent the spiritual. In general, abstract art is seen as carrying a moral dimension, in that it can be seen to stand for virtues such as order, purity, simplicity and spirituality. Pioneers of abstract <u>painting</u> were Wassily Kandinsky, Kasimir Malevich and Piet Mondrian from about 1910–20. A pioneer of abstract <u>sculpture</u> was the Russian <u>Constructivist</u> Naum Gabo. Since then abstract art has formed a central stream of modern art.

Abstract Expressionism A term applied to new forms of <u>abstract art</u> developed by American painters in the 1940s and 1950s. The Abstract Expressionists were mostly based in New York City, and also became known as the <u>New York School</u>. The name evokes their aim to make abstract art that was also expressive or emotional in its effect. They were inspired by the <u>Surrealist</u> idea that art should come from the unconscious mind, and by the <u>Automatism</u> of Joan Miró. Within Abstract Expressionism were two broad groupings. These were the so-called Action painters led by Jackson Pollock and Willem de Kooning (see <u>gestural</u>) and the <u>Colour Field painters</u>, notably Mark Rothko, Barnett Newman and Clyfford Still. The Action painters worked in a spontaneous improvisatory manner, often using large brushes to make sweeping gestural marks. Pollock

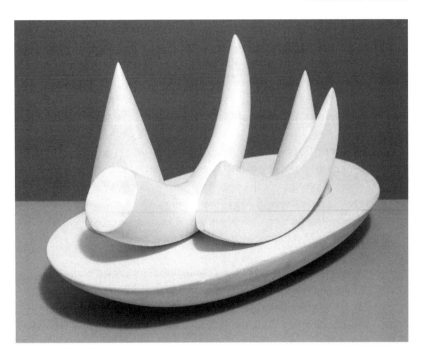

famously placed his <u>canvas</u> on the ground and danced around it, pouring paint direct from the can or trailing it from the brush or a stick. In this way they placed their inner impulses directly onto the canvas. The Colour Field painters were deeply interested in religion and myth. They created simple compositions with large areas of a single colour intended to produce a contemplative or meditational response in the viewer.

Abstraction-Création Association of <u>abstract</u> artists set up in Paris in 1931 with the aim of promoting abstract art through group exhibitions. It rapidly acquired membership of around 400. Leaders were Auguste Herbin and Georges Vantongerloo, but every major abstract painter took part including such figures as Naum Gabo, Wassily Kandinsky and Piet Mondrian. In Britain members of the <u>modernist</u> groupings the <u>Seven and Five Society</u> and <u>Unit One</u>, kept in close touch with Abstraction-Création. Abstraction-Création

Abstraction-Création

Paule Vézelay
Five Forms 1935
Plaster
28 × 38 × 25
Tate. Presented by the Patrons of British Art through the Tate Gallery Foundation 2000

embraced the whole field of abstract art, but tended towards the more austere forms represented by Concrete art, Constructivism and Neo-Plasticism. Regular exhibitions were held until 1936 and five annual publications were issued.

Academia Altamira see School of Altamira

academic art Art made according to the teachings of an art academy. In the nineteenth century the art academies of Europe became extremely conservative, resisting change and innovation. They came to be opposed to the avant-garde and to modern art generally. The term 'academic' has thus come to mean conservative forms of art that ignore the innovations of modernism.

Académie Colarossi Art school in Paris established in the nineteenth century as an alternative to the official Ecole des beaux-arts. Comparable to and slightly less famous than the Académie Julian. Like the Julian, the Colarossi admitted women and allowed them to draw from the nude male model. Artists who attended include John Banting, William Gear, George Grosz, Elsie Henderson, Hans Hofmann and Samuel Peploe.

Académie Julian Art school in Paris established in 1868 by Rodolphe Julian. It became a major alternative training centre to the official Ecole des beaux-arts, especially for women who were not admitted to the Ecole des beaux-arts until 1897. Also, at the Julian women were permitted to draw from the nude male model. In 1888–9 Pierre Bonnard and Edouard Vuillard were students there and, together with some others, formed the symbolist group the Nabis. The Académie Julian was popular with foreign art students and many leading modern artists spent time there.

academy The first art academies appeared in Italy at the time of the Renaissance. They were groupings of artists whose aim was to improve the social and professional standing of artists, as well as to provide teaching (see Ecole des beaux-arts). To this end they sought where possible to have a royal or princely patron. Previously, painters and sculptors had been organised in guilds, and were considered mere artisans or craftsmen. Academies became widespread by the seventeenth century, when they also began to organise group exhibitions of their members' work. This was a crucial innovation, since for the first time it provided a market place, and began to some extent to free artists from the restrictions of direct royal, church or private patronage. The most powerful of the academies was the French Académie Royale de Peinture et de Sculpture, established in 1648 and housed in the Palais du Louvre in Paris. The Académie began holding exhibitions in 1663 and opened these to the public from 1673. After the French Revolution the name was changed to plain Académie des Beaux Arts. The London Royal Academy was founded in 1768 with Joshua Reynolds (later Sir Joshua) as its first president. By the mid-nineteenth century the academies had become highly conservative and, by their monopoly of major exhibitions, resisted the rising tide of innovation in naturalism, Realism, Impressionism and their successors. The result was that alternative exhibiting societies were established and private commercial art galleries began to appear (see salon). The academies were bypassed and the term 'academic art' now has the pejorative connotation of conservative or old-fashioned.

acrylic paint A dispersion of pigments in a synthetic acrylic resin produced from acrylates and/or methacrylates. Acrylic paint dries as the liquid vehicle evaporates, and the resulting polymer-chains then deform and coalesce to form the paint film. While acrylic paints are generally thought to be very fast drying, thick applications may take months or even years to fully dry. Artist acrylic paints were first made in the 1950s using poly (n-butyl methacrylate) resin dissolved in solvent (mineral spirits or turpentine) with pigments and other minor components. The next type developed in the 1960s was the acrylic emulsion paint which remains so popular today. These are thinned (and brushes cleaned) using water; however, once dry, the paint films are water-resistant.

Actionism English version of a general German term for Performance art, but it was specifically used for the name of the Vienna-based group Wiener Aktionismus founded in 1962. The principal members of the group were Gunter Brus, Hermann Nitsch and Rudolph Schwarzkogler. Their 'actions' were intended to highlight the endemic violence of humanity and were deliberately

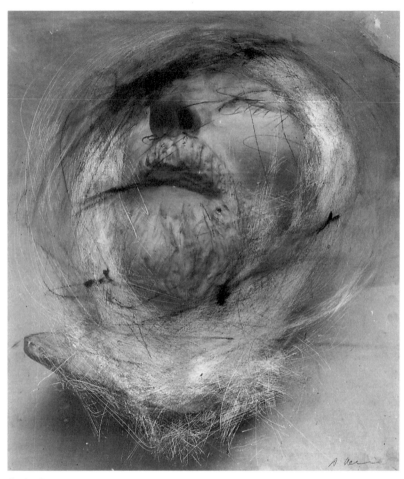

Actionism

Arnulf Rainer
Untitled (Death Mask) 1978
Oil pastel and photograph on
paper
60.9 × 50.5
Tate. Purchased 1982

shocking, including self-torture and quasi-religious ceremonies using the blood and entrails of animals. Nitsch gave his ceremonies the general title of Orgies-Mysteries Theatre. In America, Dennis Oppenheim and in Britain, Stuart Brisley performed actions in a spirit that can be related to Wiener Aktionismus. A less violent but no less anguished Vienna Actionist of the time was Arnulf Rainer.

activist art A term used to describe art that is grounded in the act of 'doing', the aim being to create art that is a form of political or social currency, actively addressing cultural power structures rather than representing them or simply describing them. This often requires the artist to work closely with a community to generate the art in question and is about empowering individuals and communities. Some artists concerned with activist art are also involved in direct action, like the Women on Waves Foundation, a feminist art collective that runs a floating abortion clinic carrying out abortions in places where they are not legal. Activist art has its roots in Performance art and feminist art and is generally situated in the public arena.

Aesthetic Movement Flourishing in Britain in the 1870s and 1880s and later popular in the USA, the Aesthetic Movement was important in both fine and applied arts. Critic Walter Hamilton published his book *The Aesthetic Movement in England* in 1882. Promoting the cult of pure beauty in art and design, its rallying cry was 'art for art's sake', meaning art foregrounding the purely visual and sensual, free of practical, moral or narrative considerations. Examples of the style in painting can be found in J.A.M. Whistler and Albert Moore and certain works by Frederic Leighton. Japan was an important influence especially on Whistler and on Aesthetic design (see japonisme). In applied arts it was part of the revolution in design initiated by William Morris with the foundation of Morris & Co. in 1862. From 1875 the style was commercialised by the Liberty store in London, which later also popularised Art Nouveau.

aesthetics A branch of philosophy that is concerned with the nature of beauty and taste. The term is derived from the Greek word 'aesthesis' meaning perception and was first used by the German philosopher Alexander Baumgarten in 1735 when, having asked the question 'what is beauty', he used the word 'aesthetics' to describe what he was doing. He wanted to understand what makes something beautiful or ugly and how we make these judgements. Later, the philosopher Immanuel Kant sought to clarify what aesthetics meant by writing a 'Critique of Judgement', in which he tried to work out how to analyse beauty, as well as taste and the sublime.

Afrapix A photographers' collective and agency founded in South Africa in 1982 which encouraged its members to use photography as activism. Afrapix played a seminal role in the development of socially informed documentary photography in South Africa, producing some of the most compelling images of apartheid in the 1980s. The group challenged the role of the photographer as a witness to events by establishing underground political organisations that formed part of the resistance art movement. They believed in using their skills as photographers to bring about change within the country and became leading proponents of what became known as struggle photography. The collective dissolved in 1991, but many of its members continued to work as documentary photographers including Santu Mofokeng, Omar Badsha, Lesley Lawson, Paul Weinberg, Biddy Partridge, Mxolise Mayo, Gille de Vlieg and Guy Tillim.

AfriCOBRA Founded in 1969 by Jeff Donaldson, Barbara Jones-Hogu, Wadsworth Jarrell and Gerald Williams, the African Commune of Bad Relevant Artists (AfriCOBRA) was a Chicago-based group of black artists who wanted to develop their own aesthetic in the visual arts in order to empower black communities. Rather than bringing about change through political revolt, these artists used the black identity, its style, attitude and worldview to foster solidarity and self-confidence throughout the African diaspora. It was a revolution of the mind, body and spirit and the art reflected this. An example of AfriCOBRA art is Jae Jarrell's *Revolutionary Suit* 1970 in which the artist is wearing a two-piece matching outfit with an ammunition belt sewn into the jacket.

Afrofuturism A term used to describe a cultural aesthetic that has its origins in African-American science fiction. It is used today to explore the African-American experience, and in particular the role

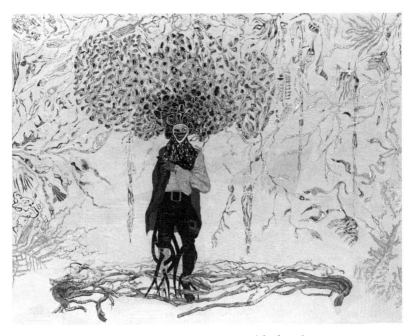

Afrofuturism

Ellen Gallagher
Bird in Hand 2006
Oil paint, ink, paper, polymer, salt
and gold leaf on canvas
238.3 × 307.2
Tate. Presented anonymously 2007

of slavery in that experience, with the aim of connecting those from the Black diaspora with their forgotten African ancestry. Central to the concept of Afrofuturism are the science-fiction writers Octavia Butler and Samuel R. Delany and the Jazz musician Sun Ra, who created a mythical persona that merged science fiction with Egyptian mysticism. It is this otherness that is at the heart of Afrofuturism. Those inspired by Afrofuturism include the musician George Clinton, the artist Ellen Gallagher and the film director Wanuri Kahiu.

Agit-prop A contraction of the Russian words *agitatsiia* and *propaganda* in the title of the Department of Agitation and Propaganda set up in 1920 by the Central Committee of the Soviet Communist Party. From then on Agit-prop was an omnipresent activity in the Soviet Union. Intended to control and promote the ideological conditioning of the masses, it took many forms such as palaces of culture, Agit-prop trains and cars covered with slogans and posters, poster campaigns, and countless agitation centres, or 'agitpunkts'. Books and libraries also played an important role in the Agit-prop enterprise. In the early years avant-garde artists, particularly those associated with the Constructivists, contributed to Agit-prop manifestations, especially poster designs. Today the term has come to refer to any cultural manifestation with an overtly political purpose.

airbrushing The airbrush was invented in the late nineteenth century, but it was not until the mid-twentieth century that it became a popular tool in painting. It is a small, hand-held instrument connected to a canister of compressed air that sprays paint in a controlled way. Pioneers of airbrushing were the graphic illustrators George Petty and Alberto Vargas (or Varga) in the 1930s and 1940s. Later, Pop artist James Rosenquist used it to evoke the qualities of advertising. In Britain, the artist Barrie Cook became one of the leading practitioners to use airbrushing. Today, it is the sci-fi artist H.K. Giger who is most commonly associated with the medium. There is also an airbrushing computer program, invented in the early 1980s, which creates a similar effect in a digital format.

AkhRR The Association of Artists of Revolutionary Russia, founded in Moscow in 1922, depicted everyday life among the working people of Russia after the Bolshevik Revolution in a realistic, documentary manner. Opposed to the non-realist innovations of the avant-garde, the association quickly became the most influential artistic group in Soviet Russia. In 1928 it was renamed the Association of Artists of the Revolution (AkhR) and in the following year established the journal *Art of the Masses*. Though abolished in 1932, the association was an influential precursor of Socialist Realism.

alabaster A fine-grained marble-like variety of gypsum, alabaster is a soft stone often white or translucent.

albumen print A type of photographic print made from paper coated with albumen (egg white). Invented in 1850, the albumen print was the most common form of print in the late nineteenth century because it produced a rich, sharp image. The process involves coating a sheet of paper with albumen, making the paper's surface glossy and smooth. Then it is coated in a solution of silver nitrate. The albumen and the silver nitrate form light sensitive silver salts on the paper. When a glass negative is placed directly on the paper and exposed to light, it forms an image on the paper.

allegory An allegory is when an image has another meaning besides the visible one and has been used in art over the centuries to tell stories. In relation to modern art, allegory is when one narrative might mean another, something that was first proposed in Craig Owen's book *The Allegorical Impulse: Toward a Theory of Postmodernism*. An example of this use of allegory would be Sarah Lucas's *Two Fried Eggs and a Kebab* 1992 in which food is a signifier of sexual politics. Owens argues that artists who use allegory are revealing how objects can hold not one, but many meanings.

Altermodern Coined by curator Nicolas Bourriaud on the occasion of the Tate Triennial 2009, Altermodern is an in-progress redefinition of modernity in the era of globalisation, which focuses on cultural translations and time-space crossings. Against cultural standardisation and massification but also opposed to nationalisms and cultural relativism, Altermodern artists position themselves within the world's cultural gaps. Cultural translation, mental nomadism and format crossing are the main principles of

Altermodern art. Viewing time as a multiplicity rather than as a linear progress, the Altermodern artist navigates history as well as all the planetary time zones producing links between signs far away from each other. Altermodern is 'docufictional' in that it explores the past and the present to create original paths where boundaries between fiction and documentary are blurred. Formally speaking, it favours processes and dynamic forms to one-dimensional single objects and trajectories to static masses.

American Abstract Artists (AAA) An organisation founded in 1936 to promote the appreciation of abstract art in the USA. It held its first annual exhibition in April 1937. Early members included Josef Albers, Willem de Kooning, Lee Krasner, Jackson Pollock and David Smith.

American Social Realist photography During America's Great Depression of the 1930s and 1940s, photographers were employed by the Farm Security Administration (FSA) to document the rural poverty and exploitation of sharecroppers and migrant labourers in an attempt to garner support for President Franklin D. Roosevelt's New Deal. The photographs were distributed free of charge to newspapers across the country and brought the plight of displaced farming communities to the public's attention. The most famous images were made by Dorothea Lange and Walker Evans, whose black and white stills of starving fruit-pickers in California became iconic symbols of the Great Depression. (See also Social Realism)

Analytical Cubism In an attempt to classify the revolutionary experiments made by Pablo Picasso, Georges Braque and Juan Gris when they were exponents of Cubism, historians have tended to divide Cubism into two stages. The early phase, generally considered to run from 1908 to 1912, is called Analytical Cubism and the second is called Synthetic Cubism. Analytical Cubism was so-called because of its structured dissection of the subject, viewpoint-by-viewpoint, resulting in a fragmentary image of multiple viewpoints and overlapping planes. Other distinguishing features of Analytical Cubism were a simplified palette of colours, so the viewer was not distracted from the structure of the form, and the density of the image at the centre of the canvas.

Angry Penguins Title of Australian <u>modernist</u> literary journal founded in 1940 at the University of Adelaide by four poets: D.B. Kerr, M.H. Harris, P.G. Pfeiffer and G. Dutton. At this time the University of Adelaide was a focus of modernist writing and debate under the influence of the poet, playwright and teacher C.R. Jury, who acted as patron to the magazine. The name became that of the modernist literary and artistic movement, centred around Harris, that sought to shake up the entrenched cultural establishment of Australia in the 1940s. They were seen as 'angry' young men – the rebels of their day. *Angry Penguins* represented the new language and the new <u>painting</u> of Australia. They were forthright and unapologetic, demanding to be heard and seen. The artists included Arthur Boyd, Sidney Nolan and Albert Tucker. In 1944 *Angry Penguins* was the victim of a famous literary hoax when two opponents concocted a set of modernist poems by a writer they invented called 'Ern Malley'. Harris published them and a storm ensued when the hoax was revealed. Harris was tried and convicted for publishing obscenities and the cause of modernism in Australia was substantially set back.

animation The rapid display of sequences of static imagery in such a way as to create the illusion of movement. The history of animation dates back to early Chinese shadow lanterns and the optical toys of the eighteenth century, but it was not until the beginning of the twentieth century that illustrators like Émile Cohl began drawing cartoon strips on to celluloid. The most famous animator was Walt Disney, best known for his cartoon feature films like *Fantasia* and *The Jungle Book* and whom Salvador Dalí believed to be the heir to <u>Surrealism</u>. Computer animation began in the 1960s and is animation's digital successor. Using software programs like Adobe Flash, animators build up sequences on a computer to be used as special effects in film, called Computer Generated Imagery (CGI), or as animated sequences in their own right. Computer animation has distinct advantages for artists: it is cheap to make, fast, and the artist is able to control every aspect of the process, unlike the vagaries of shooting film which cannot be viewed until developed. Sites like YouTube and Vimeo have become forums for computer animation, bypassing the traditional galleries and museums as the spaces for artistic enterprise.

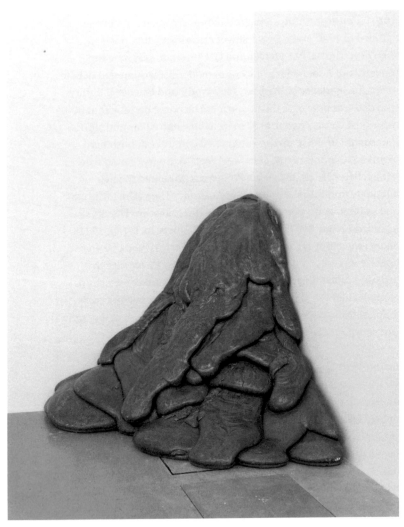

anti-form

Lynda Benglis
Quartered Meteor 1969, cast 1975
Lead and steel on steel base
150 × 168 × 158
Tate. Presented by the American
Fund for the Tate Gallery, partial
purchase and partial gift of John
Cheim and Howard Read 2010

anthropophagia Meaning cannibalism, as an art term it is associated with the 1960s Brazilian art movement <u>Tropicália</u>. Artists Hélio Oiticica, Lygia Clark, Rogério Duarte and Antonio Dias used anthropophagia in the sense of a cultural and musical cannibalism of other societies. Embracing the writings of the poet Oswald de Andrade (1890–1954), who wrote the *Manifesto Antropófago* (Cannibal Manifesto) in 1928, they argued that Brazil's history of cannibalising other cultures was its greatest strength and had been the nation's way of asserting independence over European colonial culture. The term also alluded to cannibalism as a tribal rite that was once practised in Brazil. The artworks made as a result of this concept stole their influences from Europe and America but, ultimately, were rooted in the cultural and political world of 1960s and 1970s Brazil.

anti-art Refers to art that challenges the existing accepted definitions of art. It is generally agreed to have been coined by Marcel Duchamp around 1913 when he made his first <u>readymades</u>, which are still regarded in some quarters as anti-art (for example by the Stuckist group). In 1917 Duchamp submitted a urinal, titled *Fountain*, for an exhibition in New York, which subsequently became notorious and eventually highly influential. Anti-art is associated with <u>Dada</u>, the artistic and literary movement founded in Zurich in 1916 and simultaneously in New York, in which Duchamp was a central figure. Since Dada there have been many art movements that have taken a position on anti-art, from the low-fi mail art movement to the <u>Young British Artists</u>, some of whom have embraced the absurdities of Dada and Duchamp's love of irony, paradox and punning.

anti-form A term associated with <u>Post-Minimalism</u> and a group of artists working in the USA in the late 1960s who embraced chance and other organic processes in their minimal sculptures. They worked from the principle that form should be derived from the inherent qualities of the chosen material, as opposed to the earlier Minimalist sculptors who imposed order on their materials and confined themselves to fixed geometrical shapes and structures (see <u>Minimal art</u>). An example of anti-form is Robert Morris's sculpture *Untitled* 1967 in which hanging strips of industrial felt were

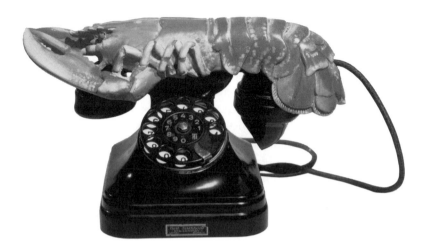

appropriation

Salvador Dalí
Lobster Telephone
1936
Steel, plaster, rubber,
resin and paper
17.8 × 33 × 17.8
Tate. Purchased 1981

allowed to tumble to the ground in an arbitrary fashion. In this way the artist had to relinquish control of the final appearance of the artwork. Other artists associated with anti-form include Lynda Benglis and Eva Hesse.

apartment art A place for underground experimental art, apartment art is usually found in countries where there are strict governmental controls on the type of art that can be exhibited publicly. In China between 1970 and the mid-1990s there were few civic spaces for exhibiting and creating art, so artists turned their state-run apartments into exhibition spaces, holding <u>salons</u>, exhibitions and <u>performances</u> in secret. A similar thing occurred in the former Eastern bloc during the 1970s and 1980s, where one-off events would be held in private spaces, usually an artist's state-run apartment for which the publicity would be limited to word of mouth only. Apartment art reflects a culture in which art is forced to hide away, it is an art of confinement, aerated by international contacts, but ultimately forced to do everything – painting, sculpting, performing, recording, projecting, exhibiting – in the same limited space.

appropriation As a term in art history and criticism, this refers
to the taking over, into a work of art, of a real object or even an
existing work of art. The practice can be tracked back to the Cubist
constructions and collages of Pablo Picasso and Georges Braque
made from 1912 onwards, in which real objects, such as newspapers,
were included to represent themselves. Appropriation was developed
much further in the readymades created by the French Dada artist
Marcel Duchamp from 1913. Most notorious of these was *Fountain*,
a men's urinal signed, titled and presented on a pedestal. Later,
Surrealism also made extensive use of appropriation in collages and
objects, such as Salvador Dalí's *Lobster Telephone*. In the late 1950s
appropriated images and objects appear extensively in the work of
Jasper Johns and Robert Rauschenberg, and in Pop art. However,
the term seems to have come into use specifically in relation to
certain American artists in the 1980s, notably Sherrie Levine and
the artists of the Neo-Geo group, particularly Jeff Koons. Sherrie
Levine reproduced other works of art as her own work, including
paintings by Claude Monet and Kasimir Malevich. Her aim was
to create a new situation, and therefore a new meaning or set of
meanings, for a familiar image. Appropriation art raises questions
of originality, authenticity and authorship, and belongs to the long
modernist tradition of art that questions the nature or definition of
art itself. Appropriation artists were influenced by the 1936 essay
by the German philosopher Walter Benjamin, 'The Work of Art in
the Age of Mechanical Reproduction', and received contemporary
support from the American critic Rosalind Krauss in her 1985
book *The Originality of the Avant-Garde and Other Modernist Myths*.
Appropriation has been used extensively by artists since the 1980s.

aquatint An intaglio printmaking technique, used to create tonal
effects rather than lines. Fine particles of acid-resistant material,
such as powdered rosin, are attached to a printing plate by heating.
The plate is then immersed in an acid bath, just like etching. The
acid eats into the metal around the particles to produce a granular
pattern of tiny indented rings. These hold sufficient ink to give the
effect of an area of wash when inked and printed. The extent of
the printed areas can be controlled by varnishing those parts of
the plate to appear white in the final design. Gradations of tone
can be achieved by varying the length of time in the acid bath;

longer periods produce more deeply bitten rings, which print darker areas of tone. The technique was developed in France in the 1760s, and became popular in Britain in the late eighteenth and early nineteenth centuries. It is often used in combination with other intaglio techniques.

Arab Image Foundation (AIF) A not-for-profit organisation established in Beirut in 1997 to preserve, exhibit and study <u>photographs</u> from the Middle East, North Africa and the Arab <u>diaspora</u> from the nineteenth century to today. Founded by artist Akram Zaatari, the AIF currently holds a collection of more than 600,000 images, including <u>negatives</u> and <u>prints</u> sourced by its artist-members. Rather than using these images to present a linear history of photography or as evidence of societies in the grips of modernisation, the artists use these images in exhibitions to discuss the role of photography in Arab societies.

archive Traditionally an archive is a store of documents or artefacts of a purely documentary nature. The rise of <u>Performance art</u> in the twentieth century meant that artists became heavily reliant on documentation as a record of their work. A similar problem arose in relation to the <u>Land art</u> movement of the 1960s whose <u>interventions</u> in the landscape were often eradicated by the elements. <u>Conceptual art</u> often consisted of documentation. In practice the documentation – <u>photograph</u>, <u>video</u>, map, text – was rapidly adapted to have the status of artwork. Some artists have used the actual structure of the archive for their work. In 1999 Mark Dion sifted the silt beds of the Thames and displayed the contents in mahogany cabinets at Tate Britain. Over six years Jeremy Deller, together with Alan Kane, collated his epic Folk Archive, which documents popular culture around Britain and Ireland.

Art & Language A pioneering <u>Conceptual art</u> group founded in Coventry, England, in 1968. The four founder members were Michael Baldwin, David Bainbridge, Terry Atkinson and Harold Hurrell. The critic and art historian Charles Harrison and the artist Mel Ramsden both became associated in 1970. In *A Provisional History of Art & Language,* Charles Harrison and Fred Orton recorded that between 1968 and 1982, up to fifty people were associated in some way with the activities around the name Art & Language and they identified three main phases of the group: the early years, up to 1972, which chiefly found public expression in the publication *Art-Language*; a middle period divided between New York and England and linked to the publication of the journal *The Fox* (discontinued in 1976); and the period since 1977, during which paintings have been produced. In that period, Art & Language has mainly concerned three people, the artists Michael Baldwin and Mel Ramsden, and the critic Charles Harrison. From the beginning, Art & Language questioned the critical assumptions of mainstream modern art practice and criticism. Much of their early work consisted of detailed discussion of these issues, presented in their journal or in an art gallery context. However, they also made exemplary works of Conceptual art such as *Map Not to Indicate* of 1967. The paintings they have made since 1977 examine the critical issues that concern them through the actual practice of painting. For a more detailed account of Art & Language see the full catalogue text for the work Gustave Courbet's *'Burial at Ornans'; Expressing a Sensuous Affection .../Expressing a Vibrant Erotic Vision .../ Expressing States of Mind that are Vivid and Compelling.*

Art Brut French term translating as 'raw art', which was invented by the French artist Jean Dubuffet to describe art made outside the tradition of fine art, dominated by <u>academic</u> training, which he referred to as *art culturel* (cultural art). Art Brut included <u>graffiti</u>, the work of patients in psychiatric hospitals, prisoners, children, and <u>naïve</u> or <u>primitive</u> artists. What Dubuffet valued in this material was the raw expression of a vision or emotions, untrammelled by convention. These qualities he attempted to incorporate into his own art, to which the term Art Brut is also sometimes applied. Dubuffet made a large collection of Art Brut, and in 1948 founded the Compagnie de l'Art Brut to promote its study. His collection is now housed in a museum, La Collection de l'Art Brut in the Swiss city of Lausanne. Another major collection, using the term <u>outsider art</u>, is the Musgrave Kinley Outsider Art Collection, now on loan to the Irish Museum of Modern Art, Dublin.

Art Deco Design style of the 1920s and 1930s in furniture, pottery, textiles, jewellery, glass, etc. It was also a notable style of cinema and hotel architecture. Named after the International Exhibition of

Modern Decorative and Industrial Arts held in Paris in 1925, it can be seen as successor to and a reaction against Art Nouveau. The chief difference from Art Nouveau is the influence of Cubism, giving Art Deco design generally a more fragmented, geometric character. However, imagery based on plant forms and sinuous curves remained in some Art Deco design, for example that of Clarice Cliff in Britain. Art Deco was in fact highly varied, showing influences from ancient Egyptian art, Aztec and other ancient Central American art, and the design of modern ships, trains and motor cars. Art Deco also drew on the modern architecture and design of the Bauhaus, and of architects such as Le Corbusier and Mies van de Rohe.

art fair The rise of the art fair is a phenomenon of recent years. Until the millennium, art fairs were small, industry-only events showcasing artists represented by commercial galleries to a select number of international collectors. Today there are more than 200 art fairs worldwide and they have evolved into big, bold, glamorous art happenings offering special VIP openings, programmes of talks, commissioned artist projects, events and parties. Commercial galleries pay a sizeable fee for their booths and the leading art fairs operate a strict selection policy.

Art Informel French term describing a wide swathe of related types of abstract painting highly prevalent, even dominant, in the 1940s and 1950s, including tendencies such as Tachisme, matter painting and Lyrical Abstraction. It mainly refers to European art, but embraces American Abstract Expressionism. The term was used by the French critic Michel Tapié in his 1952 book *Un Art Autre* to describe types of art that were based on highly improvisatory (i.e. informal) procedures and were often highly gestural. Tapié saw this art as 'other' because it appeared to him as a complete break with tradition. An important source of this kind of painting was the Surrealist doctrine of Automatism. An exhibition titled *Un Art Autre* was organised in Paris the same year as Tapié's book and included Karel Appel, Alberto Burri, Willem de Kooning, Jean Dubuffet, Jean Fautrier, Jean-Paul Riopelle and Wols. Other key figures were Henri Michaux, Hans Hartung and Pierre Soulages. The term 'Art Autre', from the title of Tapié's book, is also used for this art, but Art Informel seems to have emerged as the preferred name.

art intervention Art designed specifically to interact with an existing structure or situation, be it another artwork, the audience, an institution or in the public domain; it is most commonly associated with Conceptual art and Performance art. The popularity for art interventions emerged in the 1960s, when artists attempted to radically transform the role of the artist in society, and thereby society itself. The French filmmaker and writer Guy Debord, founder of situationism (see Situationist International), wished to eliminate the spectator's position. In 1960 he devised a raid on an international art conference in Belgium. Other collectives, like the Artist Placement Group (APG) in London attempted to reposition the role of the artist in a wider social and political context using art interventions. They acted outside the conventional gallery system, placing artists within industry and government departments in order to effect change. Such interventions served as a catalyst for artist-in-residence schemes and community programmes.

Art Nouveau Complex international style in architecture and design, parallel to symbolism in fine art. It developed through the 1890s and was brought to a wide audience by the 1900 *Exposition Universelle* in Paris. The style was characterised by sinuous linearity and flowing organic shapes based on plant forms. In Britain, Charles Rennie Mackintosh contained these qualities within severe but eccentric geometry. Art Nouveau was exemplified by the Paris Metro station entrances by Hector Guimard, Tiffany glass, Mackintosh's chairs and his Glasgow School of Art, and book designs of Aubrey Beardsley, Charles Ricketts and followers such as Arthur Rackham. The style flourished until it was killed off by the First World War.

Art Workers' Coalition (AWC) A group of activists, including Carl Andre, Lucy Lippard and Robert Smithson, who came together in 1969, in New York, to promote artists' rights and to challenge the art establishment to take political positions against discrimination and inequality.

Arte de los medios de comunicación de masas Formed in Argentina in 1966 by Eduardo Costa, Roberto Jacoby and Raúl Escari, Arte de los medios de comunicación de masas (Art of the mass media) was an experimental arts group. Its members were inspired by the writer Oscar Masotta who had used the theorist Marshall McLuhan's argument that the medium was now the message in an essay. One of the works the group undertook was to use different types of mass media to publicise and create documentation of a happening that had, in fact, never taken place. Known as *Happening for a Dead Boar*, or *The Happening that did not exist*, this work, according to Jacoby in his essay 'Against the Happening', set out to question issues around truth and invention in the media. The work is now seen as a crucial aspect of Conceptual art.

Arte Madí One of two artistic groups formed in Buenos Aires in 1944 devoted to pure geometric abstraction (the other being the Asociation Arte Concreto-Invencion) (see abstract art). Founded by the artists Gyula Kosice, Rhod Rothfuss and Carmelo Arden Quin, Arte Madí had a commitment to expressing the reality of modern life through non-figurative Concrete art. In 1946 they published a manifesto in which they declared the importance of 'the true constructive spirit which has spread though all countries and cultures'. Their style was more playful and inventive than that of the Asociation Arte Concreto-Invencion. They painted on irregular shaped canvases and experimented with three-dimensional objects. They also published a journal, *Arte Madí Universal*, that encouraged exchange with fellow abstract artists across the world. The group was to have an influence on the Neo-Concrete movement that emerged in Brazil in the 1950s.

Arte Nucleare Refers to the work of the Movimento d'Arte Nucleare, founded by the Italian artist Enrico Baj, together with Sergio Dangelo and Gianni Bertini, in Milan in 1951. Gianni Dova was a later member. Their first manifesto was issued the following year and another in 1959. The name might be translated as 'art for the nuclear age', since the group specifically set out to make art in relation to this. Their manifestos warned of the dangers of the misapplication of nuclear technology. They declared opposition to geometric abstract art and proposed instead the use of automatic techniques; they were thus closely aligned with Art Informel. In the early 1950s Baj was making paintings with suggestions of mushroom clouds and devastated landscapes. In his later painting and collage works he gave the name 'heavy water' to the enamel paint and distilled water emulsion he used. Several exhibitions were held but the movement petered out around 1960.

Arte Povera A term introduced by the Italian art critic and <u>curator</u>, Germano Celant, in 1967. His pioneering texts and a series of key exhibitions provided a collective identity for a number of young Italian artists based in Turin, Milan, Genoa and Rome. Arte Povera emerged from within a network of urban cultural activity in these cities, as the Italian economic miracle of the immediate postwar years collapsed into a chaos of economic and political instability. The name means literally 'poor art' but the word poor here refers to the movement's signature exploration of a wide range of materials beyond the quasi-precious traditional ones of <u>oil paint</u> on <u>canvas</u>, or bronze, or carved marble. Arte Povera therefore denotes not an impoverished art, but an art made without restraints, a laboratory situation in which any theoretical basis was rejected in favour of a complete openness towards materials and <u>processes</u>. Leading artists were Giovanni Anselmo, Alighiero Boetti, Pier Paolo Calzolari, Luciano Fabro, Piero Gilardi, Jannis Kounellis, Mario Merz, Marisa Merz, Giulio Paolini, Pino Pascali, Giuseppe Penone, Michelangelo Pistoletto, Emilio Prini and Gilberto Zorio. The heyday of the movement was 1967–72, but its influence on later art has been enduring. It can also be seen as the Italian contribution to <u>Conceptual art</u>.

artist-curator The name given to a practising artist who also curates shows or runs not-for-profit spaces from which they exhibit their art and that of other artists (see also <u>curator</u>). Inspired by the artist-led initiatives in New York in the 1960s, these spaces are often housed in temporary places – shops, warehouses, soon-to-be demolished buildings – which can be inhabited for free or for a nominal rent for a short period of time. The artist-curator tends to remain outside the commercial art world, and within a community of artists – often ones with whom they studied, or of a similar generation – who are frustrated by the perceived impenetrability of the art world. For some artist-curators, it is the freedom to create art, control its output and have a say in how it is exhibited that appeals; for others it is a means of survival, a way of gaining exposure for the art that they and others do.

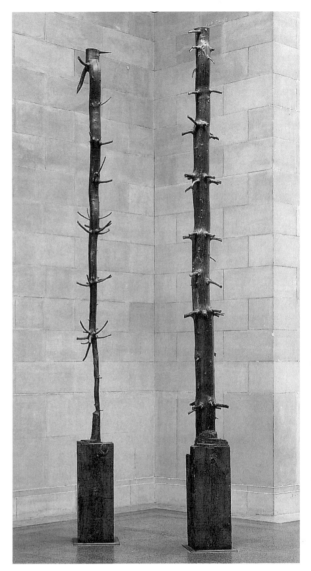

Arte Povera

Giuseppe Penone
Tree of 12 Metres
1980–2
Wood
600 × 50 × 50
Tate. Purchased 1989

artist-in-residence An artist who has been given time, space and financial aid by an institution or a community in order to create art. Residencies can exist anywhere, but they are usually attached to some kind of institution; a gallery, a museum, an arts centre, a university or a college, although increasingly there are artist-in-residence programs being established in large corporations, science laboratories, hospitals and airports. The subject matter the artist chooses to work with is often inspired by the organisation in which the artist is in residence, but not always. Residencies are for a specified time and are not meant to be endless.

Artist Placement Group (APG) Founded by Barbara Steveni with her husband John Latham, emerged from the idea that artists are a human resource underused by society. Artists are isolated from the public by the gallery system, and in the ghetto of the art world are shielded from the mundane realities of industry commerce and government. The idea was that artists, designated Incidental Persons by Latham, would bring completely alternative ways of seeing and thinking to bear on the organisations they were placed in. APG would thus recognise the artist's outsider status and turn it to positive social advantage. In 1966 Steveni and Latham were joined by Jeffrey Shaw and Barry Flanagan, soon followed by Stuart Brisley, David Hall and Ian MacDonald Munro. Among the placements made by APG was one in 1975–6 of Latham himself at the Scottish Office in Edinburgh. This resulted in radical proposals for the future of the huge industrial spoil tips, known as bings, found in the region. Latham proposed retaining them as works of art and marking them with beacons.

Artists International Association (AIA) An exhibiting society founded in London in 1933 and active until 1971. It was principally a left-of-centre political organisation and it embraced all styles of art both modernist and traditional. Its aim was the 'Unity of Artists for Peace, Democracy and Cultural Development'. It held a series of large group exhibitions on political and social themes, beginning in 1935 with the exhibition *Artists Against Fascism and War*. The AIA supported the left-wing Republican side in the Spanish Civil War (1936–9) through exhibitions and other fund-raising activities. It tried to promote wider access to art through travelling exhibitions and public <u>mural</u> paintings. In 1940 it published a series of art <u>lithographs</u> titled *Everyman Prints* in large and therefore cheap <u>editions</u>.

Arts and Crafts Movement Movement in design emerging from the Pre-Raphaelite circle and initiated by William Morris in 1861 when he founded his design firm Morris & Co. in London. He recruited Dante Gabriel Rossetti, Ford Madox Brown and Edward Burne-Jones as artist-designers and their key principle was to raise design to the level of art. They also tried to make good design available to the widest possible audience. The Arts and Crafts Movement was seen as leading to modern design, for example by Nikolaus Pevsner in *Pioneers of Modern Design: William Morris to Walter Gropius*, first published in 1936. Morris emphasised simple functional design without the excess ornament and imitation of the past, which was typical of Victorian styles. Wallpapers and fabrics were based on natural motifs, particularly plant forms, and treated as flat pattern. A key influence on the <u>Aesthetic Movement</u> and <u>Art Nouveau</u> as well as later modern design.

Ashcan School A group of North American artists who used <u>realist</u> techniques to depict social deprivation and injustice in the American urban environment of the early twentieth century. Spearheaded by the painter Robert Henri, the artists described themselves as urban realists, devoted to the realistic depiction of life in the same way journalists and novelists were writing about the harsh conditions of the poor. The group's name came from a drawing by the artist George Bellows depicting three vagrants scrutinising the contents of an ash can. The movement lost momentum in 1913 when European <u>modernism</u> exploded onto the American art scene and the group's <u>realism</u>, in the face of <u>Cubism</u> and <u>Fauvism</u>, began to look dated and out of touch. Artists associated with the Ashcan School include Robert Henri, George Bellows, William Glackens, George Luks, Everett Shinn, Ernest Lawson, Maurice Prendergast and Arthur B. Davies.

Asociación Arte Concreto-Invención Founded by Tomás Maldonado in 1944, the Asociación Arte Concreto-Invención (Concrete-Invention Art Association) was one of two artistic groups formed in Buenos Aires devoted to pure geometric <u>abstraction</u>

(the other being Arte Madí). Like their fellow Constructivists they embraced the purist aesthetics of Piet Mondrian and Theo van Doesburg, and created paintings on irregular shaped canvases. They were less experimental than the Arte Madí artists due to the tight creative constraints placed upon them by their Marxist leader Maldonado who had utopian ambitions for art in a new revolutionary society. Artists associated with the group include Tomás Maldonado, Manuel Espinosa, Lidy Prati, Enio Iommi, Alfredo Hlito and Raúl Lozza. (See also Manifesto invencionista)

Asociación de Arte Constructivo Founded in Uruguay in 1935 by Constructivist artist and writer Joaquín Torres-García, the Asociación de Arte Constructivo (Association of Constructivist Art) was an attempt to create a truly Latin American art. While living in Paris in the 1920s, Torres-García had been involved with the Neo-Plasticist movement led by Piet Mondrian. When Torres-García returned to his hometown of Montevideo in 1934, he sought to create a revolutionary movement inspired by his theory of universalismo constructivo (universal constructivism). This was a revolutionary Constructivist art that had its roots in pre-Colombian art while also embracing the utopian spirit and geometric forms of modern, urban South America. The group dissolved in 1939 after the members found it impossible to maintain the ideals of the Asociación. Other artists associated with the group include Rosa Acle, J. Álvarez Marqués, Carmelo de Arzadum, Alfredo Cáceres, María Cañizas, Luis Castellanos, Amalia Nieto, Héctor Ragni, Lia Rivas, Carmelo Rivello, Alberto Soriano, Augusto Torres, Horacio Torres and Nicolás Urta.

assemblage Art made by assembling disparate elements often scavenged by the artist (see found object), sometimes bought specially. The practice goes back to Pablo Picasso's Cubist constructions, the three-dimensional works he began to make from 1912. An early example is his *Still Life* 1914, which is made from scraps of wood and a length of tablecloth fringing, glued together and painted. Picasso himself remained an intermittent practitioner of assemblage. It was the basis of Surrealist objects, became widespread in the 1950s and 1960s and continues to be extensively used, for example by the Young British Artists.

atelier A literal translation of the French word atelier is studio or workshop. The individual artist's studio was also a place where the teaching of young artists took place but this function was gradually supplanted by the rise of the academy. At the beginning of the twentieth century, some ateliers developed into places of communal production, particularly in Germany, where there emerged a desire to unify art with industrial production. In 1919 Walter Gropius founded the Bauhaus in an attempt to marry the arts with the technology of the mechanical age. Atelier often denotes a group of artists, designers or architects working collectively. Atelier 5 is a Swiss architectural firm founded in 1955 and inspired by the visions of Le Corbusier; the Rotterdam-based Atelier Van Lieshout, founded by Joep van Lieshout, is a group of artists who devise alternative modes of living and working.

attribute This term has different meanings as a noun and a verb. In art an attribute (noun) is an object or animal associated with a particular personage. The most common attributes are those of the ancient Greek gods. For example doves are attributes of the goddess of love, Aphrodite or Venus. So a female nude with a dove or doves may be identified as Venus. The ancient musical instrument known as a lyre is an attribute of Apollo, god of music and the arts. A bow and arrows and/or a spear, together with hounds, are attributes of the goddess Diana, who was famous as a huntress. She was also goddess of the moon, so often has a crescent in her hair. To attribute (verb) a work of art is to suggest that it may be by a particular artist, although there is no hard evidence for that.

aura The term used by Walter Benjamin in his influential 1936 essay 'The Work of Art in the Age of Mechanical Reproduction', where it is identified as a quality integral to an artwork that cannot be communicated through mechanical reproduction, such as photography.

authenticity Referring to Water Benjamin's use of the word 'authenticity' in his essay 'The Work of Art in the Age of Mechanical Reproduction'. Benjamin describes an original work of art as having authenticity. It has a presence in time and space, its unique existence in the place it happens to be. A reproduction of a work of art lacks 'authenticity', as it is not possible, when reproducing the work of art, to establish the exact conditions in which the original artwork was created. But it is possible, by reproducing a work of art, to call into question the original artwork's authenticity, as reproducing it has undermined the artwork. For this reason an original work of art is considered by the art market to have a higher value over a reproduction because it contains this authenticity. Authenticity can also relate to forgery (see fake), in order to establish whether or not a work of art was actually created by the artist it pertains to be by.

Auto-Destructive art A term invented by the artist Gustav Metzger in the early 1960s and put into circulation by his article 'Machine, Auto-creative and Auto-destructive Art' in the summer 1962 issue of the journal *Ark*. From 1959 he had made work by spraying acid on to sheets of nylon as a protest against nuclear weapons. The procedure produced rapidly changing shapes before the nylon was all consumed, so the work was simultaneously auto-creative and auto-destructive. In 1966 Metzger and others organised the 'Destruction in Art Symposium' in London. This was followed by another in New York in 1968. The Symposium was accompanied by public demonstrations of Auto-Destructive art including the burning of *Skoob Tower*s by John Latham. These were towers of books (skoob is books in reverse) and Latham's intention was to demonstrate directly his view that Western culture was burned out. In 1960 the Swiss artist Jean Tinguely made the first of his self-destructive machine sculptures, *Hommage à New York*, which battered itself to pieces in the Sculpture Garden of the Museum of Modern Art, New York.

Autograph ABP An influential photography collective set up by Sunil Gupta, Monika Baker, Roshini Kempadoo and Rotimi Fani-Kayode in 1988 to support photographers from racial minorities, and also to confront the lack of visual representation of marginalised groups in British society. Originally called the Association of Black Photographers, the group changed its name in 2002 to Autograph ABP. The organisation works internationally and embodies ideas of cultural representation and how photography can define and explore the meaning of the sub-cultures we inhabit. An image archive documenting the cultural history of Britain and its diverse communities is based in Autograph ABP's offices in east London.

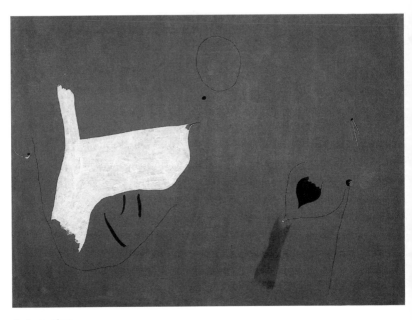

Automatism

Joan Miró
Painting 1927
Tempera and oil paint on canvas
97.2 × 130.2
Tate. Purchased with assistance
from the Friends of the Tate Gallery
1971

Automatism The central method of <u>Surrealism</u>, this movement was launched by the French poet André Breton in the *Manifesto of Surrealism* published in Paris in 1924. He was strongly influenced by the ideas of Sigmund Freud, the founder of psychoanalysis. Automatism is the same as free association, the method used by Freud to explore the unconscious mind of his patients. In the manifesto, Breton actually defined Surrealism as 'Pure psychic automatism ... the dictation of thought in the absence of all control exercised by reason and outside all moral or aesthetic concerns'. The aim was to access material from the unconscious mind. The earliest examples are the automatic writings of Breton and others, produced by simply writing down as rapidly as possible whatever springs to mind. Surrealist <u>collage</u>, invented by Max Ernst, was the first form of visual Automatism, in which he put together images clipped from magazines, product catalogues, book illustrations, advertisements and other sources to create a strange new reality. In painting various forms of Automatism were then developed by artists such as Joan Miró, André Masson and Max Ernst. Later it led to the <u>Abstract Expressionism</u> of Jackson Pollock and others and was an important element in the European movements of <u>Art Informel</u> and <u>Arte Nucleare</u>.

avant-garde Originally a French term, meaning vanguard or advance guard (the part of an army that goes forward ahead of the rest). Applied to art, it means that which is in the forefront, is innovatory, which introduces and explores new forms and in some cases new subject matter. In this sense the term first appeared in France in the first half of the nineteenth century and is usually credited to the influential thinker Henri de Saint-Simon, one of the forerunners of socialism. He believed in the social power of the arts and saw artists, alongside scientists and industrialists, as the leaders of a new society. In 1825 in his book *Opinions littéraires, philosophiques et industrielles* he wrote: 'We artists will serve you as an avant-garde ... the power of the arts is most immediate: when we want to spread new ideas we inscribe them on marble or <u>canvas</u> ... What a magnificent destiny for the arts is that of exercising a positive power over society, a true priestly function and of marching in the van [i.e. vanguard] of all the intellectual faculties!' Avant-garde art can be said to begin in the 1850s with the <u>Realism</u> of Gustave Courbet, who was strongly influenced by early socialist ideas. This was followed by the successive movements of modern art, and the term avant-garde is more or less synonymous with modern. Some avant-garde movements, for example Cubism, have focused mainly on innovations of form; others, such as Futurism, De Stijl or Surrealism, have had strong social programmes. The notion of the avant-garde enshrines the idea that art should be judged primarily on the quality and originality of the artist's vision and ideas.

AWC see Art Workers' Coalition

b

Baghdad Modern Art Group A highly influential postwar modern art group founded by Jawad Salim and Shakir Hassan al Said in 1951 with the intention of promoting an Iraqi form of modernism. Both artists had trained in Europe and Salim had also worked in the Department of Antiquities in Baghdad and was well versed in pre-Islamic and Islamic art. By incorporating Assyrian, Babylonian and Abbasid motifs into their art they helped define an Iraqi aesthetic after the 1958 revolution. The group published two manifestos, one in 1951 and one in 1955, in which they attempted to assert a distinctive Iraqi identity. Artists associated with the group include Jawad Salim and Shakir Hassan al Said and the painter and novelist Jabrā Ibrahīm Jabra.

The Baroda Group A pioneering art collective formed in Baroda, India, in 1956 by a group of artists who had taught or studied at the Faculty of Fine Arts at MSU Baroda. The art school was central to the formation of the group, having been established in 1950 – post Indian independence – as a progressive institution that wanted to distance itself from its colonial predecessors. Under the tutelage of the artists N.S. Bendre and K.G. Subramanyan, the school promoted experimentation and sought a distinctive modernist Indian aesthetic. The group's desire to look to indigenous roots and use different media and styles of painting to non-European regions, while also using the mythologies of Indian folklore, reflected the social impulses of the times and as a result the group became hugely influential. Artists associated with the group include G.R. Santosh, Ratan Parimoo, K.G. Subramanyan, Prabha Dongre, Shanti Dave, K. Patel, Triloke Kaul, Vinay Trivedi, N.S. Bendre, Balkrishna Patel, Jyoti Bhatt, Prafull Dave and Ramesh Pandya. The group disbanded in 1962.

Bauhaus Revolutionary school of art, architecture and design established by the pioneer modern architect Walter Gropius at Weimar, Germany in 1919. Its teaching method replaced the traditional pupil-teacher relationship with the idea of a community of artists working together. Its aim was to bring art back into contact with everyday life, and design was therefore given as much weight as fine art. The name is a combination of the German words for building (*bau*) and house (*haus*) and may have been intended to evoke the idea of a guild or fraternity working to build a new society. The Bauhaus moved to Dessau in 1925–6 where Gropius created a new building for it. In 1932 it moved to Berlin where it was closed by the Nazis. Teachers included Wassily Kandinsky, Paul Klee, László Moholy-Nagy and Josef Albers. Its influence was immense, especially in the USA where Moholy-Nagy opened the New Bauhaus in Chicago in 1937. In 1933 Albers took its methods to <u>Black Mountain College</u> in North Carolina and in 1950 to Yale University.

beauty A combination of shape, colour and form that pleases the eye. What constitutes beauty has been a much-debated topic in Western art. In Grecian times, the philosopher Aristotle thought beauty was about function and <u>proportion</u>, while in the early 1700s, the Earl of Shaftesbury argued that goodness and beauty are one and the same. In 1735, the German philosopher Alexander Baumgarten posed the question 'What is beauty?' and it is from this moment that our modern reading of the word begins to evolve. The philosopher Immanuel Kant responded by saying there is no scientific rule for determining what beauty is, as it is subjective, and in the eye of the beholder. (See also <u>aesthetics</u>)

Beijing East Village A short-lived, politically motivated, Chinese arts <u>collective</u> that came to prominence in the early 1990s. The collective formed soon after the Tiananmen Square protests, colonising an impoverished area of East Beijing that became known as Beijing East Village. Much of the art produced was <u>performance</u> based with an emphasis on collective action. This was partly due to the political climate at the time: with <u>avant-garde</u> artistic practice outlawed, artists found the temporary nature of Performance art a relatively secure outlet for dissident expression. The group also used performance to blur the boundaries between art and life in order to question, counter and respond to the violent shifts in Chinese culture. Their use of <u>photography</u> instigated a rise in photo and <u>video art</u> produced in China since 1990. One of the leading figures of the movement was Zhang Huan, who was known for his torturous durational pieces including *65 Kilograms* in which he hung upside down while doctors drew 250 ml of blood from his body. The movement ended in 1994 with a police raid and enforced evictions. Artists associated with Beijing East Village are Cang Xin, Yingmei

Duan, Gao Yang, Li Guomin, Ma Liuming, Ma Zongyin, Rong Rong, Tan Yeguang, Wang Shihua, Xu Shan, Zhang Binbin, Zhang Huan, Zhu Ming and Zuoxiao Zuzhou.

biennial In the art context biennial has come to mean a large international exhibition held every two years. The first was the Venice Biennale in 1895, which was situated in the Giardini, a public park, and now houses thirty permanent national pavilions and many smaller temporary structures. The early years were dominated by European art, but the exhibition now includes contributions from countries in South America, Africa, Asia and the Middle East. The late twentieth century saw a dramatic increase in biennials and by 2007 there were some fifty across the world, including the Beijing Biennial, the Liverpool Biennial, the Prague Biennale, the São Paulo Biennial and the Sharjah Biennial in The Gulf. This explosion of large-scale international art exhibitions mirrors the financial boom in international art buying.

Big Tail Elephant Group An art <u>collective</u> formed in Guangzhou in China in the early 1990s in response to rapid urbanisation. Founded by Lin Yilin, Chen Shaoxiong and Liang Juhui, the group set out to address the problems caused by rapacious modernisation. Their art, made in a variety of media, addressed the key issues facing a country that was transforming beyond recognition: the environmental, social damage caused by a population expansion, pollution, traffic, construction and corruption. An example of art created by Big Tail Elephant Group is Lin Yilin's *The Result of 1,000 Pieces* 1994, an installation featuring an unstable brick wall that was built around the artist.

bio art Art that uses biotechnology as its medium. The creations of bio art become part of evolution and, provided they are capable of reproduction, can last as long as life exists on earth. They raise questions about the future of life, evolution, society and art. Currently the dominant aspect of bio art is genetic art, as represented by the Brazilian-born artist Eduardo Kac, who genetically engineered a green fluorescent rabbit in 2000. As scientists continue their pioneering work into biotechnology, artists are also experimenting with cell and tissue cultures and neurophysiology. An example of

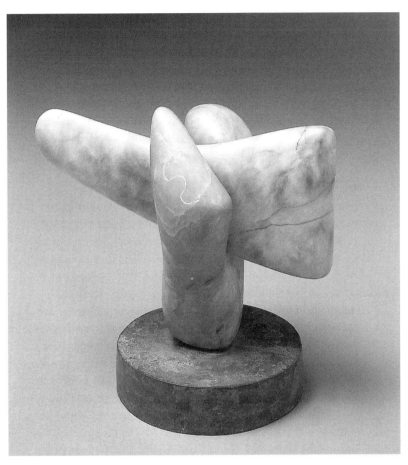

biomorphic

Barbara Hepworth
Two Forms 1933
Alabaster on limestone base
26 × 29.6 × 17.6
Tate. Purchased 1996

this is the Australian-based duo Oron Catts and Ionat Zurr who have attempted to grow a quarter-scale replica of an artist's ear.

biomorphic In painting and sculpture biomorphic <u>forms</u> or images are ones that, while <u>abstract</u>, nevertheless refer to, or evoke, living forms such as plants and the human body. The term comes from combining the Greek words *bios* (life) and *morphe* (form). Biomorphic seems to have come into use around the 1930s to describe the imagery in the more abstract types of <u>Surrealist</u> painting and sculpture, particularly in the work of Joan Miró and Jean Arp (see <u>Automatism</u>). Henry Moore and Barbara Hepworth also produced some superb biomorphs at that time and, later, so did Louise Bourgeois.

black aesthetic A cultural ideology that promoted black separatism in the arts, which developed in the USA alongside the civil rights movement in the 1960s. The theorist Larry Neal argued in 1968 that young writers and artists should confront the contradictions arising out of the African-American's experience of racism and marginalisation in the West. The development of a black aesthetic was seen as crucial to the development of an African-American identity at this revolutionary moment in American politics. Artists were called upon to seek a new aesthetic in opposition to the white Western one, and to acknowledge their black communities (see <u>aesthetics</u>). Early artworks took the form of <u>murals</u> that confronted social issues and sought to galvanise local black communities. They were colourful and rich with <u>symbolic</u> imagery and often depicted members of the black community, from Jazz musicians to politicians. Artists associated with the black aesthetic include the Visual Arts Workshop group, Dana Chandler, Gary Rickson, William Walker, Jeff Donaldson, Eugene Wade, Jae Jarrell, Wadsworth Jarrell, Barbara Jones-Hogu and Gerald Williams, many of who went on to form <u>AfriCOBRA</u>.

black arts movement An ideological movement that emerged in America the early 1960s when black artists and intellectuals came together to organise, study and think about what a new black art and black politics might be. It was inspired by the revolutions in China, Cuba and successful African and Asian independence movements, as well as the rise of the black power movement in America. The deaths of Malcolm X, Martin Luther King and Patrick Lumumba and the politicisation of black students together with the Watts uprising in 1965 resulted in unprecedented opportunities for radical black arts and politics. Despite victories in civil rights, there was anger over continuing oppression which caused regular uprisings. The movement reached its peak in the early 1970s, producing radical music, art, drama and poetry. In the visual arts, many artists associated with the movement addressed issues of black identity and black liberation. While there was not a distinctive aesthetic, many artists used appropriation, photo-screen printing and collage. Artists associated with the black arts movement include Benny Andrews, Cleveland Bellow, Kay Brown, Marie Johnson Calloway, Jeff Donaldson, Ben Hazard, Jae Jarrell, Wadsworth Jarrell, Ben Jones, Carolyn Lawrence, Dindga McCannon, Lev Mills and John T. Riddle.

Black Atlantic In 1993 the cultural critic Paul Gilroy published the book *The Black Atlantic: Modernity and Double Consciousness*, in which he used the term 'Black Atlantic' to describe a fusion of black cultures with other cultures from around the Atlantic. He argued that the Atlantic world has been deeply shaped by slavery and the slave trade. Between 1492 and 1820 about two-thirds of the people who crossed the Atlantic to the Americas were African, and this violently brutal migration played a key role in the development of a black consciousness in the Americas and Europe. Yet Gilroy argues that this black consciousness is ambivalent; it doesn't just reject white culture, but actively engages with it. Essentially it found a way of re-crossing the Atlantic creatively and, as a result, has had a central role in the formation of modernism. (See also négritude)

Black Audio Film Collective A pioneering arts initiative founded in Portsmouth in 1982 by seven undergraduates, which then re-located to east London in 1983. In response to the civil disturbances in Brixton in 1981, there was a concerted effort to provide financial and technical support to black media initiatives in order to promote a black cultural presence in the British media. One of the recipients of this assistance was Black Audio Film Collective and, in the five years in which they operated, they produced a number of groundbreaking documentaries, films, slide-tape texts and <u>videos</u> that chronicled and cross-examined Britain's new multicultural reality. Characterised by an interest in memory and history and the power of certain iconic figures like Malcolm X and Martin Luther King, the <u>collective</u> created a series of defiantly experimental works that engaged with black popular and political culture in Britain. The group were also instrumental in bringing an awareness of <u>avant-garde</u> film from Africa, India and South America to London. Artists, filmmakers and writers associated with the group include John Akomfrah, Lina Gopaul, Avril Johnson, Reece Auguis, Trevor Mathison, Edward George and Claire Johnson, who was replaced by David Lawson in 1985.

black box This term relates to <u>Performance art</u>, and is the name for a square room painted black in which artists performed experimental work . The black box became popular in the late 1960s, when artists began using abandoned warehouses as their studios. The appeal of the black box was that it was cheap to maintain and had few technical requirements apart from some simple lighting. The absence of colour on the walls, together with the lack of a set or backdrop, focused attention directly onto the performer. Black box can also be another word for a cinema, where films are screened. (See also <u>white cube</u>)

Black Mountain College Highly influential college founded at Black Mountain, North Carolina, USA, in 1933. Its progressive principles were based on the educational theories of John Rice, its founder. Drama, music and fine art were given equal status in the curriculum to all other academic subjects. Teaching was informal and stress was laid on communal living and outdoor activities. Most of the work of running the college and maintaining the buildings was done by students and faculty. Among its first teachers of art was Josef Albers, who had fled Nazi Germany after the closure of the <u>Bauhaus</u> that same year. Black Mountain quickly became an extraordinary powerhouse of modern culture in America. Its board of advisers included Albert Einstein and among its teachers at one time or another were some of the greatest luminaries of modern American culture including the founder of the Bauhaus, the architect Walter Gropius, the <u>Abstract Expressionist</u> painters Willem de Kooning and

Robert Motherwell, the composer John Cage and the dancer Merce Cunningham. In 1949 Albers and others left as a result of internal divisions. The college was reconstituted under the poet Charles Olson but eventually closed in 1953. Among its most notable artist students were Kenneth Noland and Robert Rauschenberg.

Der Blaue Reiter German Expressionist group. In English, The Blue Rider. It originated in 1909 in Munich, where the Neue Künstlervereiningung, or New Artists' Association (NKV), was founded by a number of avant-garde artists. The most important of these were the Russian-born Wassily Kandinsky and the German, Franz Marc. In 1911 Kandinsky and Marc broke with the rest of the NKV and in December that year held in Munich the first exhibition of Der Blaue Reiter. This was an informal association rather than a coherent group like Brücke. Other artists closely involved were Paul Klee and August Macke. In 1912 Marc and Kandinsky published a collection of essays on art with a woodcut cover by Kandinsky. This was the *Almanach Der Blaue Reiter*. Why the name was chosen is not entirely clear. Franz Marc adored horses and his many paintings of them and other animals is symptomatic of the turning back to nature (an aspect of primitivism) of many early modern artists. Kandinsky had apparently always been fascinated by riders on horseback (horses are symbols of power, freedom and pleasure). A Kandinsky painting of 1903 is actually called *The Blue Rider*. Blue is a colour that has often seemed of special importance to artists and for Kandinsky and Marc, whose favourite colour it was, it seems to have had a mystical significance. Der Blaue Reiter was brought to an end by the First World War in which both Macke and Marc were killed.

Blk Art Group Formed in Wolverhampton in 1979 by a small association of young black artists who had been inspired by the black arts movement, Blk Art Group raised questions about what black art was, its identity and what it could become in the future. All of the members were children of Caribbean migrants raised in the industrial landscape in and around the West Midlands. Their first exhibition, *Black Art An' Done* was held at Wolverhampton Art Gallery and focused on the concerns of the black community and racial prejudice. The group sought to empower black artists as well as encouraging young white artists to be more socially relevant

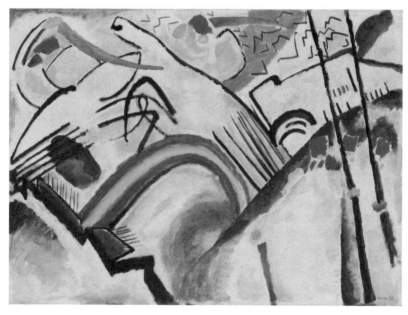

Der Blaue Reiter

Wassily Kandinsky
Cossacks 1910–11
Oil paint on canvas
94.6 × 130.2
Tate. Presented by Mrs Hazel
McKinley 1938

in their practice. Artists associated with the group include Eddie Chambers, Dominic Dawes, Lubaina Himid, Claudette Johnson, Wenda Leslie, Ian Palmer, Keith Piper, Donald Rodney and Marlene Smith. Many of the artists associated with Blk Art Group went on to participate in the British black arts movement.

Bloomsbury A district of quiet squares near central London. Its name is commonly used to identify a circle of intellectuals and artists who lived there in the period 1904–40. The intellectuals included the biographer Lytton Strachey, the economist John Maynard Keynes, the novelist Virginia Woolf and the art critic Clive Bell. The principal artists were Vanessa Bell, Roger Fry, who was also a highly influential critic, and Duncan Grant. Bloomsbury was in revolt against everything Victorian and played a key role in introducing many modern ideas into Britain. In 1910 Fry organised the London exhibition *Manet and the Post-Impressionists*, which brought modern French art to the attention of the British public. Visitors to the show were duly scandalised by the many works by Paul Cézanne, Paul Gauguin, Vincent van Gogh, Henri Matisse and Pablo Picasso. The Bloomsbury painters created their own distinctive brand of Post-Impressionism and around 1914 experimented with abstract art. Fry also founded the design firm Omega Workshops for which the Bloomsbury artists designed pottery, furniture, fabrics and interiors. Note that Bloomsbury resisted being categorised as a group.

body art Used to describe art in which the body, often that of the artist, is the principal medium and focus. It covers a wide range of art from about 1960 onwards, encompassing a variety of approaches. It includes much Performance art, where the artist is directly concerned with the body in the form of improvised or choreographed actions, happenings and staged events. However, the term body art is also used for explorations of the body in a variety of other media including painting, sculpture, photography, film and video. Body art has frequently been concerned with issues of gender and personal identity. A major theme has been the relationship of body and mind, explored in work consisting of feats of physical endurance designed to test the limits of the body and the ability of the mind to suffer pain. Body art has often highlighted the visceral or abject aspects of the body, focusing on bodily substances or the

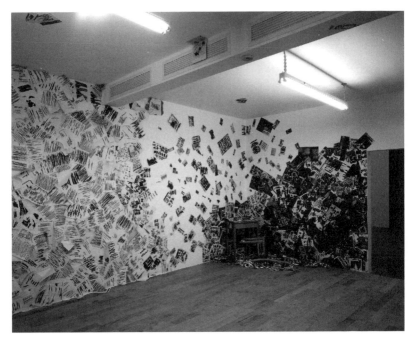

bricolage

Tomoko Takahashi
Drawing Room 1998
Wooden desk, wooden chair, staple gun, stainless
steel ashtray, cigarette butts, 2 marker pens,
cigarette boxes, tooth brush box, printed papers
and other materials
Tate. Presented by the Patrons of New Art
(Special Purchase Fund) 2002

theme of nourishment. It has also highlighted contrasts such as those between clothed and nude, internal and external, parts of the body and the whole. In some work, the body is seen as the vehicle for language. In 1998 the art historian Amelia Jones published a survey titled *Body Art*. (See also Conceptual art; feminist art)

Bombay Progressive Artists' Group A short-lived progressive art group founded in 1947 in Bombay (now Mumbai) by a group of artists who challenged India's existing conservative art establishment. Founded in the year of Indian independence, these artists sought to create an Indian form of modernism that celebrated traditional Indian painting while also acknowledging the pioneering developments in art in Europe and America. Ostracised by the Indian art establishment, the group staged their own exhibitions and events, aided financially by a group of refugees from war-torn Europe, in particular the Expressionist painter Walter Langhammer. The founder members were K.H. Ara, F.N. Souza, S.H. Raza and M.F. Husain with Sadanand Bakre, H.K. Gade, Krishen Khanna and V.S. Gaitonde joining later. Their first exhibition was held in 1948, but the group disbanded soon after, with Raza moving to Paris and Souza to London. Husain was publicly attacked for his work during the rise of Hindu nationalism in the 1980s, and was forced into exile in London.

bricolage The best translation of the French word bricolage is do-it-yourself and the creative core of bricolage in an art context is an ability to make art out of any materials that come to hand. This approach became popular in the early twentieth century when resources were scarce and aspects of Surrealism, Dada and Cubism have a bricolage character. But it was not until the early 1960s, with the formation of the Italian movement Arte Povera, that bricolage took on a political aspect and it was used by artists to bypass the commercialism of the art world. Arte Povera artists constructed sculptures out of rubbish in an attempt to devalue the art object and assert the value of the ordinary and everyday. Since then, artists have continued to make art out of detritus; Tomoko Takahashi constructs vast sculptures of junk found on the streets as a comment on the disposable nature of our culture and society.

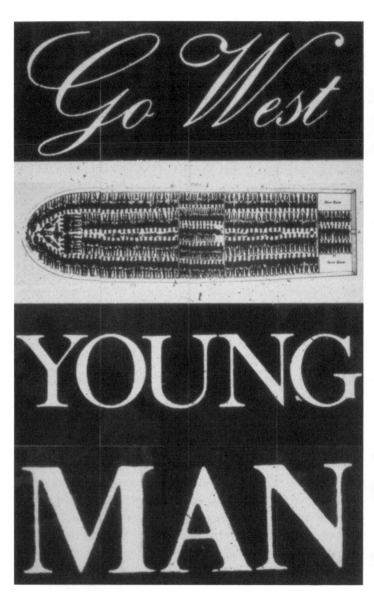

British black arts movement

Keith Piper
Go West Young Man 1987
14 photographs, gelatin silver print on
paper mounted onto board
In fourteen parts, each: 84 × 56
Tate. Purchased 2008

British black arts movement A radical political art movement founded in 1982 around the time of the First National Black Art Convention held at Wolverhampton Polytechnic, organised by <u>Blk Art Group</u>. Inspired by anti-racist discourse and feminist critique, the movement sought to highlight issues of race and gender and the politics of representation. Their work was both inspired and promoted by the cultural theorist Stuart Hall, who was one of the main proponents of <u>reception theory</u>, particularly in relation to race and the media. The group were highly influential, instrumental in de-imperialising the institutional mind and in changing the nature and perception of British culture. A key moment in the British black arts movement was the exhibition *The Other Story* staged at the Hayward Gallery in 1989, curated by Rasheed Araeen. Featuring modern artists of African, Caribbean and Asian ancestry, the show revealed how these artists had been marginalised in the West through discrimination. Artists and <u>curators</u> associated with the movement include Rasheed Araeen, David A Bailey, <u>Black Audio Film Collective</u>, Sonia Boyce, Eddie Chambers, Shakka Dedi, Denzil Forrester, Lubaina Himid, Claudette Johnson, Remi Kapo, Eugene Palmer, Keith Piper, Donald Rodney, Mark Sealy, Marlene Smith and Maud Sulter.

browser art A sub-genre of <u>net art</u> and relates specifically to a renegade artwork made as part of a URL that uses the computer as raw material, transforming the codes, the structure of the websites and the links between servers into visual material. Some browser artworks automatically connect to the internet and then proceed to mangle the web pages by reading the computer's 'code' the wrong way. The duo Joan Hermskerk and Dirk Paesmans, known as Jodi, have devised a program which the net art writer Tilman Baumgärtel has described as transforming a PC 'into an unpredictable, terrifying machine that seems to have a life of its own'. Other artists, like the British-based duo Tom Corby and Gavin Baily, reduce image-rich web pages to stark white text and the American artist Maciej Wisniewski has developed a browser that transforms the interactive experience of surfing the net into a passive activity, staring at floating images and texts. (See also <u>software art</u>)

Brücke German Expressionist group founded in Dresden in 1905. The name means bridge and may have been intended to convey the idea of a bridge between the artist, seen as a special person, and society at large. Also, Brücke recruited members who were not artists but patrons, paying a subscription entitling them to an annual portfolio of prints. The name may thus refer to this direct bridge between artist and patron. The manifesto of 1906 stated 'we want to achieve freedom of life and action against the well established older forces'. In art this freedom involved blending elements of old German art and African and South Pacific tribal art with Post-Impressionism and Fauvism to create a distinctive modern style. In life they sought a return to a more direct relationship with nature (another bridge). This is vividly expressed in their pictures of themselves bathing nude in the lakes near Dresden. Chief artists were Ernst Ludwig Kirchner, Karl Schmidt-Rottluff, Fritz Bleyl and Erich Heckel, joined in 1910 by Otto Müller. Emil Nolde was also briefly a member.

brushwork A word used in relation to painting to describe the characteristics of the paint surface resulting from its application with a brush. Brushwork can range from extremely smooth – as, for example, in the work of the German Neue Sachlichkeit painters – to extremely thick, as in the various forms of Expressionism, and what is called gestural (see also impasto). Brushwork, like handwriting, can be highly individual and can be an important factor in identifying an artist's work. It can also be highly expressive – that is, the application of the paint itself plays a role in conveying the emotion or meaning of the work. In modern art theory, emphasis is placed on the idea that a painting should have its own reality rather than attempting to imitate the three-dimensional world. Value is therefore placed on distinctive brushwork because it asserts the two-dimensional surface of the work and the reality of the paint itself. Distinctive brushwork is also seen as valuable because it foregrounds the role of the medium itself. The painter Robert Ryman has devoted his entire career to an exploration of brushwork.

Brutalism Coined by the British architectural critic Reyner Banham to describe the approach to building particularly associated with the architects Peter and Alison Smithson in the 1950s and 1960s. The term originates from the use by the pioneer modern architect and painter Le Corbusier of *beton brut* (raw concrete). Banham gave the French word a punning twist to express the general horror with which this concrete architecture was greeted in Britain. Typical examples of Brutalism are the Hayward Gallery and National Theatre on London's South Bank. The term Brutalism has sometimes been used to describe the work of artists influenced by Art Brut.

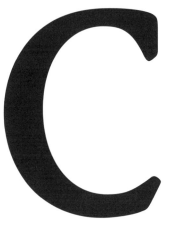

cadavre exquis Invented in 1925 in Paris by the <u>Surrealists</u> Yves Tanguy, Jacques Prévert, André Breton and Marcel Duchamp, cadavre exquis (exquisite corpse) is similar to the old parlour game consequences, in which players write in turn on a sheet of paper, fold to conceal part of the writing and pass it on to the next player. The Surrealists adapted the game by drawing parts of the body. The name cadavre exquis was derived from a phrase that resulted when they first played the game, 'Le cadavre/ exquis/ boira/ le vin/ nouveau' ('The exquisite corpse will drink the new wine').

Calligraphic School of Art By the second half of the twentieth-century, a new art movement began to take shape in the Arab world. Arab artists, well versed in Western aesthetics, wanted to create an art that was truly original, using a style that related to their cultural history while also embracing modernism. The answer was the Calligraphic School of Art (al-Madrasa al-Huruffiyah). Inspired by traditional Islamic calligraphy, these artists incorporated the Arabic alphabet into their predominantly abstract artworks. The school emerged as individual young artists, working in isolation of each other, developed this artistic tradition into a truly modern form. There are several pioneers of the movement, including the Syrian/Iraqi artist Madiha Omar who wrote a declaration of the style entitled *Arabic Calligraphy: An Element of Inspiration in Abstract Art*. Other artists to embrace calligraphy are Jamil Hamoudi and later Shakir Hassan Al-Said who founded the <u>One-Dimension group</u> (Al Bu'd al Wahad) dedicated to modern calligraphy in Arabic art. (See also <u>Khartoum School</u>)

Camden Town Group British <u>Post-Impressionist</u> group founded by Walter Sickert in London in 1911. Other members were Robert Bevan, Spencer Gore, Harold Gilman and Charles Ginner. They painted <u>realist</u> scenes of city life and some <u>landscape</u> in a range of Post-Impressionist styles. The group was named after the seedy district of north London where Sickert had lived in the 1890s and again from 1907. His series of Camden Town nudes and his paintings of alienated couples in interiors, such as *Ennui*, are his outstanding contribution to Camden Town art.

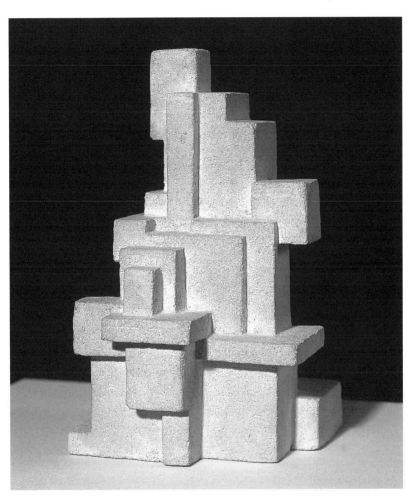

Cercle et Carré

Georges Vantongerloo
Interrelation of Volumes
1919
Sandstone
22.5 × 13.7 × 13.7
Tate. Purchased 1978

canvas Strong, woven cloth traditionally used for artists' supports. Commonly made of either linen or cotton thread, but also manufactured from man-made materials such as polyester.

Capitalist Realism A movement formed in Berlin in Germany in 1963 to challenge the pervasiveness of American Pop art in the Western world. Capitalist Realism is sometimes thought of as German Pop art because the artists associated with it were similarly interested in the banal and the mass media. Yet unlike

Pop art, its cultural value was political, not economical, using Germany's postwar society as its starting point. The movement was founded during the Cold War in Berlin, and it is important to see the development of Capitalist Realism in relation to this. The Eastern bloc had Socialist Realism and the West had Pop art: both were essentially art for the masses. For artists living in Berlin, a city straddling both artistic ideologies, Capitalist Realism represented their unique situation. Artists associated with Capitalist Realism included Sigmar Polke, Gerhard Richter, Manfred Kuttner and Konrad Lueg.

caricature A caricature is a painting, or more usually drawing, of a person or thing in which the features and form have been distorted and exaggerated in order to mock or satirise the subject.

carving see direct carving; sculpture

cast A form created by pouring liquid material, such as plaster or molten metal, into a mould.

Cercle et Carré French abstract group founded in Paris in 1929 by critic and artist Michel Seuphor and artist Joaquín Torres García. They published a periodical of the same name and held a major group exhibition in 1930. This included 130 works by a wide range of abstract artists. The group strongly supported new developments in abstract art and in particular promoted the mystical tendency within it. Cercle et Carré (Circle and Square) was absorbed by Abstraction-Création when the latter was founded in 1931, but Torres García continued the publication in Montevideo in his native Uruguay.

chalk White or off-white inorganic material composed of calcium carbonate. Naturally occurring, although also produced industrially throughout the twentieth century.

charcoal One of the most basic drawing materials, known since antiquity. It is usually made of thin peeled willow twigs that are heated without the presence of oxygen. This produces black crumbly sticks, which leave microscopic sharp-edged particles in the paper or textile fibres, producing a line denser at the pressure point, but more diffuse at the edges. The overall result is less precise than hard graphite

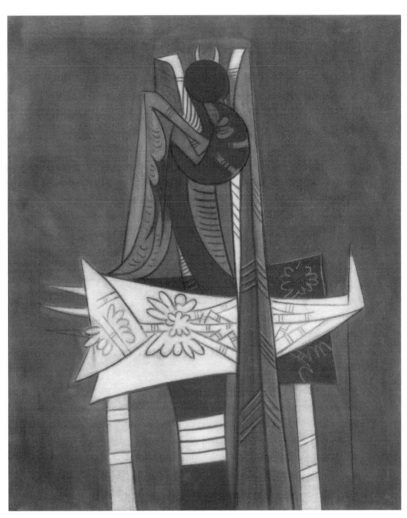

pencils, suited to freer studies. Charcoal smudges easily and is often protected with a sprayed fixative. It is used to make both sketches and finished works, and as under-drawing for paintings. In the twentieth century a processed version was developed, called compressed charcoal.

chiaroscuro
Wifredo Lam
Ibaye 1950
Oil paint on canvas
104.5 × 87.6
Tate. Purchased 1952

chiaroscuro Italian term used in that form in English. It translates as light-dark, and refers to the balance and pattern of light and shade in a painting or drawing. Chiaroscuro is generally only remarked upon when it is a particularly prominent feature of the work, usually when the artist is using extreme contrasts of light and shade.

cinematic Of, or pertaining to, the characteristic of film. The word cinematic is sometimes used to describe a form of tableau photography where the artist has used dramatic lighting and scene-setting to heighten the tension and create an atmosphere that is similar to that of a movie. It is a technique used by artists to blur fact and fiction. Cindy Sherman's *Untitled Film Stills*, a series of black and white photographs made between 1977 and 1980, depict the artist playing fictitious characters. Using vintage clothing, make-up and wigs, she created a range of female personae in scenarios that resembled moments in a film. Since the advent of digital film-making, and the decline of analogue film, the word 'cinematic' can also be used to describe a piece of digital film that has the stylistic look and ambition of analogue film.

Círculo y Cuadrado see Cercle et Carré

CoBrA Group formed in 1948 by artists from Copenhagen, Brussels and Amsterdam and taking its name from the first letters of those cities. However, they welcomed the coincidental reference to the snake, since animal imagery was common in CoBrA painting. They were also interested in the art of children. Leading members of CoBrA were Karel Appel, Asger Jorn and Constant Nieuwenhuys (known as Constant). In style their painting was highly expressionist. As a group they had active social and political concerns. CoBrA held a major exhibition in 1949 at the Stedelijk Museum in Amsterdam under the title *International Experimental Art*, but the group dissolved in the early 1950s.

collaborative A term meaning to work together, or in conjunction with another, to engage in united labour. The most common way for artists to collaborate is with other artists (see also collective). Duos like Marina Abramović and ULAY created works that relied on mutual dependency. Other artists collaborate with individuals from different skill backgrounds, like a musician or a scientist, or with a wider community. Collaborative practices gained momentum in the 1960s when artists began questioning the idea of the artist as the sole creator. When artists collaborate they intentionally blur the boundaries of individual effort and ego and this can have an impact on the reception of the work of art, and sometimes its financial status as it makes attribution difficult. Collaborative practices also suggest a paradigm shift in contemporary art production, because the process of making can sometimes be the work itself (see process art).

collage Used to describe both the technique and the resulting work of art in which pieces of paper, photographs, fabric and other ephemera are arranged and stuck down to a supporting surface. Collage can also include other media such as painting and drawing, and may contain three-dimensional elements. The term collage derives from the French words papier collé or découpage, used to describe techniques of pasting paper cut-outs on to various surfaces. It was first used as an artists' technique in the twentieth century.

collective Loosely defined, an art collective is a group of artists working together to achieve a common objective. They are united by shared ideologies, aesthetics or political beliefs. In the early modern period, there were roughly two forms of art collective. Those who sought to bring about social change by cultural means like the Futurists. They looked towards the future where they envisioned a radically new way of life. Others, like the Dada artists, represented the psychological consequences of the loss of a pre-modern existence and reflected that in their art. They spoke for a collective group, in this case those mentally and physically scarred by the First World War. Today, thanks to social media, art collectives have an extraordinary global reach, giving them the power to bring about change through direct action.

Colour Field painting Originally used to describe the work from about 1950 of the Abstract Expressionist painters Mark Rothko, Barnett Newman and Clyfford Still, which was characterised by large areas of a more or less flat single colour. 'The Colour Field Painters' was the title of the chapter dealing with these artists in the American scholar Irving Sandler's groundbreaking history, *Abstract Expressionism*, published in 1970. Around 1960 a more purely abstract form of Colour Field painting emerged in the work of Helen Frankenthaler, Sam Gilliam, Morris Louis, Kenneth Noland, Alma Thomas and others. It differed from Abstract Expressionism in that these artists eliminated the emotional, mythic or religious content and the highly personal and painterly or gestural application associated with of the earlier movement. In 1964 an exhibition of thirty-one artists associated with this development was organised by the critic Clement Greenberg at the Los Angeles County Museum of Art. He titled it *Post-Painterly Abstraction*, a term often also used to describe the work of the 1960 generation and their successors. In Britain there was a major development of Colour Field painting in the 1960s in the work of Robyn Denny, John Hoyland, Richard Smith and others. (See also Post-Painterly Abstraction)

comic strip art In the 1960s a group of Pop artists began to imitate the commercial printing techniques and subject matter of comic strips. The American painter Roy Lichtenstein became notorious for creating paintings inspired by Marvel comic strips and incorporating and enlarging the Ben Day dots used in newspaper printing – surrounding these with black outlines similar to those used to conceal imperfections in cheap newsprint. At the same time Andy Warhol was also using images from popular culture, including comic strips and advertising, which he repeatedly reproduced, row after row, on a single canvas until the image became blurred and faded. The German painter Sigmar Polke also manipulated the Ben Day dot, although, unlike the slick graphic designs of Lichtenstein, Polke's dots were splodges that looked like rogue accidents in the printing room. In a similar vein, Raymond Pettibon undermined the innocent spirit of the comic strip with his ink-splattered drawings and sardonic commentary.

complementary colours Colours which complete each other – hence the name. The effect of this completing is to enhance the colours – they look stronger when placed together. This is because they contrast with each other more than with any other colours, and we can only see colour by contrast with other colours. The more contrast the more colour. If you stay in a room entirely painted one colour, after about ten minutes it will fade to grey. The complementary colours are the three primary colours, red, blue and yellow, and their secondaries. Secondary colours are the colours obtained by mixing the primaries in all their combinations of pairs. So the three secondary colours are green, orange and violet. The complementary pairs are red-green, blue-orange and yellow-violet. Artists began to become particularly aware of the significance of complementary colours after the development of scientific colour theory in the nineteenth century. This theory played an important part in the development of Impressionism and Post-Impressionism as well as Fauvism and much modern painting thereafter. The Impressionists were the first to note that shadows are not neutral but are the complementary colour of the light that throws them. So yellow sunlight throws a violet shadow. This can be seen very well in Monet's *Woman Seated on a Bench* in the crease of her arm and the pool of shadow at her feet.

composition In a general sense any piece of music or writing, or any painting or sculpture, can be referred to as a composition. More specifically, the term refers to the way in which an artist has arranged the elements of the work so as to bring them into a relationship satisfactory to the artist and, it is hoped, the viewer. The idea that composition was the adjustment of the relationships of elements within the border of the canvas remained unchallenged through the upheavals of the early modern movements such as Cubism and abstract art. Then in the late 1940s the American Abstract Expressionist painter, Jackson Pollock, introduced what came to be called allover composition, and the traditional concept became known as relational composition. Pollock still generally seems to be composing within the canvas but, at the same time, the Abstract Expressionist Barnett Newman began making paintings in which large blocks of colour ran from top to bottom of the canvas. These were relational to the extent that the proportions of the colours were adjusted against each other, but they were compositionally radical in that the blocks of colour simply ran off the top and bottom edges of the canvas, which Newman deliberately left unframed. It was Frank Stella in the late 1950s who achieved a composition that was allover and at the same time broke out of the confines of the canvas.

computer animation see animation

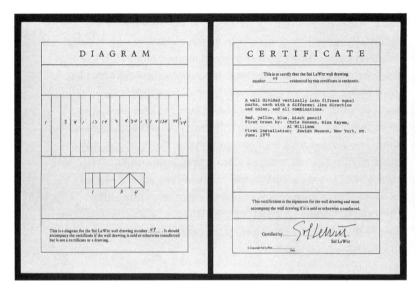

Conceptual art

Sol LeWitt
*A Wall Divided
Vertically into Fifteen
Equal Parts, Each
with a Different Line
Direction and Colour,
and All Combinations*
1970
Graphite on wall
Tate. Purchased
1973

Conceptual art This term came into use in the late
1960s to describe a wide range of types of art that
no longer took the form of a conventional art object.
In 1973 a pioneering record of the early years of the
movement appeared in the form of a book, Six Years
by the American critic Lucy Lippard. The 'six years'
were 1966–72. The long subtitle of the book referred
to 'so-called Conceptual or information or idea art'.
Conceptual artists do not set out to make a painting
or a sculpture and then fit their ideas to that existing
form. Instead they think beyond the limits of those
traditional media, and then work out their concept
or idea in whatever materials and whatever form is
appropriate. They were thus giving the concept priority
over the traditional media: hence Conceptual art.
From this it follows that Conceptual art can be almost
anything, but from the late 1960s certain prominent
trends appeared such as Performance (or Action)
art, Land art, and the Italian movement Arte Povera
(poor art). Poor here meant using low-value materials
such as twigs, cloth, fat, and all kinds of found objects
and scrap. Some Conceptual art consisted simply
of written statements or instructions. Many artists

began to use photography, film and video. Conceptual art was initially a movement of the 1960s and 1970s but has been hugely influential since. Artists include Art & Language, Joseph Beuys, Marcel Broodthaers, Victor Burgin, Michael Craig-Martin, Gilbert & George, Yves Klein, Joseph Kosuth, John Latham, Richard Long, Piero Manzoni and Robert Smithson.

Conceptual photography The rise of Conceptual photography in the 1960s coincided with the early explorations into video art. Using cameras, artists like Richard Long and Dennis Oppenheim began recording their performances and temporary artworks in a manner that is now often described as deadpan. The aim was to make simple, realistic images of the artwork that looked as documentary as possible. It was the pedestrian nature of photography, its unshakable capacity to photograph everything the same, that the artists liked, believing it was the art depicted in the photograph that was important. Precedents for Conceptual photography can be found as far back as the early twentieth century when Alfred Stieglitz photographed Marcel Duchamp's readymade, *Fountain*, for an exhibition in New York. The original *Fountain* was lost, but the photographs by Stieglitz remain and have become works of art in themselves.

Concrete art A term introduced by Theo Van Doesburg in the 1930 *Manifesto of Concrete Art* published in the first and only issue of magazine *Art Concret*. He called for a type of abstract art that would be entirely free of any basis in observed reality and that would have no symbolic implications. He stated that there was nothing more concrete or more real than a line, a colour or a plane (a flat area of colour). The Swiss artist Max Bill later became the flag bearer for Concrete art, organising the first international exhibition in Basel in 1944. In practice Concrete art is very close to Constructivism and there is a museum of Constructive and Concrete art in Zurich, Switzerland. (See also Neo-Concrete)

Constructionism An extension of Constructivism in Britain from about 1950 in the work of Victor Pasmore, Kenneth Martin, Mary Martin and Anthony Hill. Naturally occurring proportional systems and rhythms underpinned their geometrical art. They were inspired by the theories of the American artist Charles Biederman and explored the legacy of the 'Constructive art' made in the 1930s by Ben Nicholson and Barbara Hepworth; also Naum Gabo, whose contribution to Russian Constructivism was exemplary. Hill insisted on using the term Constructionism for the British phenomenon, but Constructivism is more commonly found.

Constructivism Particularly austere branch of abstract art founded by Vladimir Tatlin and Alexander Rodchenko in Russia around 1915. The Constructivists believed art should directly reflect the modern industrial world. Tatlin was crucially influenced by Pablo Picasso's Cubist constructions, which he saw in Picasso's studio in Paris in 1913. These were three-dimensional still lifes made of scrap materials. Tatlin began to make his own but they were completely abstract and made of industrial materials. By 1921 Russian artists who followed Tatlin's ideas were calling themselves Constructivists and in 1923 a manifesto was published in their magazine *Lef*: 'The material formation of the object is to be substituted for its aesthetic combination. The object is to be treated as a whole and thus will be of no discernible "style" but simply a product of an industrial order like a car, an aeroplane and such like. Constructivism is a purely technical mastery and organisation of materials.' Constructivism was suppressed in Russia in the 1920s but was brought to the West by Naum Gabo and his brother Antoine Pevsner and has been a major influence on modern sculpture.

contemporary art A term loosely used to denote art of the present day and of the relatively recent past, of an innovatory or avant-garde nature. In relation to contemporary art museums, the date of origin for the term contemporary art varies. The Institute of Contemporary Art in London, founded in 1947, champions art from that year onwards. Whereas The New Museum of Contemporary Art in New York chooses the later date of 1977. In the 1980s, Tate planned a Museum of Contemporary Art in which contemporary art was defined as art of the past ten years on a rolling basis.

content Content generally refers to the subject matter, meaning or significance of a work of art, as opposed to its form. In modern art the dramatic succession of innovations in form from Impressionism onwards have meant that discussion of this has often taken precedence over that of content. In the 1960s and early 1970s the particularly radical flight from traditional forms of art that resulted in what became known as Conceptual art, gave rise to work in which form and content were fused in a new way.

conversation piece Informal group portrait, usually small in scale, showing people – often families, sometimes groups of friends – in domestic interior or garden settings. Sitters are shown interacting with each other or with pets, taking tea, playing games.

C-print Also know as C-type print or Chromogenic print, this is a photographic print made from a colour negative or slide, which is exposed to photographic paper that contains three emulsion layers, each of which is sensitised to a different primary colour. After the image has been exposed it is submerged in a chemical bath, where each layer reacts to the chemicals to create a full-colour image. Because the chemicals are so complex, the image continues to react even after the process is completed. The chemicals are also extremely sensitive to water, light and heat, making it difficult to protect C-prints from deterioration. (See also digital C-print)

craft In the past, craft was considered to be a lesser form of art than painting and sculpture because the objects made had a domestic function; you could wear them, drink or eat from them. They were also creative techniques that tended to be practiced by women, which contributed to their lesser status. In the mid-1800s William Morris began to question the differences between art and craft by bringing an artist aesthetic to a craft object, like wallpaper design. During the twentieth century, the boundaries between art and craft became blurred, particularly at the Bauhaus, as artists started to experiment with craft practices in their art. The artist Sonia Delaunay created geometric abstracts using textiles. Today many contemporary artists use craft techniques like Grayson Perry and Tracey Emin.

creolisation Originally a Caribbean concept, creolisation describes the mixing together of different people and cultures to become one. The term comes from the word Creole, used to describe people born in the Americas as opposed to those who were African-born.

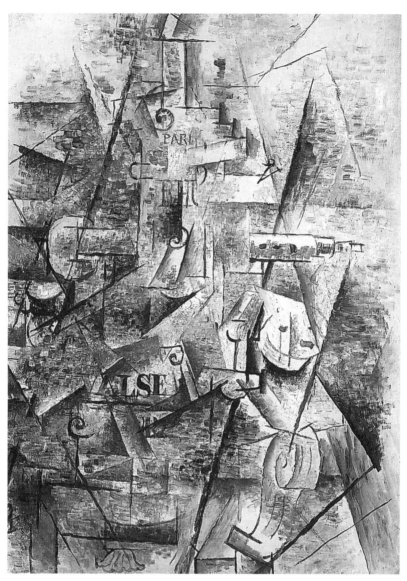

Cubism

Georges Braque
Clarinet and Bottle of Rum on a Mantelpiece 1911
Oil paint on canvas
81 × 60
Tate. Purchased with assistance from a special
government grant and with assistance from
The Art Fund 1978

The idea of creolisation gained prominence during the Second World War, when scholars, such as the Martinique poet and politician Aimé Césaire wrote about the ambiguities of Caribbean life and the cultural identity of black Africans in a colonial setting. In this respect, creolisation can be related to négritude. Today the term creolisation is sometimes used to describe the cultural complexity of the world we live in and of the many diverse societies that exist within it.

Crystalist Group A Conceptual art group founded in Khartoum at the College of Fine Arts in 1971 by the Sudanese artists Kamala Ibrahim Ishaq and her students Muhammad Hamid Shaddad and Nayla El Tayib. In 1978 they published the *Crystalist Manifesto* in which they argued that the universe is like a crystal cube: transparent and constantly changing according to the viewer's position. The manifesto was intended to challenge the dominance of the older, more established art movement in Sudan known as the Khartoum School and also sought to question the dominating masculine vision of art in the country. The group was multi-disciplinary, painting pictures, staging performances and installations. Kamala Ibrahim Ishaq has become a highly respected artist in the Arab world and participated in the 2002 exhibition *Breaking the Veils: Women Artists from the Islamic World*.

Cubism A new way of representing reality in art invented by Pablo Picasso and Georges Braque from 1907–8. A third core Cubist was Juan Gris. It is generally agreed the beginning of Cubism was Picasso's celebrated *Demoiselles d'Avignon* of 1907. The name seems to have derived from the comment of the critic Louis Vauxcelles that some of Braque's paintings exhibited in Paris in 1908 showed everything reduced to 'geometric outlines, to cubes'. Cubism was partly influenced by the late work of Paul Cézanne in which he can be seen to be painting things from slightly different points of view. Picasso was also influenced by African tribal masks which are highly stylised, or non-naturalistic, but nevertheless present a vivid human image. In their Cubist paintings Braque and Picasso began to bring different views of single objects together on the picture surface – the object became increasingly fragmented and the paintings became increasingly abstract. They countered this by incorporating words, and then real elements, such as newspapers, to represent themselves (see appropriation). This was Cubist collage, soon extended into three dimensions in Cubist constructions, and it was the start of one of the most important ideas in modern art – that you can use real things directly in art. Cubism was the starting point for much abstract art including Constructivism and Neo-Plasticism. It also, however, opened up almost infinite new possibilities for the treatment of reality in art. (See also Analytical Cubism; Synthetic Cubism)

cultural democracy A concept that emerged after the Second World War, and seeks to democratise culture. Culture was traditionally divided into two parts; high art and low art. High art being opera, music, ballet, painting, sculpture, poetry and drama, and low art being culture that has mass appeal, sometimes known as popular culture. The high arts tend to be defined and enjoyed by one small section of society and this is considered undemocratic. Cultural democracy seeks to break down the boundaries between high and low culture in order to bring about an awareness of art and an appreciation of it to as wide a section of society as possible. Community art evolved out of cultural democracy.

Cultural Revolution A social-political movement that took place in China between 1966 and 1976 in order to rid the country of the middle classes. The Communist leader Mao Zedong believed the intelligentsia were trying to restore capitalism to China and so instigated a drive to enforce communism and remove capitalist, traditional and cultural elements from Chinese society. Historical relics and artefacts considered anti-socialist or too closely associated with the old order were destroyed. Museums, art galleries, theatres and art educational establishments were closed down and many artists were persecuted and prevented from working. The only art acceptable during this time was that which promoted the benefits of socialism.

curator Museums and galleries typically employ numbers of curators who are concerned with staging temporary loan exhibitions, arranging displays of the museum's own collection and making acquisitions for that collection. In the past twenty years the role of the curator has evolved: now there are freelance or independent curators who are not attached to an institution and who have their own idiosyncratic ways of making exhibitions. Such curators are invited to curate, or themselves propose, exhibitions in a wide range of spaces, both within and outside the established gallery system, and online. The Swiss curator Harald Szeemann who was the director of the Venice Biennale in 1999 and 2001 is a good example of an independent curator, as is the artist and curator Matthew Higgs who is known for his low-budget, DIY exhibitions that have included the publication *Imprint 93*, an art exhibition that was posted to people rather than exhibited in a gallery space.

Cynical Realism A term coined by the art critic Li Xianting in 1992 to describe a group of Beijing artists who painted the psychological fallout felt by the population in response to China's rapid growth and ambiguous political ideology. Cynical Realism was humorous and satirical in tone and adopted the style of Socialist Realist painting (the only officially sanctioned artistic style at the time), but the content is far from idealistic. Paintings by Yue Minjun depict bright pink heads grinning manically against crystal blue skies, their heightened colour palette suggestive of the disquiet the artist feels in the wake of the student riots of 1989. Other artists associated with Cynical Realism include Fang Lijun, Liu Wei, Zhang Xiaogang and Wang Jinsong.

d

Dada The Dada movement began in Zurich, in neutral Switzerland, during the First World War. It can be seen as a reaction by artists to what they saw as the unprecedented horror and folly of the war. They felt it called into question every aspect of the society capable of starting and then prolonging it, including its art. Their aim was to destroy traditional values in art and to create a new art to replace the old. In 1916 the writer Hugo Ball started a satirical nightclub in Zurich, the Cabaret Voltaire, and a periodical of the same name. In it he wrote of publishing an international review that would bear the name '"DADA" ("Dada") Dada Dada Dada.' This was the first of many Dada publications. Dada became an international movement and eventually formed the basis of Surrealism in Paris after the war. Leading artists associated with it include Hans Arp, Marcel Duchamp, Francis Picabia and Kurt Schwitters. Duchamp's questioning of the fundamentals of Western art had a profound subsequent influence (see readymade).

Danseakhwa: the Korean monochrome movement

A formidable movement formed in South Korea in the 1970s in an effort to reconcile the influence of Western modernism on Korean artistic culture. Stylistically the artists of Danseakhwa rejected realism and formalism for modernist abstraction, choosing to paint only in monochrome and in a style that emphasised the flatness of the canvas. The movement highlighted the postwar struggle within Korea over national identity, belonging and tradition. By using repetitive patterns and gestures in their pictures, they attempted to create an aesthetic style that was universal and belonged to no one. Artists associated with Danseakhwa are Ha Chong-hyun, Hur Hwang, Lee Dong-Youb, Lee Ufan, Park Seo-bo and Yun Hyong-keun.

Dashanzi Art District see 798 Art Zone

data visualisation A term used to describe the visual representation of information, often statistical. In the past this was usually in map or graph form, but computers make it possible to represent data in animated and interactive form. Artists use data visualisation as a way of revealing and exploring hidden aspects of society as manifested in new forms of social representation such as web logs. An example of this is *The Dumpster*, an online artwork devised by Golan Levin with Kamal Nigam and Jonathan Feinberg, which uses data from web logs to plot the romantic lives of teenagers.

Decadence Phase or branch of symbolism in the 1880s and 1890s and many artists and writers are seen as exponents of both. The term, which came into use in the 1880s (for example the French journal *Le Décadent*, 1886), generally refers to extreme manifestations of symbolism emphasising the spiritual, the morbid and the erotic. Decadents are inspired partly by disgust at the corruption and rampant materialism of the modern world, partly by the concomitant desire to escape it into realms of the aesthetic, fantastic, erotic or religious. In art key influences were Dante Gabriel Rossetti and then Edward Burne-Jones. Key artists are Fernand Khnopff, Gustave Moreau, Félicien Rops; and from Britain Aubrey Beardsley and Simeon Solomon. Key books associated with Decadence are Joris Karl Huysmans's *A Rebours* (Against Nature) and Oscar Wilde's *Dorian Gray*.

decalcomania A popular technique used by the Surrealists, decalcomania is a blotting process whereby paint is squeezed between two surfaces to create a mirror image. The most common example of decalcomania involves applying paint to paper then folding it, applying pressure and then unfolding the paper to reveal a mirror pattern. Decalcomania is most commonly associated with the surrealist painters Max Ernst and Oscar Dominguez, who would use the technique and then turn the resulting patterns into landscapes and mythical creatures. Decalcomania can be seen as a form of Automatism.

décollage French word meaning literally to unstick. The term is generally associated with the Nouveau Réalisme (New Realism) movement, although the first time it appeared in print was in the *Dictionnaire Abrégé du Surréalisme* in 1938. In the context of Nouveau Réalisme it meant making artworks from posters ripped from walls, exhibiting them as aesthetic objects and social documents. The artists involved, such as Raymond Hains, often sought out sites with many layers of posters so that the process of décollage took on an archeological character and was seen as a means of uncovering historical information. From 1949 Hains made work from posters that he tore from the walls of Paris. In 1963 the German artist Wolf Vostell appropriated the term, staging a series of happenings under the title *Nein – 9 Decollagen*. These involved television images that he had *decollé* – unstuck from the screen – and re-presented. In 1962 Vostell had founded *Dé-coll/age: Bulletin Aktueller Ideen*, a magazine devoted to the theoretical writings of artists involved in happenings, Fluxus, Nouveau Réalisme and Pop art.

decolonisation A term used to describe the process by which a country that was previously a colony becomes politically independent. In the context of art, the word decolonisation is often used to describe the process of reversing the dominance of Western art and a move towards a truly global art world.

deconstruction A form of criticism that involves discovering, recognising and understanding the underlying – and unspoken and implicit – assumptions, ideas and frameworks of cultural forms such as works of art. First used by the French philosopher Jacques Derrida in the 1970s, deconstruction asserts that there is not one single intrinsic meaning to be found in a work, but rather many, and often they can be conflicting. In Derrida's 1978 book *La Vérité en peinture* (The truth in painting) he uses the example of Vincent van Gogh's painting *Old Shoes with Laces*, arguing that we can never be sure whose shoes are depicted in the work, making a concrete analysis of the painting difficult. Since Derrida's assertions in the 1970s, the notion of deconstruction has been a dominating influence on many writers and Conceptual artists.

degenerate art The English translation of the German phrase *Entartete Kunst*. In 1933 the National Socialist (Nazi) party, under its leader Adolf Hitler, came to power in Germany and began to bring art under its control. All modern art was labelled degenerate and Expressionism was particularly singled out. In 1937, German museums were purged of modern art by the government, a total of some 15,550 works being removed. A selection of these was then put on show in Munich in an exhibition titled *Entartete Kunst*. This was carefully staged so as to encourage the public to mock the work. At the same time an exhibition was held of traditionally painted and sculpted work which extolled the Nazi party and Hitler's view of the virtues of German life: 'Kinder, Küche, Kirche' – roughly, 'family, home and church'. Ironically, this official Nazi art was a mirror image of the Socialist Realism of the hated Communists. Some of the degenerate art was sold at auction in Switzerland in 1939 and more was disposed of through private dealers. About five thousand items were secretly burned in Berlin later that year.

destruction The act of destroying or mutilating a work of art. During the English Reformation in the sixteenth century, attacks on artworks were carried out for religious reasons and this is known as iconoclasm. In the twentieth century the women's suffrage movement attacked paintings – slashing the <u>canvases</u> – for political purposes in order to effect change. These acts revealed to subsequent artists that destroying an art object does not necessarily eradicate it, but replaces it with something else, a concept which inspired a number of artists to use destruction as a creative force. In 1953 Robert Rauschenberg rubbed out an ink drawing by the abstract artist Willem de Kooning and exhibited it under the title *Erased de Kooning Drawing*. Jake and Dinos Chapman have courted controversy by adding their own cartoon characters to artworks by Francisco Goya and William Hogarth: *Insult to Injury* 2004 defaced a series of etchings by Goya, adding Mickey Mouse heads and grinning clowns. The act was condemned as vandalism, although the Chapmans responded by arguing that it was their attempt to eclipse an artist that obsessed them. (See also <u>Auto-Destructive art</u>)

diaspora A term used to describe movements in population from one country to another. Diaspora is often cited in discussions about identity. In his essay 'Cultural identity and Diaspora', 1990, the theorist Stuart Hall explained that the experience of the migrant – one of dislocation, displacement and hybridity – is seen as a <u>postmodern</u> condition. Through his investigations into identity based on the experiences of the Caribbean diaspora, he came to the conclusion that individuals have more than one identity, one that is based on commonalities and one that is based on an active process of identification. This has become a potent subject in art and can be related to movements in art like <u>relational aesthetics</u> and <u>Altermodern</u>.

Diez Pintores Concretos A radical group formed in Havana, Cuba in the late 1950s, Diez Pintores Concretos (Ten Concrete Painters) consisted of ten artists devoted to geometric <u>abstraction</u>. There is some debate as to whether their belief in abstraction was championed by the Cuban Revolution or at odds with it. Some argue that the artists associated with Diez Pintores Concretos were heralding a new art for a new Cuba, and there is plenty of evidence to support this including posters supporting the Revolution in their new abstract style. Others argue that the group were attacked during the Revolution for adopting a style that was foreign, superficial and dehumanising. Artists associated with the group were Pedro Álvarez, Wifredo Arrcay, Salvador Corratgé, Sandú Darié, Luis Martínez Pedro, Alberto Menocal, José Mijares, Pedro de Oraá, Loló Soldevilla and Rafael Soriano.

digital art The first use of the term digital art was in the early 1980s when computer engineers devised a paint program that was used by the pioneering digital artist Harold Cohen. This became known as AARON, a robotic machine designed to make large drawings on sheets of paper placed on the floor. Since this early foray into artificial intelligence, Cohen has continued to fine-tune the AARON program as technology becomes more sophisticated. Digital art can be computer-generated, scanned or drawn using a tablet and a mouse. In the 1990s, thanks to improvements in digital technology, it was possible to download video onto computers, allowing artists to manipulate the images they had filmed with a video camera. This gave artists a creative freedom never experienced before with film, allowing them to cut and paste within moving images to create visual collages. In recent times some digital art has become interactive, allowing the audience a certain amount of control over the final image.

digital C-print A digital C-print is the same as a C-print except that the process is digital. The picture is made from a printer that uses lasers or LEDs to expose an image from a digital file onto light-sensitive photographic paper. The picture is then developed in a processor using conventional, silver-based photographic chemicals. Just like C-prints, the materials used to create a digital C-print are complex compounds that continue to have chemical reactions after the process is completed making it difficult to protect the print from deterioration.

diptych A painting made up by two panels.

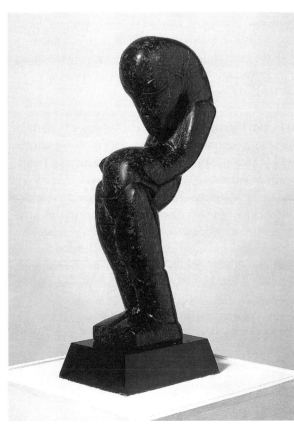

direct carving
Jacob Epstein
*Female Figure in
Flenite* 1913
Serpentine
45.7 × 9.5 × 12.1
Tate. Purchased 1972

direct carving A new approach to making carved sculpture
introduced by Constantin Brancusi from about 1906. Before that,
carved sculpture had always been based on a carefully worked out
preliminary model. Often it was then actually carved by craftsmen
employed by the artist: the marble sculptures of Auguste Rodin
were made in this way. In direct carving there is no model and the
final form evolves through the process of carving. An important
aspect of direct carving was the doctrine of truth to materials (see
also impasto). This meant that the artist consciously respected
the nature of the material, working to bring out its particular
properties and the beauty of colour and surface. Direct carvers
used a wide variety of types of marble, stone and wood. They kept
to simple forms that respected the original block or tree trunk.
Surfaces were kept uncluttered by detail in order to expose the
material itself and were often carefully polished to enhance the

colour and markings. The results were often highly abstract. In introducing this approach Brancusi brought about a revolution in the tradition of carved sculpture. After Brancusi, notable direct carvers were Jacob Epstein, Henri Gaudier-Brzeska, Barbara Hepworth and Henry Moore.

disability arts movement A movement that emerged in the mid-1970s following the groundswell of political activity among disabled people in the West during the previous decade. The disquiet over the prevalence of negative disablist imagery in popular culture and the arts among the disabled community prompted the development of a positive alternative, which is now known as the disability arts movement. In Britain, television programmes, theatre companies and arts organisations were set up and Shape was founded in 1977 to develop opportunities for disabled artists and enable deaf and disabled people access to the arts. Pioneers of the disability arts movement include the artists Mat Fraser, Colin Hambrook, Tony Heaton, Nikki Hewish, David King, Julie McNamara, Zoe Partington-Sollinger, Allan Sutherland, Joy Tudor and artist and academic Paul Darke.

divisionism see Neo-Impressionism

Documenta An exhibition of international contemporary art held in Kassel in Germany, originally every four years, and from 1972 every five years. It is perceived as one of the world's most important art exhibitions. Founded by the artist, teacher and curator Arnold Bode in 1955, the first Documenta featured, among others, Pablo Picasso, Barbara Hepworth, Ben Nicholson and Max Beckmann. It was created in order to herald a new era after the reactionary aesthetic values of the Nazi period. Sometimes called the Hundred Day Museum, it appoints a new director for every exhibition and the format is often re-invented.

documentary photography A style of photography that offers an insight into people, places and events, sometimes over many years. Until the mid-twentieth century, photography was a vital way of bearing witness to world events: from the shoot-from-the-hip photographs of the Spanish Civil War by Robert Capa to the considered <u>portraits</u> of poor farmers by Dorothea Lange. With the rise of television and digital technology there was less demand for published photography and it began to go into decline, but has since found a new audience in <u>photobooks</u>, art galleries and museums. Robert Frank's seminal book *The Americans*, which documented the photographer's journey across the USA, is an example of this. Documentary photography is at the centre of a debate surrounding the power of the photograph, based on claims of its objectivity. The choice of subject matter, the perspective from which the photograph was taken and the context in which it is shown or reproduced feed into this debate and raise questions about photographers' motivations and subjectivities.

doual'art A not-for-profit cultural laboratory in Douala, Cameroon founded in 1991 by the socio-economist Marilyn Douala-Bell and the art historian Didier Schaub. The organisation is community orientated, promotes a vision of art as a catalyst for social change and has a strong commitment to cultural development. In 1994 they opened the arts centre L'Espace doual'art that promotes ongoing dialogues between artists, local authorities and residents of the city. In 2007 doual'art founded the Salon Urbain de Douala, SUD, a <u>triennial</u> arts festival featuring a month long program of cultural activities across the city.

drawing Essentially, drawing is a technique in which images are depicted on a flat surface by making lines, though drawings can also contain <u>tonal</u> areas, washes and other non-linear marks. <u>Ink</u>, <u>pen</u>, pencil (see <u>graphite</u>), crayon, <u>charcoal</u> and <u>chalk</u> are the most commonly used materials, but drawings can be made with or in combination with paint and any other wet or dry <u>media</u>.

drypoint An <u>intaglio</u> process in which incised lines are drawn on a plate with a sharp, pointed needle-like instrument (not the <u>engraving</u> burin). Drypoint is usually done on copper plates as the softer metal lends itself to this technique. The process of incising creates a slightly raised ragged rough edge to the lines, known as the burr. Both the incised line and specifically the burr receive <u>ink</u> when the plate is wiped, giving the printed line a distinctive velvety look. Due to the delicate nature of the burr, drypoint is usually made in small editions, stopping before the burr is crushed by the pressure of the intaglio press. Drypoint is often combined with other etching techniques.

Dumb Type A Japanese multi-media Performance art collective founded in 1984 by students from Kyoto Art University. Called Dumb Type because they do not use language, the group became internationally recognised for their ambitious site-specific performances that combined video, music, lighting, digital technology and dance. Inspired by New York Performance artists Laurie Anderson and Robert Wilson – artists who sought to expand the borders of art through the use of technology – Dumb Type created performances that examined the effects of globalisation, technology and identity on Japanese society. Their most ambitious perhaps being *Pleasure Life*, a dystopian vision of a future Japanese society inspired by the pleasure gardens of the Japanese Heira period. One of the group's founders, Teiji Furuhashi, died of AIDS in 1995, and their work has since confronted the AIDS crisis and issues surrounding homosexuality in Japanese society. Artists associated with Dumb Type are Teiji Furuhashi, Toru Koyamada, Yukihiro Hozumi, Shiro Takatani, Takayuki Fujimoto and Hiromasa Tomari.

The Düsseldorf School of Photography A group of students at the Kunstakademie Düsseldorf in the mid 1970s who studied under the influential photographers Bernd and Hiller Becher, known for their rigorous devotion to the 1920s German tradition of Neue Sachlichkeit (New Objectivity). The Bechers' photographs were clear, black and white pictures of industrial archetypes (pitheads, water towers, coal bunkers). Andreas Gursky, Candida Höfer, Axel Hütte, Thomas Ruff and Thomas Struth modified the approach of their teachers by applying new technical possibilities and a personal and contemporary vision, while retaining the documentary method their tutors propounded.

dye destruction print (Cibachrome print, Ilfochrome print) A photographic printing process in which colour dyes embedded in the paper are selectively bleached away (destroyed) to form a full-colour image. The paper has at least three emulsion layers and each layer is sensitised to a primary additive colour of light. The layers contain a dye related to that colour. During exposure to a colour transparency, each layer records different information about the colour make-up of the image and in development the silver and unnecessary dyes are destroyed to form the image. Dye destruction prints are characterised by their vibrant colour and durability.

e

Earth art see Land art

Ecole de Dakar A term used to describe a period of intense creative activity in Senegal between 1960 and 1974. The president of Senegal, Leopold Senghor, established a lively, well supported cultural system, creating art schools, a national museum, cultural festivals and touring exhibitions in order to promote a distinctly modern African voice in the arts, free from colonial influences. This patronage resulted in the art school Ecole de Dakar where many of Senegal's radical artists taught, notably Iba N'Diaye, Papa Ibra Tall and Pierre Lods who sought to ally painting, sculpture and craft with the literary négritude movement. These artists promoted a particular African aesthetic that became known as Africanité. The school was instrumental in opening up a discourse on the arts in post-independent Senegal and on the role of the modern artist in the making of a new nation.

Ecole des beaux-arts French term meaning school of fine arts. The original Ecole des beaux-arts emerged from the teaching function of the French Académie Royale de Peinture et de Sculpture, established in Paris in 1648 (see academy). In 1816 the Académie Royale school moved to a separate building and in 1863 was renamed the Ecole des beaux-arts. The basis of the teaching was the art of ancient Greece and Rome, that is, classical art. Subsequently most major French cities established their own Ecole des beaux-arts. By the end of the nineteenth century the Ecole des beaux-arts had become deeply conservative and independent; rival schools sprang up in Paris, such as the Académie Julian and the Académie Colarossi. The Ecole remained the basic model for an art school until the foundation of the Bauhaus in 1919 (see also Black Mountain College). Most of the illustrious names in French art passed through the Ecole up to and including some of the young Impressionists.

edition A series of identical impressions from the same printing surface. Since the late nineteenth century the number of prints produced has usually been restricted and declared as a 'limited edition'; before this prints were often produced in as many numbers as the process would allow. Modern artists' prints are usually limited to a specified number. Sometimes the quantity is dictated by the process – the plate wears out – but more commonly it is restricted by the artist or publisher, in which case the printing surface is usually destroyed. Editioned prints are usually signed, numbered and often dated by the artist. An edition of twenty-five will be numbered 1/25, 2/25, etc. These are usually accompanied by a number of proof prints, identical to the edition; those produced for the artist are marked 'AP' (Artist's Proof), those for the printer or publisher are marked 'PP' (Printer's Proof). A number of working proofs may also be made. 'Bon à tirer' (good to print) proofs provide a standard to guide the printer.

educational turn A theme that emerged in the mid-1990s, educational turn refers to collaborative or research-based art where the impetus is on the process rather than an object-based artwork. Much of the focus is on finding new methodologies for creating art outside the existing traditional educational and institutional structures. Questions are raised about authorship, exhibition display, audience participation and collaboration. The idea was inspired by the radical organisations of the 1960s that aimed to revolutionise educational and museum practice, like Joseph Beuys's Free International University in Düsseldorf and the AntiUniversity in London, a short-lived experiment set up in 1968 promoting self-organised education and communal living. A contemporary example of educational turn is The Useful Art Association set up by the artist Tania Bruguera. It is a long-term project that aims to explore the idea of usefulness and promotes the idea of art as a process that should have real effect in society, as part of everyday life, not as a rarefied spectator experience.

electronic media The most common examples of electronic media are video recordings, audio recordings (see sound art), slide presentations, CD-ROM and online content (see browser art; net art; software art). The term also incorporates the equipment used to create these recordings or presentations; television, radio, telephone, computer. Much of the theory surrounding the use of electronic media by artists is based on Walter Benjamin's seminal essay of 1936, 'The Work of Art in the Age of Mechanical Reproduction', which discussed the democratisation of art, freed from its confines as a unique entity thanks to the development of photographic reproduction and forms such as cinema, where there is no unique original. (See also digital art)

embossed In printmaking this describes any process used to create a raised or depressed surface. It is sometimes used to create false plate-marks in lithographs or screenprints.

emotional architecture A style of modernist architecture conceived by the Mexican architect Luis Barragán and the sculptor and painter Mathias Goéritz. Frustrated by the cold functionalism of modernism, Barragán devised a style of modernist architecture that embraced space, colour and light, creating buildings that encouraged meditation and reflection. In 1954 Barragán and Goéritz published *The Emotional Architecture Manifesto* in which they argued that architecture needed to be spiritually uplifting. Luis Barragán's house on the outskirts of Mexico City is an example of emotional architecture.

emulation The process of recreating works of digital art to keep it alive. As technology becomes more sophisticated, the early video cameras, software programs and computers of the 1970s and 1980s are virtually obsolete. Conservators have had to emulate artworks made on outdated technology – such as an old Spectrum computer – in existing technology. This process has caused considerable debate about the nature of conservation in this context and about technological nostalgia in contemporary art.

engraving An intaglio technique in which a metal plate is manually incised with a burin, an engraving tool like a very fine chisel with a lozenge-shaped tip. The burin makes incisions into the metal at various angles and with varying pressure, which dictates the quantity of ink the line can hold – hence variations in width and darkness when printed. Photoengraving is a process using acid to etch a photographically produced image onto a metal plate that can then be printed from. (See also wood engraving)

entropy The inevitable and steady deterioration of a system or society. The concept is articulated by the Second Law of Thermodynamics (the tendency for all matter and energy in the

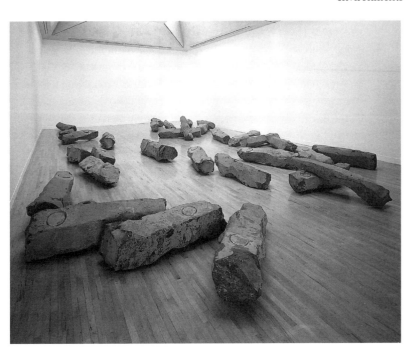

universe to evolve towards a state of inert uniformity). In an art context the term became popular in the late 1960s when the artist Robert Smithson used entropy in relation to Postmodernism, he also described the shattering of Marcel Duchamp's *The Large Glass* and the artist's attempt to put it back together again, as an attempt to overcome entropy.

environmental art From about the late 1960s the term environmental art became applied specifically to art – often, but not necessarily, in the form of installation – that addressed social and political issues relating to the natural and urban environment. One of the pioneers of this was the German artist Joseph Beuys and a notable recent practitioner is Lothar Baumgarten. (See also Land art)

environments see installations

environmental art

Joseph Beuys
The End of the Twentieth Century
1983–5
Basalt, clay and felt
90 × 700 × 1200
Tate. Purchased with assistance from Edwin C. Cohen and Echoing Green 1991

ephemeral art A type of art that lasts for a short amount of time. There are many forms of ephemeral art, from <u>sculpture</u> to <u>performance</u>, but it is usually used to describe a work of art that only occurs once, like a <u>happening</u>, and cannot be embodied in any lasting object to be shown in a museum or gallery. Ephemeral art first came to prominence in the 1960s with the <u>Fluxus</u> group, when artists like Joseph Beuys were interested in creating works of art that existed outside the gallery and museum structure and had no financial worth. Happenings, performances and <u>sound</u> sculptures were all part of ephemeral art, as were flyers and cheap, mass-produced items that carried subversive messages out into the world. Examples of ephemeral art include Richard Long's walks, Sarah Lucas's early mobiles and Joseph Beuys's Social Sculptures.

Estridentismo An <u>avant-garde</u> movement founded in Mexico City in 1921 by the poet Manuel Maples Arce. Estridentismo (or <u>Stridentism</u>) shared some of the characteristics of <u>Futurism</u> and <u>Dada</u>, in that the group celebrated technology and modernity and also attempted to transform everyday experiences through <u>performance</u>, pranks and absurdist events. The group emerged during the Mexican Revolution and the art they produced sought to reinvent and re-invigorate Mexican cultural life. The movement dispersed in 1928. Artists associated with Estridentismo include Fermín Revueltas, Ramón Alva de la Canal, Leopoldo Méndez, Jean Charlot and Germán Cueto.

etching An <u>intaglio</u> technique that uses chemical action to produce incised lines in a metal printing plate. The plate, traditionally copper but now usually zinc, is prepared with an acid-resistant ground. Lines are drawn through the ground, exposing the metal. The plate is then immersed in acid and the exposed metal is 'bitten', producing incised lines. Stronger acid and longer exposure produce more deeply bitten lines. The resist is removed and ink applied to the sunken lines, but wiped from the surface. The plate is then placed against paper and passed through an intaglio press with great pressure to transfer the ink from the recessed lines. Sometimes ink may be left on the plate surface to provide a background <u>tone</u>. Etching was used for decorating metal from the fourteenth century, but was probably not used for printmaking much before the early sixteenth century.

Since then many etching techniques have been developed, which are often used in conjunction with each other: soft-ground etching uses a non-drying resist or ground, to produce softer lines; spit bite involves painting or splashing acid onto the plate; open bite in which areas of the plate are exposed to acid with no resist; photo-etching (also called photogravure or heliogravure) is produced by coating the printing plate with a light-sensitive acid-resist ground and then exposing this to light to reproduce a photographic image. Foul biting results from accidental or unintentional erosion of the acid-resist.

ethnography see experimental ethnography; visual ethnography

Euston Road School British Modern Realist group formed in 1938 of artists all of whom either taught or studied at the School of Painting and Drawing at 316 Euston Road in London. They were in conscious reaction against avant-garde styles. Instead they asserted the importance of painting traditional subjects in a realist manner. This attitude was based on a political agenda to create a widely understandable and socially relevant art. Some of them were members of the Communist Party but their work was not propagandist in the manner of Socialist Realism. Artists were Graham Bell, William Coldstream, Lawrence Gowing, Rodrigo Moynihan, Victor Pasmore and Claude Rogers.

expanded cinema In the mid-1960s, the American filmmaker Stan Van Der Beek coined the term expanded cinema to describe an immersive environment that pushed the boundaries of cinema and film, rejecting the traditional one-way relationship between the audience and the screen. Through the use of multi-screen projections, performances and installations, artists created more participatory roles for the viewer. Many of these works were shown not in the cinema, but in art galleries, warehouses and out in the open air. *Light Music* 1975 by Lis Rhodes, comprised of two films projected into a misty room accompanied by an intense soundtrack created from the flickering patterns on the screen. Other proponents of expanded cinema are Carolee Schneeman, William Raban, Malcolm Le Grice, Annabel Nicolson, Gill Eatherley and, more recently, Mark Leckey. (See also moving image; video art)

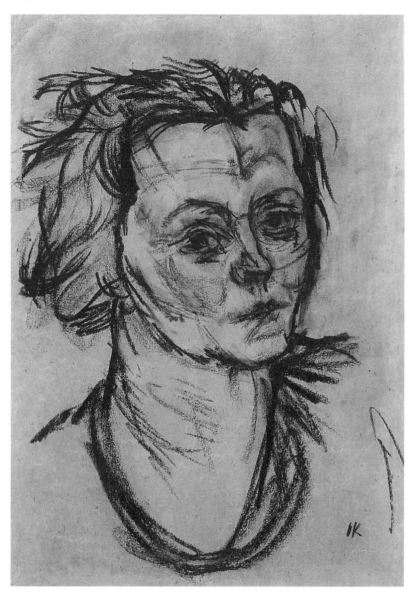

expressionism

Oskar Kokoschka
Dr Fannina W. Halle c.1910–12
Chalk on paper
45.1 × 30.5
Tate. Bequeathed by Dr Leopold
Rubinstein 1977

experimental ethnography A radical alternative to conventional
ethnographic film, experimental ethnography uses the techniques
of experimental filmmaking, like <u>montage</u>, <u>found</u> footage and
<u>Surrealism</u>, to create new ways of seeing the world around us. As
opposed to traditional ethnographic film, which tended to divide
the world into those 'out there' being watched by those 'in here',
experimental ethnography searches for new ways of representation
that reflect the complexities of the multicultural world in which
we live. Chantal Akerman's feature-film *D'Est* 1995 – a continuous
montage of images and sounds of everyday life in Germany, Poland
and Russia – privileged the personal over the national or the
political in reflecting a post-communist world.

Experiments in Art and Technology (E.A.T.) A <u>collective</u>
formed in 1967 in New York, with the engineers Billy Klüver and
Fred Waldhauer and the artists Robert Rauschenberg and Robert
Whitman, to promote collaboration between the arts and new
technology. During the group's existence, <u>performances</u> were
held that incorporated pioneering technology in <u>video</u> projection,
wireless sound transmission and Doppler sonar. Other artists
associated with the group include Deborah Hay, David Tudor,
Yvonne Rainer and Steve Paxton.

Expressionism Specifically, and with a capital letter, the term is
associated with modern German art, particularly the <u>Brücke</u> and
<u>Der Blaue Reiter</u> groups, but this is best referred to as German
Expressionism.

expressionism Expressionism as a general term, and with a lower
case 'e', refers to art in which the image of reality is distorted in
<u>form</u> and colour in order to make it expressive of the artist's inner
feelings or ideas about it. In expressionist art colour can be highly
intense and non-naturalistic, <u>brushwork</u> is typically free and paint
application tends to be generous and highly textured (see <u>impasto</u>).
Expressionist art tends to be emotional and sometimes mystical. It
can be seen as an extension of romanticism. In its modern form it
may be said to start with Vincent van Gogh and then form a major
stream of modern art embracing, among many others, Edvard
Munch, <u>Fauvism</u> and Henri Matisse, Georges Rouault, the <u>Brücke</u>

and <u>Der Blaue Reiter</u> groups, Egon Schiele, Oskar Kokoschka, Paul Klee, Max Beckmann, most of Pablo Picasso, Henry Moore, Graham Sutherland, Francis Bacon, Alberto Giacometti, Jean Dubuffet, Georg Baselitz, Anselm Kiefer and the New Expressionism of the 1980s. It went <u>abstract</u> with <u>Abstract Expressionism</u>.

f

fairy painting A fascination with fairies and the supernatural was a phenomenon of the Victorian age and resulted in a distinctive strand of art depicting fairy subjects drawn from myth and legend and particularly from Shakespeare's play *A Midsummer Night's Dream*. Richard Dadd created keynote paintings, but the most consistent and compelling artist in the genre is John Anster Fitzgerald. Other contributions came from many painters including Edwin Henry Landseer and J.M.W. Turner and illustrators such as Richard Doyle. There was a final flowering in the illustrated books of Arthur Rackham around 1900–14. The influence of fairy painting can be seen to continue in some aspects of Surrealism and Fantastic Realism.

fake A fake or forgery is a copy of a work of art, or a work of art in the style of a particular artist, that has been produced with the intention to deceive. The most infamous forger of the twentieth century was the Dutch painter Han Van Meegren who made a number of paintings purporting to be by Jan Vermeer. (See also replica)

Fantastic Realism Johann Muschik first used the term *Phantastischer Realismus* (Fantastic Realism) in the late 1950s to describe a group of painters working in Vienna who had met at the Akademie der Bildenden Künste after the Second World War. The group consisted of Arik Brauer, Ernst Fuchs, Rudolf Hausner, Wolfgang Hutter and Anton Lehmden and was inspired by their teacher Albert Paris Gütersloh, who painted pictures that combined the painterly precision of the old masters with an interest in modern art movements and psychoanalysis. The resulting images were dreamlike visions from the subconscious painted in a realistic manner. Much of the art was rooted in the traumatic experiences of the Second World War, from which the artists attempted to escape in their fantastic paintings.

Fauvism Name given to the painting of Henri Matisse, André Derain and their circle from 1905 to about 1910. They were called *les fauves* (the wild beasts) because of their use of strident colour and apparently wild brushwork. Their subjects were highly simplified so their work was also quite abstract. Fauvism can be seen as an extreme extension of the Post-Impressionism of Vincent van Gogh combined with the Neo-Impressionism of Georges Seurat. It can also be seen as a form of Expressionism. The name was coined by the critic Louis Vauxcelles when the work of *les fauves* was shown for the first time at the Salon d'automne in Paris in 1905. Other members of the group included Georges Braque, Raoul Dufy, Georges Rouault and Maurice de Vlaminck.

Federal Art Project Short for Works Progress Administration Federal Art Project, an American government programme to give work to unemployed artists during the Great Depression of the 1930s. It was one of a succession of art programmes set up under President Roosevelt's New Deal policy to combat the Depression. In 1933 he set up the Public Works of Art Project, which in five months employed 3,749 artists who produced 15,633 works of art for public institutions. Pictures were expected to be American scenes but otherwise artists were given complete freedom. From 1934 to 1943 the Treasury Section of Painting and Sculpture employed artists to create paintings, murals and sculpture for the embellishment of federal buildings. From 1935 to 1939 the Treasury also ran a parallel scheme, the Treasury Relief Art Fund. The Federal Art Project, administered by the Works Progress Administration (WPA), ran from 1935 to 1943 and within a year of the start was employing some 5,500 artists, teachers, designers, craftsmen, photographers and researchers. Some of the most important works that came out of these projects were murals in public buildings, inspired by the example of the Mexican Muralists. These programmes gave an enormous boost to art in America – not least by raising the morale of artists – and are now considered to have been a crucial factor in the explosion of creativity in American art following the Second World War (see Abstract Expressionism). (See also American Social Realist photography)

feminist art May be defined as art by women artists made consciously in the light of developments in feminist art theory since about 1970. In 1971 the art historian Linda Nochlin published a groundbreaking essay 'Why Have There Been No Great Women Artists?' In it she investigated the social and economic factors that had prevented talented women from achieving the same status as

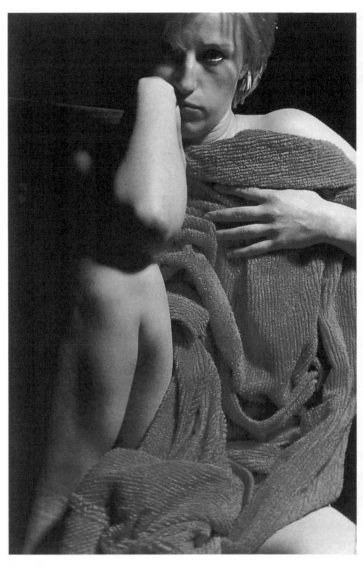

feminist art

Cindy Sherman
Untitled #97 1982
Colour photograph on paper
115 × 76
Tate. Purchased 1983

their male counterparts. By the 1980s art historians such as Griselda Pollock and Rozsika Parker were going further, to examine the language of art history with its gender-loaded terms such as 'old master' and 'masterpiece'. They questioned the central place of the female nude in the Western canon, asking why men and women are represented so differently. In his 1972 book *Ways of Seeing* the Marxist critic John Berger concluded 'Men look at women. Women watch themselves being looked at'. In other words Western art replicates the unequal relationships already embedded in society. Feminist art followed a similar trajectory. In what is sometimes known as First Wave Feminist art, women artists revelled in feminine experience, exploring vaginal imagery and menstrual blood, posing naked as goddess figures and defiantly using media such as embroidery that had been considered 'women's work'. One of the great iconic works of this phase of feminist art is Judy Chicago's *The Dinner Party* 1974–9. Later feminist artists rejected this approach and attempted to reveal the origins of our ideas of femininity and womanhood. They pursued the idea of femininity as a masquerade – a set of poses adopted by women to conform to social expectations of womanhood.

Festac (Second Festival of Black Arts and Culture)

An ambitious festival of arts, music, dance, literature and culture held in Lagos in 1977. This was the second Black and African Festival of Arts and Culture (see World Festival of Negro Arts in Dakar in 1966) and brought together artists from all over Africa and its diaspora. The participants used the event to devise a strategy of cultural empowerment; they wanted to protect black culture from being destroyed by other cultures and stop it from being seen only in the context of primitive museum artefacts. Today many see Festac as the turning point in the development of a black global consciousness. It enabled artists to talk about identity, discuss issues of cultural awakening and think about their collective survival, yet there was also criticism at the time, with some African nations refusing to take part due to the political situation in Nigeria, while the President of Senegal, Leopold Senghor, abdicated his position as co-patron of the festival.

figurative Since the arrival of <u>abstract art</u> the term figurative has been used to refer to any form of modern art that retains strong references to the real world and particularly to the human figure. In a general sense figurative also applies retrospectively to all art before abstract art. Modern figurative art can be seen as distinct from <u>modern realism</u> in that figurative art uses modern idioms, while modern realists work in styles predating <u>Post-Impressionism</u> (more or less). In fact, modern figurative art is more or less identical with the general current of <u>expressionism</u> that can be traced through the twentieth and twenty-first centuries. Pablo Picasso, after about 1920, is the great exemplar of modern figurative <u>painting</u>, and Alberto Giacometti, from about 1940, is the great exemplar of figurative <u>sculpture</u>. After the Second World War figuration can be tracked through the work of Francis Bacon, Lucian Freud and the other artists of the <u>School of London</u>, and through <u>Pop art</u>, <u>Neo-Expressionism</u> and <u>New Spirit painting</u>.

Filmaktion A loose-knit group of British filmmakers who worked and performed together in the early 1970s. Endorsing a more active, participatory experience of cinema, they re-imagined the possibilities for film projection as a live event. Because of their improvisational and participatory approach, the artists rejected conventional cinemas in favour of more immersive <u>environments</u>, screening their works in art venues and warehouses. Artists associated with Filmaktion include Gill Eatherley, Malcolm Le Grice, Annabel Nicolson and William Raban who were also active members of the influential London Filmmaker's Co-operative that ran between 1966 and 1999.

fin de siècle French phrase meaning end of century. As a historical term it applies specifically to the end of the nineteenth century and even more specifically to decade of the 1890s. It is an umbrella term embracing <u>symbolism</u>, <u>Decadence</u> and all related phenomena (for example <u>Art Nouveau</u>) that reached a peak in that decade. Almost synonymous with the terms the Eighteen-Nineties, the Mauve Decade, the Yellow Decade and the Naughty Nineties. Fin de siècle, however, expresses the apocalyptic sense of the end of a phase of civilisation. The spirit was exemplified in France by Henri de Toulouse-Lautrec, and in Britain by Aubrey Beardsley and Charles Conder. The real end came not in 1900 but with the First World War in 1914.

flâneur The nineteenth-century French poet Charles Baudelaire identified the *flâneur* (stroller) in his essay 'The Painter of Modern Life' (1863) as the dilettante observer of modern urban life, a character that features in many Impressionist paintings and was taken up in the twentieth century by the Situationists.

Fluxus An international avant-garde group or collective founded and given its name in 1960 by the Lithuanian-American artist George Maciunas (originally for an eponymous magazine featuring the work of a group of artists and composers centred around John Cage). In Latin the word means flowing; in English a flux is a flowing out. Maciunas wrote in a manifesto that the purpose of Fluxus was to 'promote a revolutionary flood and tide in art, promote living art, anti-art'. This has strong echoes of Dada with which Fluxus had much in common. The group coalesced on the continent, first in Germany where Maciunas worked for the US Army. Fluxus subsequently staged a series of festivals in Paris, Copenhagen, Amsterdam, London and New York at which activities included concerts of avant-garde music and performances often spilling out into the street. Almost every avant-garde artist of the time took part in Fluxus, such as Joseph Beuys, Dick Higgins, Alice Hutchins, Yoko Ono, Nam June Paik, Ben Vautier, Robert Watts, Emmett Williams, and the group played an important part in the opening up of definitions of what art can be, leading to the intense and fruitful pluralism seen in art since the 1960s (see Conceptual art; Performance art; Postmodernism; video art). Its heyday was the 1960s but its influence continues.

foreshortening The treatment of an object or human body in a picture seen in perspective from close to the viewpoint and at right angles to the picture surface. For example a body viewed from either the feet or the top of the head.

forgery see fake

form In relation to art the term form has two meanings. First it refers to the overall form taken by the work – its physical nature. Secondly, within an artwork form refers to the element of shape among the various elements that make up a work. Painting, for example, consists of the elements of line, colour, texture, space, scale and format as well as form. Sculpture consists almost exclusively of form. Until the emergence of modern art, when colour became its rival, form was the most important element in painting and was based above all on the human body. In treating or creating form in art, the artist aims to modify natural appearances in order to make a new form that is expressive and conveys some sensation or meaning in itself. In modern art the idea grew that form could be expressive even if largely or completely divorced from appearances. In 1914 the critic Clive Bell coined the term 'significant form' to describe this (see formalism). The idea played an important part in abstract art. (See also biomorphic)

formalism In general, the term formalism describes the critical position that the most important aspect of a work of art is its form, that is, the way it is made and its purely visual aspects, rather than its narrative, content or its relationship to the visible world. In painting, therefore, a formalist critic would focus exclusively on the qualities of colour, brushwork, form, line and composition. Formalism as a critical stance came into being in response to Impressionism and Post-Impressionism (especially the painting of Paul Cézanne) in which unprecedented emphasis was placed on the purely visual aspects of the work. In 1890 the Post-Impressionist painter and writer on art, Maurice Denis, published a manifesto titled *Definition of Neo-Traditionism*. The opening sentence of this is one of the most widely quoted texts in the history of modern art: 'Remember, that a picture, before it is a picture of a battle horse, a nude woman, or some story, is essentially a flat surface covered in colours arranged in a certain order.' Denis emphasised that aesthetic pleasure was to be found in the painting itself, not its subject. In Britain formalist art theory was developed by the Bloomsbury painter and critic Roger Fry and the Bloomsbury writer Clive Bell. In his 1914 book *Art*, Bell formulated the notion of 'significant form', that form itself can convey feeling. All this led quickly to abstract art, an art of pure form. Formalism dominated the development of modern art until the 1960s when it reached its peak in the so-called New Criticism of the American critic Clement Greenberg and others, particularly in their writings on Colour Field painting and Post-Painterly Abstraction. It was precisely at that time that formalism began to be challenged by Postmodernism.

format Traditionally used to describe the shape or proportions of the support, for example the <u>canvas</u>, of a painting or other essentially flat work of art such as a <u>relief</u>. The two commonest traditional formats for paintings are the horizontal rectangle often referred to as landscape format and the upright rectangle known as <u>portrait</u>. Another traditional but less common format is the circular one known as the <u>tondo</u>. Square formats have sometimes been used, notably for example by J.M.W. Turner and in the twentieth century Ad Reinhardt. The abstract painter Piet Mondrian occasionally used a square canvas hung by one corner as a diamond. From the 1960s on a much freer approach to format became evident in some of the work of artists such as Frank Stella and Ellsworth Kelly and the shape of the canvas became an important element in the composition of the work.

formlessness The French writer-philosopher Georges Bataille first introduced the concept of formlessness in 1929, when he wrote about 'l'informe' (formless) in the <u>Surrealist</u> journal *Documents* 1929–30. To Bataille, l'informe was about destroying categories and knocking art off its metaphorical pedestal so that it sat in the gutter. He rejected high-minded humanism, which he said elevated form to an idealised notion, and celebrated the debased. This concept was re-introduced by the cultural theorists Rosalind Krauss and Yves-Alain Bois in 1996, when they used Bataille's notion of l'informe in an exhibition at the Centre Pompidou in Paris called *Formless: A User's Guide*. They argued that artists throughout the twentieth century, from the <u>Abstract Expressionists</u> like Jackson Pollock, to <u>Postmodern</u> artists like Mike Kelly and Cindy Sherman, have used formlessness as a tool for creativity, not to elevate art, but to get it down and dirty. They gave the example of Jackson Pollock, who dripped paint onto a <u>canvas</u> that was laid out on the floor. The paint would get mixed up with the ash dropping from the artist's cigarette and other bits of detritus, all of which would end up in the final work of art.

found object A natural or man-made object (or fragment of an object) found (or sometimes bought) by an artist and kept because of some intrinsic interest the artist sees in it. Found objects may be put on a shelf and treated as works of art in themselves or provide inspiration for the artist. The sculptor Henry Moore collected bones and flints, which he seems to have treated as natural sculptures as well as sources for his

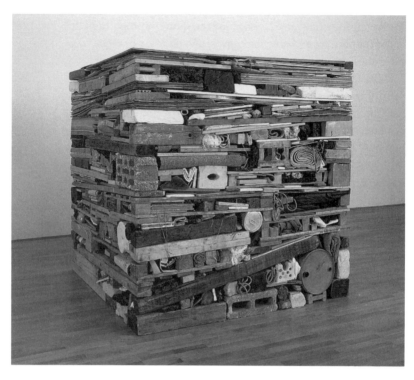

found object

Tony Cragg
Stack 1975
Wood, concrete,
brick, metal, plastic,
textile, cardboard
and paper
200 × 200 × 200
Tate. Purchased 1997

own work. Found objects may also be modified by the artist and presented as art, either more or less intact as in the Dada and Surrealist artist Marcel Duchamp's readymades, or as part of an assemblage. Pablo Picasso was an originator when, from 1912, he began to incorporate newspapers and such things as matchboxes into his Cubist collages, and to make his Cubist constructions from various scavenged materials. Extensive use of found objects was made by Dada, Surrealist and Pop artists, and by later artists such as Carl Andre, Tony Cragg, Bill Woodrow, Damien Hirst, Sarah Lucas and Michael Landy among many others.

frottage Surrealist automatist technique developed by Max Ernst in drawings made from 1925. Frottage is the French word for rubbing. Ernst was inspired by an ancient wooden floor where the grain of the planks had been accentuated by many years of scrubbing. The patterns of the graining suggested strange images to him. He captured these by laying sheets of paper on the floor and then rubbing over them with a soft pencil (see graphite). The results suggest mysterious forests peopled with bird-like creatures and Ernst published a collection of these drawings in 1926 titled *Histoire Naturelle* (Natural History). He went on to use a wide range of textured surfaces and quickly adapted the technique to oil painting, calling it grattage (scraping). In grattage the canvas is prepared with a layer or more of paint then laid over the textured object which is then scraped over. In Ernst's *Forest and Dove* the trees appear to have been created by scraping over the backbone of a fish.

fumage Invented by the Austrian Surrealist artist Wolfgang Paalen in the late 1930s, fumage is a technique in which an image is created by painting with smoke from a lighted candle into a ground of wet paint. The result is a hazy cloudy image suggestive of dreams and apparitions. *The Messenger*, created in 1941 by Paalen, depicts a ghostly form floating in deep space. Fumage was also inspired by the Surrealists' attempts to transform automatic writing into drawing and painting. Salvador Dalí appears to have used fumage in the painting *Autumnal Cannibalism* 1936.

Futurism An art movement launched by the Italian poet Filippo Tommaso Marinetti in 1909. On 20 February he published his *Manifesto of Futurism* on the front page of the Paris newspaper *Le Figaro*. Among modernist movements Futurism was exceptionally vehement in its denunciation of the past. This was because the weight of past culture in Italy was felt as particularly oppressive. In the manifesto, Marinetti asserted that 'we will free Italy from her innumerable museums which cover her like countless cemeteries'. What the Futurists proposed instead was an art that celebrated the modern world of industry and technology: 'We declare ... a new beauty, the beauty of speed. A racing motor car ... is more beautiful than the Victory of Samothrace' (a celebrated ancient Greek sculpture in the Musée du Louvre in Paris). Futurist painting used elements of Neo-Impressionism and Cubism to create compositions that expressed the idea of the dynamism, the energy and movement of modern life. Chief artists were Giacomo Balla, Umberto Boccioni and Gino Severini. Boccioni was a major sculptor as well as painter.

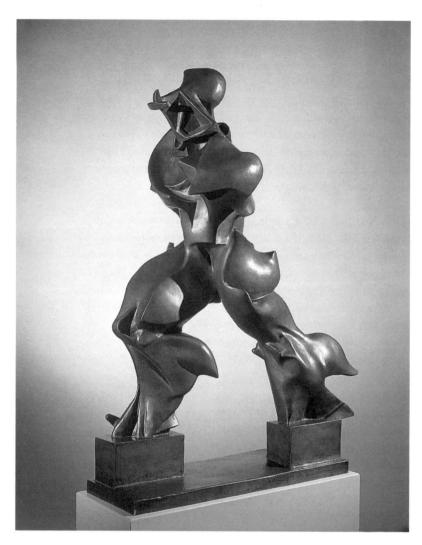

Futurism

Umberto Boccioni
Unique Forms of Continuity in Space
1913, cast 1972
Bronze
117.5 × 87.6 × 36.8
Tate. Purchased 1972

g

generative art Art made by a predetermined system that often included an element of chance. The practice has its roots in Dada, yet it was the pioneering artist Harold Cohen who was considered one of the first practitioners of generative art when he used computer-controlled robots to generate paintings in the late 1960s. More recently the Turner Prize winner Keith Tyson built *Artmachine*, a complex recursive system that generated detailed propositions for artworks for Tyson to make. Generative art is predominantly used in reference to a certain kind of art made on the net, particularly because artists devise programs that can be accessed and controlled by the public. Generative art is also associated with process art.

genres The genres, or types of painting, were codified in the seventeenth century by the French Royal Academy. In descending order of importance the genres were history, portrait, genre, landscape and still life. This league table, known as the hierarchy of the genres, was based on the notion of man the measure of all things – landscape and still life were the lowest because they did not involve human subject matter. History was highest because it dealt with the noblest events of human history and with religion.

Geometry of Fear Phrase coined by the British critic and poet Herbert Read in 1952. He used it in a review of the British Pavilion at the Venice Biennale of that year. The British contribution was an exhibition of the work of the group of young sculptors that had emerged immediately after the Second World War in the wake of the older Henry Moore. Their work, and that of Moore at that time, was characterised by spiky, alien-like or twisted, tortured, battered or blasted-looking human or animal figures. They were executed in pitted bronze or welded metal and vividly expressed a range of states of mind and emotions related to the anxieties and fears of the post-war period. The artists were Robert Adams, Kenneth Armitage, Reg Butler, Lynn Chadwick, Geoffrey Clarke, Bernard Meadows, Eduardo Paolozzi and William Turnbull. A sculpture by Moore was outside the Pavilion. In the Biennale catalogue Read wrote: 'These new images belong to the iconography of despair, or of defiance; and the more innocent the artist, the more effectively he transmits the collective guilt. Here are images of flight, or ragged claws "scuttling across the floors of silent seas", of excoriated flesh, frustrated sex, the geometry

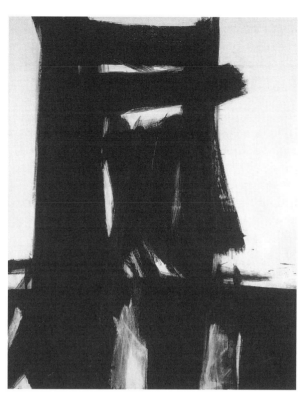

gestural
Franz Kline
Meryon 1960–1
Oil paint on canvas
235.9 × 195.6
Tate. Purchased 1967

of fear.' The quotation within Read's text is from the poet T.S. Eliot's 'Prufrock'. The use of the image of 'ragged claws "scuttling"' may have also referred to Meadows's *Black Crab* 1952.

gestural A term that originally came into use to describe the painting of the Abstract Expressionist artists Jackson Pollock, Willem de Kooning, Franz Kline, Robert Motherwell, Hans Hofmann and others. What they had in common was the application of paint in free sweeping gestures with the brush. In Pollock's case the brush might be a dried one, or a stick, dipped in the paint and trailed over the canvas. He also poured directly from the can. The idea was that the artist would physically act out his inner impulses and that something of his emotion or state of mind would be read by the viewer in the resulting paint marks. De Kooning wrote: 'I paint this way because I can keep putting more and more things into it – drama, anger, pain, love ... through your eyes it again becomes an emotion or an idea.' Such an approach to painting has its origins in <u>Expressionism</u> and <u>Automatism</u> (especially the painting of Joan Miró). In his 1970 history, *Abstract Expressionism*, Irving Sandler distinguished two branches of the movement, the 'Gesture painters' and the '<u>Colour Field painters</u>'. The term gestural has come to be applied to any painting done in this way.

Glasgow School Usually refers to the circle of artists and designers in Glasgow from the 1890s to about 1910. Most notable were the sisters, Frances and Margaret Macdonald, Herbert MacNair and Charles Rennie Mackintosh who were known as The Four. They made a distinctive and highly influential contribution to international <u>Art Nouveau</u> and are sometimes referred to as the Spook School. Another group, known as the Glasgow Boys, introduced forms of <u>Impressionism</u> to Scotland in the 1880s and 1890s, developing their own individual interpretations of it, often highly coloured. As well as <u>painting</u> in Glasgow and its environs they sought scenes of rural life and character in other parts of Scotland. Principal members of the group included Joseph Crawhall, Sir James Guthrie, George Henry, E.A. Hornel, Sir John Lavery and E.A. Walton.

globalisation Art has become increasingly internationalised through the internet and cheap air travel, and through the great international contemporary art exhibitions, such as <u>biennials</u>, and the commercial <u>art fairs</u>, such as Basel and Frieze. Artists are addressing the issues that surround this phenomenon and globalisation refers to both the unifying process that occurs when artists are exposed to the same influences and the art made in response to this. The beginnings of globalisation date back to the early twentieth-century <u>avant-gardist</u> notion of 'the primitive', when artists were influenced by artefacts brought back from Africa and the Far East and incorporated the imagery in their paintings (see <u>primitivism</u>). The term globalisation was first used in America as a way of defining the growing character of capitalism and in the 1990s an anti-globalisation movement was spawned in response to what people saw as the cultural and economic neo-imperialism of the globalising establishment.

gouache A term first used in France in the eighteenth century to describe a type of paint made from pigments bound in water-soluble gum, similar to <u>watercolour</u>. Larger percentages of binder are used than with watercolour and various amounts of inert pigments such as <u>chalk</u> are added to enhance the opacity. Gouache forms a thicker layer of paint on the <u>paper</u> surface and does not allow the paper to show through. It is often used to create highlights in watercolours. Today the term 'gouache' is often used loosely to describe any <u>drawing</u> made in body colour. Body colour is any type of opaque water-soluble pigment; used by artists from the late fifteenth century. Lead white was used until the introduction of zinc oxide, known as Chinese White, in the nineteenth century.

graffiti art Graffiti has its origins in 1970s New York, when young people began to use spray paint and other materials to create images on the sides of Subway trains. Such graffiti can range from bright graphic images (wildstyle) to the stylised monogram (tag). Graffiti as such is rarely seen in galleries and museums, yet its aesthetic has been incorporated into artists' work. Jean-Michel Basquiat and Keith Haring were both New York graffiti artists who enjoyed considerable commercial success in the 1980s. Their gallery-exhibited work incorporated graffiti styles and they were pioneers of <u>street art</u>. More recently, graffiti and street artists such as Barry McGee and Banksy have been seen exhibited in commercial spaces.

graphite A crystalline form of carbon useful as a writing and <u>drawing</u> tool, as only the slightest pressure is needed to leave a mark. However, as graphite is soft and brittle it requires some form of protective casing. The exact date and origin of the first graphite pencil is unknown but it is thought that the first graphite sticks encased in wood appeared around 1565, shortly after the discovery of natural graphite in Cumberland in Britain. Graphite also occurs naturally in Siberia, Bavaria in Germany, and in the USA. It can, however, be made artificially by heating cokes at high temperatures, known as the Asheson process. It has a greasy texture and is dull metallic grey in colour. Graphite is a stable and permanent material but can easily be removed using an eraser. Today graphite is referred to as 'pencil' or occasionally 'lead pencil'. This name came about because prior to the discovery of graphite, lead had been used since ancient times as a writing tool. Graphite was thought to be a form of lead until 1779, when K.W. Scheele, a Swedish chemist, discovered that the so-called lead used in pencils, was in fact a mineral form of carbon. It was named 'graphite' from the Greek word for writing. The term pencil derives from the Latin word 'penicillus.'

grattage see <u>frottage</u>

Group 1890 Named after the number of the house in which the artists first met, Group 1890 was a short-lived movement founded in Bhavnagar, India, in 1962. The 11 artists associated with the group sought to create a modern Indian art aesthetic in the wake of Indian independence. Many of the members were Communist sympathisers who supported the Communist Party in India and incorporated their left-leaning ideas into their manifesto. Published to coincide with their only exhibition *Surrounded by Infinity* in 1963, the manifesto set out their desire for an indigenous modern Indian art. Taking inspiration from the Pahari School of painting, a North Indian aesthetic dating back to the seventeenth century, rather than the Mughal miniatures that were a blend of Persian and Indian ideas, Group 1890 created <u>paintings</u> that embraced colour, Indian folk art and mysticism. The 11 members of the group were Jyoti Bhatt, Eric Bowen, Raghav Kaneria, Ambadas Khobragade, Rajesh Mehra, Reddappa Naidu, Jeram Patel, Nagji Patel, Himmat Shah, Ghulam Mohammed Sheikh and Jagdish Swaminathan.

Group f.64 A group of 11 <u>photographers</u> united by their desire to photograph life as it really is. Group f.64 was founded on 15 November 1932 during their exhibition at the M.H. de Young Memorial Museum in San Francisco. Their images were characterised by a clear, sharp-focus aesthetic, which was at odds with the <u>Pictorialist</u> methods in fashion at the time. The name f.64 refers to the smallest aperture on a camera, used by the group because it provided the greatest depth of field, allowing for much of the photograph to be in sharp focus. Perhaps the overarching vision of the group was their belief in the camera as a passive observer of the world, better able to depict life as it really was because it didn't project personal prejudices. The 11 members of Group f.64 were Ansel Adams, Imogen Cunningham, John Paul Edwards, Preston Holder, Consuelo Kanaga, Alma Lavenson, Sonya Noskowiak, Henry Swift, Willard Van Dyke, Brett Weston and Edward Weston.

Group of Ten see <u>Diez Pintores Concretos</u>

Group Zero see <u>Zero</u>

Grupo Frente A Brazilian <u>Concrete art</u> movement founded by the artist and teacher Ivan Serpa in Rio de Janeiro in 1954. Many of the artists associated with Grupo Frente were former pupils of Serpa at the Museum of Modern Art of Rio de Janeiro. Although the group were associated with Concrete art, they were not characterised by any single stylistic position, rather they were united in their rejection of <u>modernist</u> Brazilian painting that tended to be <u>figurative</u> and nationalistic in character. Some of the artists associated with the group, including Lygia Clark and Lygia Pape, went on to form the hugely influential <u>Neo-Concrete</u> movement in 1958. Artists associated with Grupo Frente include Aluísio Carvão, Carlos Val, Décio Vieira, João José da Silva Costa, Lygia Clark, Lygia Pape and Vicent Ibberson.

Grupo Ruptura In 1952 an exhibition called Ruptura was held at the São Paulo Museum of Modern Art marking the beginning of the <u>Concrete art</u> movement in Brazil. The exhibition had been organised by seven artists who became the Grupo Ruptura after publishing the *Ruptura Manifesto*. As the name suggests, their desire was to break with the old, which in this case referred to a form of <u>naturalist</u> painting that was prevalent in Brazil at the time. Grupo Ruptura wanted a new art for a new country, one that promoted truth and rationality, and they believed this could be done through geometric <u>abstraction</u>. The seven founding members of the group were Anatol Władysław, Leopoldo Haar, Lothar Charoux, Kazmer Féjer, Geraldo de Barros, Luiz Sacilotto and Waldemar Cordeiro. The group were later joined by Hermelindo Fiaminghi, Judith Lauand and Maurício Nogueira Lima.

Gruppo Origine Italian group (origin group) founded in Rome in 1951 by Alberto Burri, Ettore Colla, Giuseppe Capogrossi and Mario Ballocco. Critical of what they saw as the increasingly decorative quality of <u>abstract art</u> at the time, they opposed a 'troubled' consciousness of the world to the progressivist utopia of the Fronte Nuovo delle Arti neo-cubists and of the <u>formalist</u> abstraction of the

Movimento Arte Concreta and Forma I groups. In their founding manifesto they called for a return to fundamentals: 'The Gruppo Origine intends to become the most morally valid point of reference of "non-figurative" expressive needs ... By openly renouncing three-dimensional forms, by reducing colour to its simplest, peremptory and incisive expressive function, by evoking ... pure and elemental images, the Group's artists express the necessity of a rigorous, coherent, energetic vision [which is] primarily antidecorative.' They held a group exhibition in Rome at the Galleria Origine in 1951 and disbanded the same year.

Guerrilla Girls A group of anonymous American female artists who, since their formation in New York in the mid-1980s, have sought to expose sexual and racial discrimination in the art world and the wider cultural arena. The group's members protect their identities by wearing gorilla masks in public and by assuming pseudonyms taken from deceased female figures.

Gugulective A contemporary art collective founded in 2006 in Gugulethu, a township near Cape Town, South Africa. Many of the members grew up in Gugulethu, an area that was originally established to accommodate the migrant workers of Cape Town. The group consists of musicians, artists, writers, DJs, rappers and poets who believe in art as an instrument for social change. Gugulective collaborate with local communities to empower them through art. Current members include ZiphozeNkosi Dayile, Ayanda Kilimane, Athi Mongezeleli Joja, Khanyisile Mbongwa, Dathini Mzayiya and Kemang Wa Lehulere. The multi-media artist and co-founder of Gugulective, Unathi Sigenu died in 2013.

Gutai Japanese avant-garde group. Gutai Bijutsu Kyokai (Gutai Art Association) was formed in 1954 in Osaka by Yoshihara Jiro, Kanayma Akira, Murakami Saburo, Shiraga Kazuo and Shimamoto Shozo. The word has been translated into English as 'embodiment' or 'concrete'. Yoshihara was an older artist around whom the group coalesced and who financed it. In their early public exhibitions in 1955 and 1956 Gutai artists created a series of striking works anticipating later happenings and Performance art and Conceptual art. Shiraga's *Challenge to the Mud* 1955, in which the artist rolled

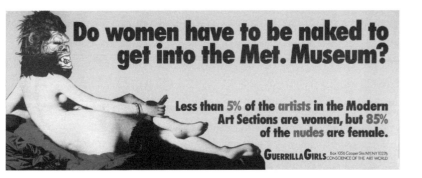

Do women have to be naked to get into the Met. Museum?

Less than 5% of the artists in the Modern Art Sections are women, but 85% of the nudes are female.

GUERRILLA GIRLS CONSCIENCE OF THE ART WORLD Box 1056 Cooper Sta. NY, NY 10276

half-naked in a pile of mud, remains the most celebrated event associated with the group. Also in 1955 Murakami created his reportedly stunning performance *Laceration of Paper*, in which he ran through a paper screen. At the second Gutai show in 1956, Shiraga used his feet to paint a large canvas sprawled across the floor. From about 1950 Shimamoto had been making paintings from layers of newspaper pasted together, painted and then pierced with holes, anticipating the pierced work of Lucio Fontana. In 1954 Murakami had made a series of paintings by throwing a ball soaked in ink at paper. In 1956 Shimamoto went on to make works called *Throws of Colour* by smashing glass jars filled with pigment onto canvases laid out on the floor. The group dissolved in 1972 following the death of Yoshihara. There was a retrospective exhibition of their work at the Jeu de Paume in Paris in 1999.

Guerrilla Girls

Guerrilla Girls
Do Women Have To Be Naked To Get Into the Met. Museum?
from *Guerrilla Girls Talk Back* 1989
Screenprint on paper
28 × 71
Tate. Purchased 2003

h

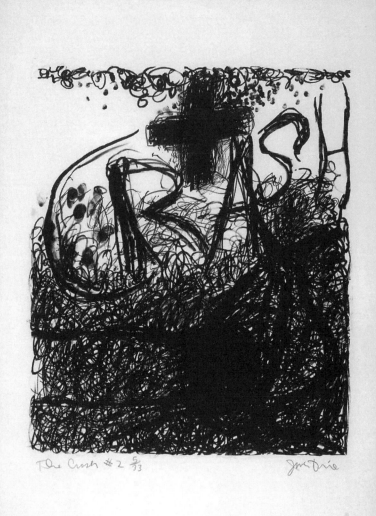

happening

Jim Dine
The Crash #2 1960
Lithograph on paper
53.5 × 44
Tate. Purchased 1990

happening A theatrical event created by artists, initially in America, in the late 1950s and early 1960s. Happenings were the forerunners of Performance art and in turn emerged from the theatrical elements of Dada and Surrealism. The name was first used by the American artist Allan Kaprow in the title of his 1959 work *18 Happenings in 6 Parts* which took place on six days, 4–10 October 1959, at the Reuben Gallery, New York. Happenings typically took place in an environment or installation created within the gallery and involved light, sound, slide projections and an element of spectator participation. Other notable creators of happenings were Claes Oldenburg, Jim Dine, Red Grooms and Robert Whitman. Happenings proliferated through the 1960s but gave way to Performance art in which the focus was increasingly on the actions of the artist. A detailed account of early happenings can be found in Michael Kirby's 1965 book, *Happenings*. Jim Dine's 1960 suite of prints *The Crash* relates to the drawings that were props for his 1960 happening, *The Car Crash*.

haptic Derived from the Greek word (*haptesthai*) meaning 'touch' or 'contact', haptic relates to the way in which humans interact by touch with the world around them. Artists use haptic technology to give the sensation of a physical presence to a virtual object. This can be manifested in several ways: via vibrations in sound installations or using computer software that has input devices that offer touch feedback. An example of this is a computer program that enables the user to paint a picture using virtual 3D brushes.

Hard Edge painting This can be seen as a subdivision of Post-Painterly Abstraction, which in turn emerged from Colour Field painting. The term was coined by the Californian critic Jules Langster in 1959 to describe those abstract painters, particularly on the West Coast, who in their reaction to the more painterly or gestural forms of Abstract Expressionism adopted a particularly impersonal paint application and delineated areas of colour with particular sharpness and clarity. This kind of approach to abstract painting became extremely widespread in the 1960s.

Harlem Renaissance Sometimes known as the New Negro Movement, the Harlem Renaissance was the flowering of black art, literature and music in the USA and in particular Harlem, New York, in the 1920s. Its predominant idea was that through the production of art, literature and music the 'New Negro' could challenge the pervading racism and stereotyping of the white community and therefore promote racial integration. Artists associated with the movement include Aaron Douglas and Lois Mailon Jones.

Heidelberg School Late nineteenth-century art movement named after the village of Heidelberg in Australia where a small group of artists would go to paint en plein air. Sometimes described as Australian Impressionism, the Heidelberg School developed an informal, evocative and naturalistic style that evoked the colours and flora of the Australian landscape. One of the leading exponents of the Heidelberg School was Tom Roberts, an artist who had studied in Europe before returning to Australia in 1885, bringing with him the new innovations in Impressionism. Other artists associated with the Heidelberg School include Arthur Streeton, Frederick McCubbin, Charles Conder and Arthur Loureiro. The group soon became synonymous with a national style of painting in Australia.

Hi-Red Centre A short-lived radical art collective that emerged in postwar Japan and was active between 1963 and 1964. Founded in Tokyo by the artists Genpei Akasegawa, Natsuyuki Nakanishi and Jiro Takamatsu, Hi-Red Centre created happenings and events that were socially reflective, anti-establishment and anti-commercial. Inspired by Japan's Neo-Dada movement and Fluxus, the group used the urban environment as their canvas, creating interventions that raised questions about centralised authority and the role of the individual in society. One of their most famous performances consisted of an ironic action in which the artists scrubbed the streets of Tokyo during the 1964 Tokyo Olympic Games, in response to the government's demands that the city should present a clean image to the world. The group disbanded in 1964.

Hudson River School The collective name given for a number of North American landscape painters active between the 1820s and 1870s who depicted scenes of natural beauty in areas that

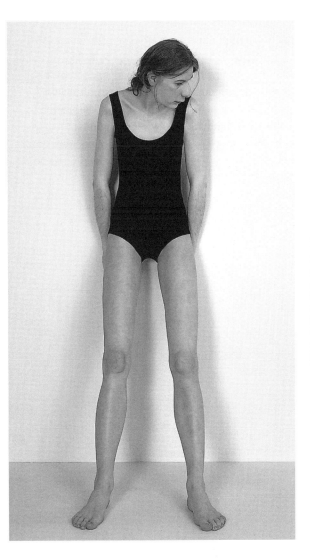

Hyper-Realism

Ron Mueck
Ghost 1998
Aluminium,
fibreglass, silicone
rubber, polyurethane
foam, polyester
resin, acrylic fibre
and fabric
201.9 × 64.8 × 99.1
Tate. Purchased 1998

included the Hudson River Valley and the Catskill Mountains. Prominent artists associated with the school include Thomas Cole and Frederic Edwin Church. (See also luminism)

Hyper-Realism Term that appeared in the early 1970s to describe a resurgence of particularly high-fidelity realism in sculpture and painting at that time. Also called Super-Realism, and in painting is synonymous with photorealism. In sculpture the outstanding practitioner was Duane Hanson, together with John de Andrea. More recently the work of Ron Mueck and some of that of Robert Gober could be seen as Hyper-Realist. Leading painters were Chuck Close, Robert Bechtle, Richard Estes, Audrey Flack and Ralph Goings.

i

iconography The iconography of a <u>painting</u> is the imagery in it. The term comes from the Greek word *ikon*, meaning image. An icon was originally a picture of Christ on a <u>panel,</u> used as an object of devotion in the orthodox Greek Church from at least the seventh century onwards. Hence the term icon has come to be attached to any object or image that is outstanding or has a special meaning attached to it. An iconography is a particular range or system of types of image used by an artist or artists to convey particular meanings. For example, in Christian religious painting there is an iconography of images such as the lamb which represents Christ, or the dove which represents the Holy Spirit. In the iconography of classical myth, however, the presence of a dove would suggest that any woman also present would be the goddess Aphrodite or Venus, so the meanings of particular images can depend on context. In the eighteenth century William Blake invented a complex personal iconography to illustrate his vision of man and God, and much scholarship has been devoted to interpreting it. In the twentieth century the iconography of Pablo Picasso's work is mostly autobiographical, while Joseph Beuys developed an iconography of substances such as felt, fat and honey to express his ideas about life and society. Iconography (or iconology) is also the academic discipline of the study of images in art and their meanings.

identity politics A political and cultural movement that gained prominence in America and Europe in the mid-1980s. It was anti-authoritarian and asked questions about identity, repression, inequality and injustice and often focused on the experiences of certain marginalised groups, like the LGBT community. The artist Lorna Simpson used the image of a black woman in her work to highlight issues surrounding racial stereotyping, gender and identity. Identity politics emerged out of the 1960s Black Civil Rights Movement, second wave feminism and gay and lesbian liberation. It was confrontational and asked questions about the kind of art that should be made, and for whom, in a post-colonial world where the history of art was being re-written to encompass a broader, less Western-dominated perspective. (See also <u>decolonisation</u>; <u>otherness</u>; <u>queer aesthetics</u>)

illusionism In Baroque art, illusionism refers particularly to decorative schemes in buildings, especially ceiling <u>paintings</u>, in which the artist uses <u>perspective</u> and <u>foreshortening</u> to create, for example, the illusion that the ceiling is open sky populated by groups of figures such as saints or angels. Such effects are also sometimes referred to as *trompe l'oeil*, a French phrase meaning 'deceives the eye'. More generally illusionism can refer to any painting that strives to achieve a high degree of mimesis, meaning imitation of reality. In modern art theory illusionism has been frowned upon on the grounds that it denies the basic truth of the flatness of the canvas. However, <u>Surrealist</u> artists such as Salvador Dalí and René Magritte have used it to great effect to evoke the alternative world of the unconscious mind.

impasto An area of thick paint or texture in a <u>painting</u>. The use of impasto became more or less compulsory in modern art as the view took hold that the surface of a painting should have its own reality rather than just being a smooth window into an <u>illusionistic</u> world beyond. With this went the idea that the texture of paint and the <u>brushwork</u> could themselves help to convey feeling, that they are a kind of handwriting, that they can directly express the artist's emotions or response to the subject (see also <u>gestural</u>). A painting in which impasto is a prominent feature can also be said to be painterly. This term carries the implication that the artist is revelling in the manipulation of the <u>oil paint</u> itself and making the fullest use of its sensuous properties. The idea that the artist should foreground the innate qualities of the materials of the work as part of its content is a central one in modern art, and is summarised in the phrase 'truth to materials'. (See also <u>direct carving</u>)

Impressionism A new way of painting <u>landscape</u> and scenes of everyday life, developed in France by Claude Monet and others from the early 1860s. Based on the practice of painting finished pictures out of doors, as opposed to simply making sketches (and actually practised in Britain by John Constable around 1813–17), the result was greater awareness of light and colour and the shifting pattern of the natural scene. <u>Brushwork</u> became rapid and broken into separate dabs to render these effects. The first group exhibition in Paris in 1874 was greeted with derision, Monet's *Impression, Sunrise*

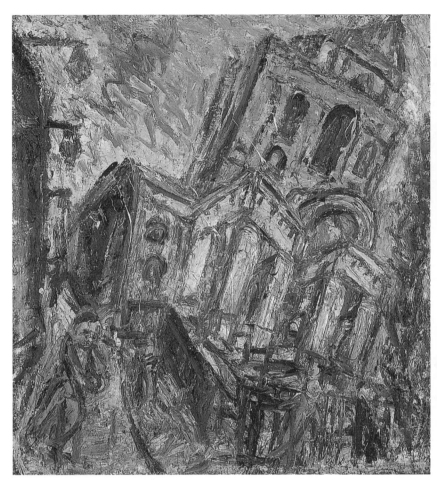

impasto

Leon Kossoff
*Christ Church,
Spitalfields,
Morning* 1990
Oil paint on board
198.6 × 189.2
Tate. Purchased 1994

being particularly singled out and giving its name to the movement. Seven further exhibitions were held at intervals up until 1886. Other core artists were Camille Pissarro, Auguste Renoir, plus Edgar Degas and Édouard Manet in a slightly tangential relationship. A second generation manifested itself in <u>Post-Impressionism</u>.

improvisation In art, improvisation refers to the act of creating a work of art without pre-planning. In the early twentieth century it was seen as a radical break away from the art establishment. Early <u>Dada</u> and <u>Futurist</u> impromptu performances were a way of re-imaging what art could be. The Surrealists also embraced improvisation, seeing it as a way to work directly from their unconscious. Their automatic drawings can be seen as a form of improvisation, and later inspired the Abstract Expressionist artist Jackson Pollock to drip paint onto a canvas tacked on the floor. He was called an action painter because he embraced improvisation and spontaneity as a style. Improvisation is also an aspect of Performance art, and was developed through the choreographical experiments of the Judson Dance Theatre in New York in the 1960s in which performances and happenings were devised through chance and improvisation. It was also embraced by the Fluxus group and continues to be used today in the performances of artists like Marvin Gaye Chetwynd.

Independent Group A radical group of young artists within the Institute of Contemporary Arts (ICA) in London. The Independent Group, or IG, was first convened in the winter of 1952–3 and then again in 1953–4. It was responsible for the formulation, discussion and dissemination of many of the basic ideas of British Pop art and of much other new British art in the late 1950s and early 1960s. Leading artists involved were Richard Hamilton, Nigel Henderson, John McHale, Eduardo Paolozzi and William Turnbull. The IG also included the critics Lawrence Alloway and Rayner Banham, and the architects Colin St John Wilson, and Alison and Peter Smithson (see Brutalism). In 1953 the IG staged the exhibition *Parallel of Art and Life* and in 1956 the ground-breaking *This is Tomorrow*. This exhibition at the Whitechapel Gallery in London was an expression of the IG's pioneering interest in popular and commercial culture and consisted of a series of installations, and a jukebox that played continuously.

indigenism There are several meanings relating to the word indigenism, but in the context of visual art the term refers to a movement that originated in Latin America during the 1920s. Artists associated with indigenism fought against the hegemony of European art in favour of making art about their own culture, which embraced pre-Colombian art. In Mexico during the Revolution, the Mexican Muralists Diego Rivera, José Clemente Orozco, David Alfaro Siqueiros and Rufino Tamayo embraced indigenism; they were committed to promoting Mexican culture and their murals depicted their country's history and its people. Art associated with indigenism is nearly always <u>figurative</u>, with subjects that focus on the country's cultural heritage and traditions as well as their spiritual beliefs. (See also <u>decolonisation</u>)

industrial design The design of mass-produced, machine-made goods. The word was first used in America in the 1920s to describe the work of specialist designers who worked on product design. Earlier, Henry Ford's introduction in 1913 of the production line to the motor car industry, and subsequently to the production of other merchandise, led to a move in the art world to attempt to weld art and technology together. <u>Constructivism</u> in Russia and the <u>Bauhaus</u> in Germany were inspired by the new machine age; putting emphasis on <u>form</u> following function they created design that had an <u>abstract</u>, geometric form.

ink An ancient <u>drawing</u> and writing <u>medium</u>, ink is still most commonly made of carbon and binders, but historically was also made from plant or animal sources such as iron gall and sepia. Inks are traditionally black or brown in colour, but can also contain coloured dyes or pigments. They are traditionally used with sable brushes or varieties of quill, reed or pen.

installation Also described as environments, the term is used to describe <u>mixed media</u> constructions or <u>assemblages</u> usually designed for a specific place and for a temporary period of time. Works often occupy an entire room or gallery space that the spectator invariably has to walk through in order to engage fully with the work of art. Some installations, however, are designed simply to be walked around and contemplated, or are so fragile that they can only be viewed from a doorway, or one end of a room. One of the originators of environments was the American artist Allan Kaprow in works made from about 1957 onwards. From that time on the creation of installations became a major strand in modern art, increasingly from about 1990, and many artists have made them. In 1961 in New York, Claes Oldenburg created an early environment, *The Store*, from which his *Counter and Plates with Potato and Ham* comes. One of the outstanding creators of installations using light is James Turrell. Miscellaneous materials (mixed media), light and <u>sound</u> have remained fundamental to Installation art.

institutional critique The act of critiquing an institution as artistic practice, the institution usually being a museum or an art gallery. Institutional criticism began in the late 1960s when artists began to create art in response to the institutions that bought and exhibited their work. In the 1960s the art institution was often perceived as a place of 'cultural confinement' and thus something to attack aesthetically, politically and theoretically. Hans Haacke is a leading exponent of institutional critique, particularly targeting funding and donations given to museums and galleries. In 1971, the Wallraf-Richartz Museum, Cologne rejected his work *Manet-Projekt 74* from one of their shows. The work was related to the museum's recent acquisition of Édouard Manet's *Bunch of Asparagus* and detailed the provenance of the painting and Nazi background of the donor. During the 1990s it became a fashion for critical discussions to be held by curators and directors within art galleries and museums that centred on this very subject, thereby making the institution not only the problem but also the solution. This has changed the nature of institutional critique, something that is reflected in the art of Carey Young, who considers this dilemma. (See also Guerrilla Girls)

intaglio Any form of printmaking in which the image is produced by incising into the printing plate and where it is the incised line or area that holds the ink. Intaglio methods include etching, drypoint, engraving and wood engraving.

interactive art A term used to describe art that relies on the participation of a spectator. Interactive art emerged in the late 1950s in parallel with artists' desires to find less alienating and exclusive environments in which to show art. As the street, the warehouse or the shop front became their choice of venue, the art also became more participatory and inclusive. Artists designed sculptures that could be touched and played with. Niki de Saint-Phalle built the monumental walk-in sculpture *Golem*, which incorporates a children's slide, in Rabinovich Park, Jerusalem. In 1971 Gordon Matta-Clark cooked a pig under Brooklyn Bridge and served 500 pork sandwiches as part of the performance. Interactive art is also computer based, with the participant responding to the technology set up by the artist like the public artworks of Rafael Lozano-Hemmer. Interactive art is also associated with relational aesthetics.

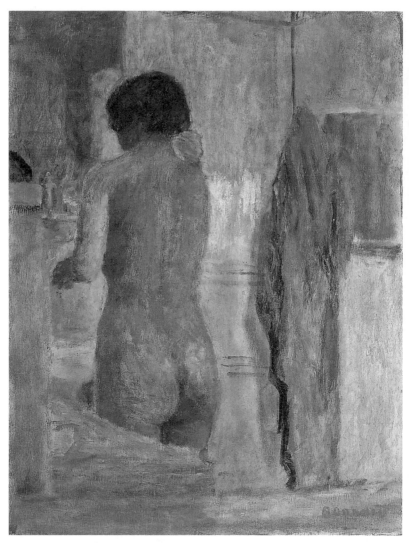

intimism

Pierre Bonnard
Bathing Woman, Seen from the Back
c.1919
Oil paint on canvas
44.1 × 34.6
Tate. Bequeathed by the
Hon. Mrs A.E. Pleydell-Bouverie through
the Friends of the Tate Gallery 1968

International Style In 1932 The Museum of Modern Art in New York held the first architectural exhibition featuring architects associated with the Modern Movement. International Style was the term coined by historian Henry-Russell Hitchcock and architect Philip Johnson for the catalogue. Most of the architects defined by International Style were European with a considerable German brigade emerging from the Bauhaus, namely Walter Gropius, Marcel Breuer, Ernst May, Erich Mendelsohn, Mies van der Rohe and Hans Scharoun; other Europeans included France's Le Corbusier, Italy's Luigi Figini and Finland's Alvar Aalto. The majority of the buildings defined by International Style were similar in that they were rectilinear, undecorated, asymmetrical and white, although after the Second World War this was modified as a matter of economy in dealing with postwar reconstruction and, later, with the introduction of industrial steel and glass. International Style is seen as single-handedly transforming the skylines of every major city in the world with its simple cubic forms.

internet art see net art

intervention art see art intervention

intimism Originally a French term (*intimisme*) applied to the quiet domestic scenes of Pierre Bonnard and Edouard Vuillard in the early twentieth century. Since then it has been applied widely to any painting of such subject matter. An outstanding example is the work of Gwen John.

Inventionist Manifesto see Manifesto invencionista

japonisme Said to have been coined by the French critic Philippe Burty in the early 1870s. It described the craze for Japanese art and design that swept France and elsewhere after trade with Japan resumed in the 1850s, the country having been closed to the West since about 1600. The rediscovery of Japanese art and design had an almost incalculable effect on Western art. The development of modern <u>painting</u> from <u>Impressionism</u> onwards was profoundly affected by the flatness, brilliant colour and high degree of stylisation, combined with the <u>realist</u> subject matter, of Japanese <u>woodcut</u> <u>prints</u>. Design was similarly affected in the <u>Aesthetic Movement</u> and <u>Art Nouveau</u>.

Jikken Kobo Founded in Tokyo in 1951, against the backdrop of the Hiroshima and Nagasaki bombs and in a time of post-war austerity, Jikken Kobo (Experimental Workshop) was an interdisciplinary group of 14 artists, musicians, choreographers and poets inspired by the European and American <u>avant-gardes</u>. Their multi-layered <u>installations</u> embraced <u>sound</u> recording, <u>photography</u> and film, together with artist-designed sets, specially composed music and dance. Many of the members associated with the group were self-taught, and as a result distanced themselves from the traditional artistic culture in Japan. Co-founder Katsuhiro Yamaguchi described them as <u>Bauhaus</u> without the building. Jikken Kobo was active between 1951 and 1958 and its members included Kazuo Fukushima, Hikaru Hayashi, Ririko Hayashi, Toshi Ichiyanagi, Keijiro Sato, Takahiro Sonoda, Hiroyoshi Suzuki, Toru Takemitsu and Joji Yuasa.

k

Khartoum School Formed in Sudan in 1960 by the painters Ahmed Shibrain, Kamala Ishag and Ibrahim El-Salahi, the Khartoum School was a modernist movement that sought to develop a new visual vocabulary to reflect the distinctive identity of the newly independent nation. As one of the most active contributors to the growth of modern art in Africa, the group was typified by its use of primitive and Islamic imagery. One of its distinctive characteristics was the use of calligraphic writing, in which the artists would simplify Arabic script into abstract shapes. This aesthetic, called huruffiyya, together with Islamic motifs, became a hallmark of the Khartoum School. The group disbanded in 1975 after Ishag broke away to found the Crystalist School and El-Salahi was accused of anti-government activities and imprisoned, later going into self-imposed exile in Britain.

kinaesthetic art Kinaesthesia is the sense that detects bodily position, weight or movement of the muscles, tendons and joints of the body. The term has come to be used in relation to art that deals with the body in movement. It was first associated with Futurism, which sought to champion the dynamism of the modern age by depicting people and things in motion. The performances of the American choreographer Merce Cunningham can also be described as kinaesthetic, because his dancers are concerned with the exploration of space through the body's movement. In 1973 Trisha Brown used the Manhattan skyline as a stage for her performance *Roof Piece* in which dancers transmitted movements to other dancers standing on rooftops across New York.

kinetic art The word kinetic means 'relating to motion'. Kinetic art depends on motion for its effects. Since the early twentieth century artists have been incorporating movement into art. This has been partly to explore the possibilities of movement, partly to introduce the element of time, partly to reflect the importance of the machine and technology in the modern world and partly to explore the nature of vision. Movement has either been produced mechanically by motors or by exploiting the natural movement of air in a space. Works of this latter kind are called mobiles. A pioneer of kinetic art was Naum Gabo with his motorised *Standing Wave* of 1919–20. Mobiles were pioneered by Alexander Calder from about 1930. Kinetic art became a major phenomenon of the late 1950s and the 1960s.

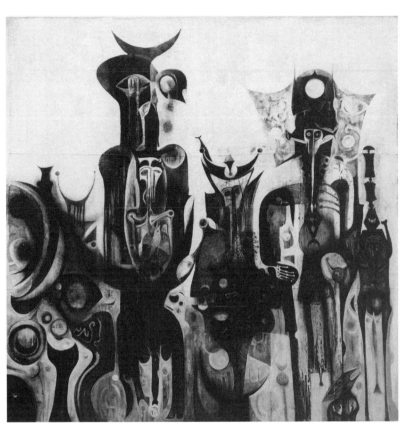

Khartoum School

Ibrahim El-Salahi
Reborn Sounds of Childhood Dreams I
1961–5
Enamel paint and oil paint on cotton
258.8 × 260
Tate. Purchased from the artist
with assistance from the Africa
Acquisitions Committee, the Middle
East North Africa Acquisitions
Committee, Tate International
Council and Tate Members 2013

kinetic art

Naum Gabo
*Kinetic Construction
(Standing Wave)* 1919–20,
replica 1985
Metal, wood and
electric motor
61.6 × 24.1 × 19
Tate. Presented by
the artist through the
American Federation of
Arts 1966

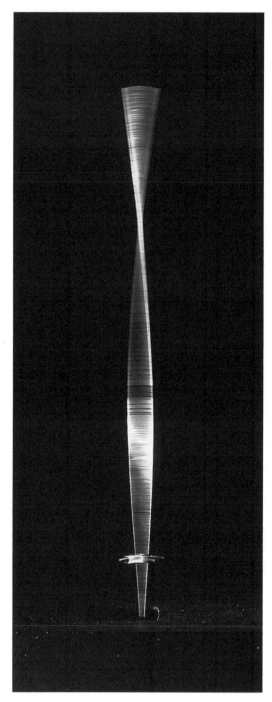

Kitchen Sink painters Originally used as the title of an article by the critic David Sylvester in the December 1954 issue of the journal *Encounter*. The article discussed the work of the British realist artists known as the Beaux Arts Quartet, John Bratby, Derrick Greaves, Edward Middleditch and Jack Smith. Sylvester wrote that their work 'takes us back from the studio to the kitchen' and described their subjects as 'an inventory which includes every kind of food and drink, every utensil and implement, the usual plain furniture and even the babies' nappies on the line. Everything but the kitchen sink? The kitchen sink too.' Sylvester also emphasised that these kitchens were ones 'in which ordinary people cooked ordinary food and doubtless lived their ordinary lives'. The Kitchen Sink painters' celebration of the everyday life of ordinary people carries implications of a social if not political comment and Kitchen Sink art can be seen to belong in the category of Social Realism. Kitchen Sink reached its apogee in 1956 when the Beaux Arts Quartet was selected to represent Britain at the Venice Biennale.

kitsch The German word for trash that came into use in English sometime in the 1920s to describe particularly cheap, vulgar and sentimental forms of popular and commercial culture. In 1939 the American art critic Clement Greenberg published a famous essay titled 'Avant-Garde and Kitsch'. In it he defined kitsch and examined its relationship to the high-art tradition as continued in the twentieth century by the avant-garde: 'Where there is an avant-garde, generally we also find a rear-guard. True enough – simultaneously with the entrance of the avant-garde, a second new cultural phenomenon appeared in the industrial West: that thing to which the Germans give the wonderful name of Kitsch: popular, commercial art and literature with their chromeotypes, magazine covers, illustrations, ads, slick and pulp fiction, comics, Tin Pan Alley music, tap dancing, Hollywood movies, etc., etc.' Some more up-to-date examples of kitsch might include plastic or porcelain models of the late Diana, Princess of Wales, Japanese manga comics and the Hello Kitty range of merchandise, many computer games, the whole of Las Vegas and Disneyland, and the high-gloss soft porn of Playboy magazine. Greenberg saw kitsch as the opposite of high art but from about 1950 artists started to take a serious interest in popular culture, resulting in the explosion of Pop art in the 1960s.

This engagement with kitsch has continued to surface in movements such as Neo-Geo and in the work of artists such as John Currin and Paul McCarthy.

kunsthalle A German term for a public art space that mounts temporary exhibitions. In Germany they are often supported by the local *kunstverein* (art association). It has come to be used internationally as a term for a publicly funded art space usually devoted to contemporary art.

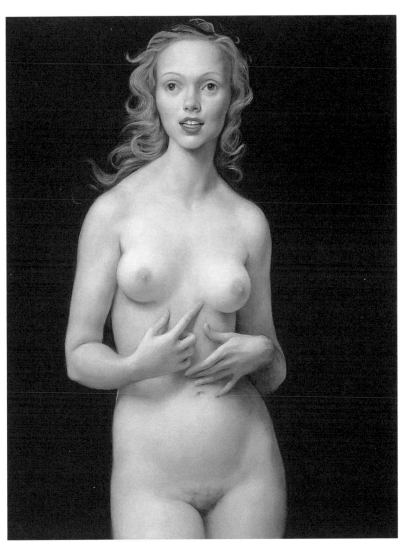

kitsch

John Currin
Honeymoon Nude 1998
Oil paint on canvas
116.8 × 91.4
Tate. Purchased with assistance
from Evelyn, Lady Downshire's
Trust Fund 1999

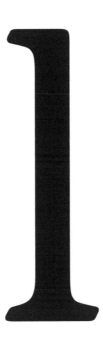

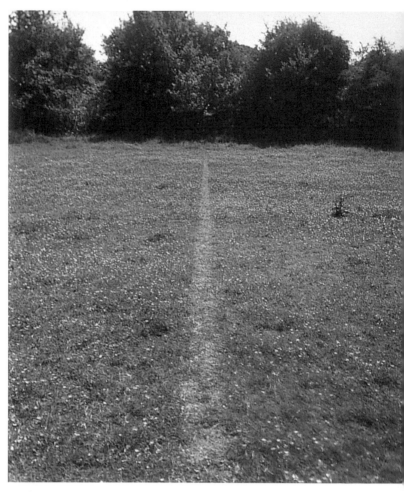

Land art

Richard Long
A Line Made by Walking 1967
Photograph and graphite on board
37.5 × 32.4
Tate. Purchased 1976

Laboratoire Agit'Art Founded in Dakar in 1974, Laboratoire Agit'Art was a revolutionary and subversive art <u>collective</u> united in critiquing and challenging the prevailing <u>négritude</u> philosophy in Senegal. Established by the artist Issa Samb, the filmmaker Djibril Diop Mambéty, painter El Hadji Sy and the playwright Youssoupha Dione, it was an interdisciplinary collective, devising street <u>performances</u>, improvisational <u>happenings</u>, <u>installations</u> and workshops that sought to combine traditional African performance and creativity with a modern aesthetic. The group's outlook was political, and community focused, publishing manifestos and creating installations out of street detritus that raised issues about African contemporary society. Today Laboratoire Agit'Art is considered to be one of the most influential African art collectives of the twentieth century.

Lacanian Referring to the thought of the prominent French psychoanalyst and theorist Jacques Lacan, who postulated a distinction between experience that is 'imaginary' – associated with the 'gaze' of an active spectator, characterised as being motivated by desire – and 'symbolic' – an area of experience that is approached through language. He had a strong influence on <u>Postmodernism</u>.

Lahore Art Circle Founded in 1952 by a group of young Pakistani artists and writers who aspired towards <u>modernism</u> and <u>abstraction</u>. The group heralded the beginning of the Pakistan modernist movement, a progressive attempt to connect Pakistani modern art to global modernism. There was no one distinct aesthetic, although Cézanne and <u>Cubism</u> were influences. Active until the late 1950s, the group disbanded when some of the members left to work in Europe and the USA. Artists associated with the group include Ali Imam, Moyene Najmi, Ahmed Parvez, S. Safdar and Anwar Jelal Shemza.

Land art Also known as Earth art. It can be seen as part of the wider <u>Conceptual art</u> movement in the 1960s and 1970s. Land artists began working directly in the landscape, sculpting into earthworks or making structures with rocks or twigs. Some of them used mechanical earth-moving equipment, but Richard Long simply walked up and down until he had made a mark in the earth. Land art was usually documented in artworks using <u>photographs</u> and maps that the artist could exhibit in a gallery. Land artists also made artworks in the gallery by bringing in material from the landscape and using it to create <u>installations</u>. Arguably, the most famous Land artwork is Robert Smithson's *Spiral Jetty* of 1970, an earthwork built out into the Great Salt Lake in the USA. Other Land artists include Walter de Maria, Michael Heizer and Dennis Oppenheim.

landscape One of the principal types or <u>genres</u> of Western art. However, the appreciation of nature for its own sake and its choice as a specific subject for art is a relatively recent phenomenon. Until the seventeenth century landscape was confined to the background of <u>paintings</u> dealing principally with religious, mythological or historical subjects. When, also in the seventeenth century, the French <u>Academy</u> classified the genres of art, it placed landscape fourth in order of importance out of five genres. Nevertheless, landscape painting became increasingly popular through the eighteenth century. The nineteenth century saw a remarkable explosion of naturalistic landscape painting, partly driven by the notion that nature is a direct manifestation of God, and partly by the increasing alienation of many people from nature by growing industrialisation and urbanisation. Britain produced two outstanding contributors to this phenomenon in John Constable and J.M.W. Turner. The baton then passed to France where, in the hands of the <u>Impressionists</u>, landscape painting became the vehicle for a revolution in Western painting and the traditional hierarchy of the genres collapsed.

Lettrisme Founded by the Romanian-born artist Isidore Isou in the mid-1940s, this French <u>avant-garde</u> movement was associated with the <u>Situationist</u> branch of the Anarchist family and became the art that dominated posters and barricades in the Parisian student riots of spring 1968. Lettrisme is a form of visual poetry: using calligraphic techniques it began by artists superimposing letters on various objects from furniture to film. This practice foreshadowed layering and other computer techniques, and because of this it is sometimes called hypergraphie. Both <u>mail art</u> and contemporary <u>graffiti art</u>, which share many of Lettrisme's basic characteristics, could be said to have evolved out of Lettrisme.

lightbox A box fitted with an internal light source, commonly a fluorescent tube or small incandescent bulbs, and a translucent white surface. Normally used for examining transparencies and negatives and tracing works made with a variety of techniques and materials. However, since the late twentieth century artists have made works in which large-scale photographic transparencies are presented fitted on a lightbox to create an integral work.

linocut A relief print produced in a manner similar to woodcut. The lino block consists of a thin layer of linoleum (a canvas backing coated with a preparation of solidified linseed oil) usually mounted on wood. The soft linoleum can be cut away more easily than a woodblock and in any direction (no grain) to produce a raised surface that can be inked and printed. Its slightly textured surface accepts ink evenly. Linoleum was invented in the nineteenth century as a floor covering; it became popular with artists and amateurs for printmaking in the twentieth century.

lithography A printing process based on the antipathy of grease and water. The image is applied to a grained surface (traditionally stone but now usually aluminium) using a greasy medium: greasy ink (tusche), crayon, pencils, lacquer or synthetic materials. Photochemical or transfer processes can be used. A solution of gum arabic and nitric acid is then applied over the surface, producing water-receptive non-printing areas and grease-receptive image areas. The printing surface is kept wet, so that a roller charged with oil-based ink can be rolled over the surface, and ink will only stick to the grease-receptive image area. Paper is then placed against the surface and the plate is run through a press. Lithography was invented in the late eighteenth century, initially using Bavarian limestone as the printing surface. Its invention made it possible to print a much wider range of marks and areas of tone than with earlier printmaking techniques. It also made colour printing easier: areas of different colours can be applied to separate stones and overprinted onto the same sheet. Offset lithography involves printing the image onto an intermediate surface before the final sheet. The image is reversed twice, and appears on the final sheet the same way round as on the stone or plate.

Live art Mainly refers to Performance art and its immediate precursor happenings, together with the developments of performance since the 1960s. In 1999 the publicly funded Live Art Development Agency was founded in London, to promote and co-ordinate activity in this field. Live art may also refer to art using living animals or plants. A major practitioner of this has been the Arte Povera artist Jannis Kounellis.

London Group In 1913 this group took over from the Camden Town Group the organising of modern art exhibitions in Britain. Its stated aim was 'to advance public awareness of contemporary visual art by holding exhibitions annually'. Its first president was Harold Gilman, one of the leading Camden Town painters. As an exhibiting society the London Group was specifically in opposition to the conservatism of the Royal Academy. It was also in opposition to the New English Art Club that, once avant-garde, had become conservative. Its strength was that it embraced the whole spectrum of modern art in Britain at the time, spanning Camden Town, Bloomsbury and Vorticism. The first exhibition was held in 1914 at the Goupil Gallery in London. This and the next few exhibitions included some of the icons of modern British art of the time. Among these was David Bomberg's *In the Hold*, Jacob Epstein's *Rock Drill* and Mark Gertler's anti-war painting *Merry-Go-Round*. The London Group flourished in the 1920s, when the Bloomsbury painter and critic Roger Fry played a prominent role, maintaining its support for the principles of modern French art. From about 1930 it gradually lost its pre-eminence as the showcase for modern art in Britain, but the Group still exists and holds exhibitions.

luminism Term meaning, roughly, 'painting of light'. Applied specifically to American landscape painters of the Hudson River School, many of their paintings were dominated by intense and often dramatic light effects. It is sometimes applied to Neo-Impressionist paintings in which the divisionist technique leads to a marked all-over luminosity.

m

Magic Realism A term invented in 1925 by German photographer, art historian and art critic Franz Roh in his book *Nach Expressionismus: Magischer Realismus* (After Expressionism: Magic Realism). It describes <u>modern realist</u> <u>paintings</u> with fantasy or dream-like subjects. In Central Europe Magic Realism was part of the reaction against modern or <u>avant-garde</u> art, known as the <u>'return to order'</u>, that took place generally after the First World War. Artists included Giorgio de Chirico, Alberto Savinio and others in Italy, and Alexander Kanoldt and Adolf Ziegler in Germany (see also <u>Neue Sachlichkeit</u>). Magic Realism is closely related to oneiric <u>Surrealism</u> and <u>Neo-Romanticism</u> in France. The term is also used of certain American painters in the 1940s and 1950s including Paul Cadmus, Philip Evergood and Ivan Albright. In 1955 the critic Angel Flores used Magic Realism to describe the writing of Jorge Luis Borges and Gabriel García Márquez, and it has since become a significant, if disputed, literary term.

Magnum Photos A photographic co-operative founded by Robert Capa, Henri Cartier-Bresson, George Rodger and David 'Chim' Seymour in New York in 1947. All four photographers had been photojournalists in the Second World War and were profoundly affected by what they had seen. These photographers believed that the most important job of a photojournalist was to record the human condition in the outside world as compassionately as possible. The agency was set up in order to give photographers the freedom to determine their own fate and not be beholden to magazine or newspaper editors with agendas that might compromise the integrity of the photographer. To fund this endeavour, photographers at Magnum retain the copyrights of their <u>photographs</u>. Today the organisation is among the most respected photographic agencies in the world and supports some 64 international photographers. It holds an extensive library of images recording major world events from the Spanish Civil War to the present day.

mail art Considered to be the predecessor of <u>net art</u>, mail art began in the 1960s when artists sent postcards inscribed with poems or drawings through the post rather than exhibiting or selling them through conventional commercial channels. Its origins can be found in Marcel Duchamp and Kurt Schwitters and the Italian <u>Futurists</u>,

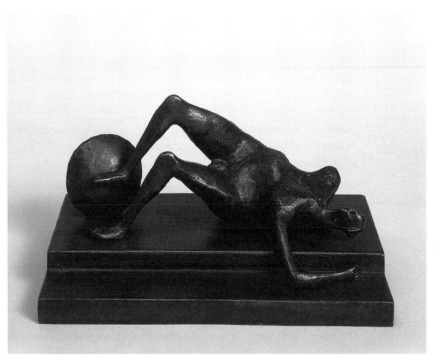

maquette

Henry Moore
*Maquette for Fallen
Warrior* 1956,
cast 1956–7
Bronze
14 × 15.5 × 26.5
Tate. Presented by
Gustav and Elly
Kahnweiler 1974,
accessioned 1994

although it was the New York artist Ray Johnson who, in the mid-1950s, posted small collages, prints of abstract drawings and poems to art world notables, giving rise to what eventually became known as the New York Correspondence School. Mail art can take a variety of forms including postcards, packages, faxes, emails and blogs. In the 1960s the Fluxus artist On Kawara sent telegrams to friends and family that informed them he was alive. In the mid-1990s, the artist and curator Matthew Higgs set up *Imprint 93*, which posted art by young British artists, among them Martin Creed, to critics and curators.

Manifesto invencionista Written by the artist Tomás Maldonado and published by the short-lived group the Asociación Arte Concreto-Invención in Buenos Aires in 1946, the *Manifesto invencionista* (Inventionist Manifesto) heralded the start of the abstraction and Concrete art movement in Argentina. It advocated experimentation and invention in the arts and scientific research. The manifesto was signed by Edgar Bayley, Antonio Caraduje, Simón Contreras, Manuel O. Espinosa, Alfredo Hlito, Enio Iommi, Obdulio Landi, Raúl Lozza, Rembrandt van Dyck Lozza, Tomás Maldonado, Alberto Molenberg, Primaldo Mónaco, Oscar Nuñez, Lidy Prati, Jorge Souza and Matilde Werbin.

maquette A model for a larger piece of sculpture. Often fascinating works in their own right, maquettes convey the immediacy of the artist's first realisation of an idea.

Market Photo Workshop Founded by the documentary photographer David Goldblatt in 1989, the Market Photo Workshop was originally set up to support black photographers in apartheid South Africa, enabling access to workshops, education and international photographers. The organisation is based in Newtown, Johannesburg, where it runs a project space, a gallery and a resource centre. Initially the school focused on social documentary photography but has since expanded its remit to include all aspects of photography. Many acclaimed photographers have emerged from the organisation including Bonile Bam, Jodi Bieber, Themba Hadebe, Sabelo Mlangeni, Zanele Muholi, Musa Nxumalo and Nontsikelelo 'Lolo' Veleko.

matter painting The term appeared in the 1950s and referred to the use of thick impasto into which other materials were often inserted. These included sand, mud, cement and shells. Matter painting was popularised by a group of Dutch and Belgian painters such as Bram Bogart, Jaap Wagemaker, Bert de Leeuw, René Guiette and Marc Mendelson. Its intention was to highlight the nature of painting and its materials. Other artists whose work is often associated with matter painting are the French painter and sculptor Jean Dubuffet, the Spanish artist Antoni Tàpies and the American painter Julian Schnabel.

medium In relation to art this term has two principal overlapping, even slightly confusing meanings. Painting, sculpture, drawing and printmaking are all media of art in the sense of a type of art. However, the term can also refer to the materials of the work. For example, a sculpture in the medium of bronze or marble; a painting in the medium of <u>oil paint</u> on <u>canvas</u>, <u>tempera</u> on <u>panel</u> or <u>watercolour</u> on <u>paper</u>; a drawing in the medium of <u>graphite</u> or crayon; a print in the medium of <u>etching</u> or <u>lithography</u>. In modern art new media in both senses have appeared. First of all, modern artists, from Pablo Picasso and Marcel Duchamp onwards, have established that art can be made of absolutely any material, so the media of modern art, in that sense, have ranged from <u>appropriated</u> or <u>found objects</u> and materials of all kinds, to the artist's own bodily excretions and the body itself. Many modern works are made from a variety of such things and the term <u>mixed media</u> has had to be coined to take account of this. This expansion of media, in the sense of materials, has given rise to new media in the overarching sense of a type of art. For example, <u>assemblage</u>, <u>installation</u> and performance are all three-dimensional art forms sufficiently distinct from traditional sculpture to become considered new media in themselves. In the case of the first two, the medium from which they are usually made is a variety of materials, that is, mixed media. <u>Performance art</u> uses the artist's own body as the material or medium. Finally, in a third meaning, the term medium also refers to the liquid in which the pigment is suspended to make paint. So the medium of the medium of oil paint is linseed oil. (See also <u>electronic media</u>; <u>multi-media</u>; <u>new media</u>; <u>time-based media</u>)

memento mori Latin phrase meaning 'remember you must die'. A memento mori <u>painting</u> or <u>sculpture</u> is one designed to remind the viewer of their mortality and of the brevity and fragility of human life in the face of God and nature. A basic memento mori painting would be a <u>portrait</u> with a skull, but other symbols commonly found are hourglasses or clocks, extinguished or guttering candles, fruit and flowers. Closely related to the memento mori picture is the vanitas <u>still life</u>. In addition to the symbols of mortality these may include other symbols such as musical instruments, wine and books to remind us explicitly of the vanity (in the sense of worthlessness) of worldly pleasures and goods. The term originally comes from the opening lines of the Book of Ecclesiastes in the Bible: 'Vanity of vanities, saith the Preacher, vanity of vanities, all is vanity.' Vanitas and memento mori pictures became popular in the seventeenth century, in a religious age when almost everyone believed that life on earth was merely a preparation for an afterlife. However, modern artists have continued to explore this <u>genre</u>.

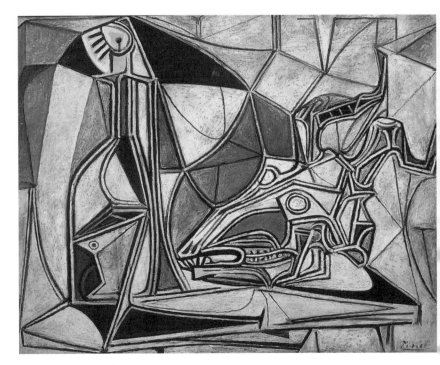

memento mori

Pablo Picasso
Goat's Skull, Bottle and Candle 1952
Oil paint on canvas
89.2 × 116.2
Tate. Purchased 1957

Merz Nonsense word invented by the German <u>Dada</u> artist Kurt
Schwitters to describe his <u>collage</u> and <u>assemblage</u> works based
on scavenged scrap materials. He made large numbers of small
collages, and more substantial assemblages, in this <u>medium</u>.
He is said to have extracted the word Merz from the name Commerz
Bank, which appeared on a piece of <u>paper</u> in one of his collages.
Schwitters founded a Dada group in Hanover where he was based
from 1919. There he created his first Merzbau (Merz building).
This was his own house, which he filled with about forty 'grottoes' –
constructions actually attached to the interior fabric of the building
and even extending through windows. In 1937 after his work had
been included in the <u>degenerate art</u> exhibition he fled Germany
for Norway. There he created a second Merzbau. In 1940 he found
refuge in England where he started a third Merzbau at Ambleside
in the Lake District. The first Merzbau was destroyed in the Second
World War, the second by fire in 1951 and the third was left
unfinished at his death in 1947. It is now preserved in the Hatton
Gallery at Newcastle University.

metal There are two families of metals: Ferrous and non-ferrous. All
ferrous metals contain iron. Non-ferrous metals include aluminium,
zinc and copper and its alloys, for example bronze. The use of bronze
for making <u>cast</u> <u>sculpture</u> is very ancient. From the early twentieth
century artists such as Pablo Picasso and the Russian <u>Constructivists</u>
began to explore the use of other metals, and Julio González
introduced <u>welded</u> metal sculpture. The use of a range of metals and
of industrial techniques became widespread in <u>Minimal art</u> and <u>New
Generation sculpture,</u> for example.

Mexican Muralism A term describing the revival of large-scale
<u>mural</u> painting in Mexico in the 1920s and 1930s. The three
principal artists were José Clemente Orozco, Diego Rivera and David
Alfaro Siqueiros. Rivera is usually considered the chief figure. All
three were committed to left-wing ideas in the politically turbulent
Mexico of the period and their painting reflects this. Siqueiros in
particular pursued an active career in politics, suffering several
periods of imprisonment for his activities. Their use of large-scale
mural painting in or on public buildings was intended to convey
social and political messages to the public. In order to make their

work as accessible as possible they all basically worked in realist styles but with distinctively personal differences – Orozco has elements of Surrealism while Siqueiros is vehemently expressionist, for example. The movement can be said to begin with the murals by Rivera for the Mexican National Preparatory School and the Ministry of Education, executed between1923 and 1928. Orozco and Siqueiros worked with him on the first of these. The Mexican Muralists carried out a number of major works in the USA that helped bring them to wide attention and had some influence on the Abstract Expressionists. Notable among these are Rivera's 1932–3 murals in the Detroit Institute of Arts depicting the Ford automobile plant (extant), and at the Rockefeller Center, New York (destroyed on Rockefeller's orders after a press scandal when a portrait of Lenin was noticed in the mural); Orozco's *The Epic of American Civilisation* at Dartmouth College, New Hampshire and his *Prometheus* at Pomona College. California (both extant); and Siqueiros's 1932 *Tropical America* in Los Angeles. This attack on American imperialism in Mexico was painted over some time after it was made, but is now undergoing restoration.

mezzotint A form of engraving where the metal printing plate is indented by rocking a toothed metal tool across the surface. Each pit holds ink, and if printed at this stage the image would be solid black. The printmaker works from dark to light by gradually rubbing down or burnishing the rough surface to various degrees of smoothness to reduce the ink-holding capacity of areas of the plate. The technique was developed in the seventeenth century, and became particularly popular in eighteenth-century England for reproducing portrait paintings. It is renowned for the soft gradations of tone and richness and velvet quality of its blacks.

Minimal art An extreme form of abstract art that developed in the USA in the second half of the 1960s. It can be seen as extending the abstract idea that art should have its own reality and not be an imitation of some other thing. It picked up too on the Constructivist idea that art should be made of modern, industrial materials. Minimal artists typically made works in very simple geometric shapes based on the square and the rectangle. Many Minimal works explore the properties of their materials. Minimal art or Minimalism

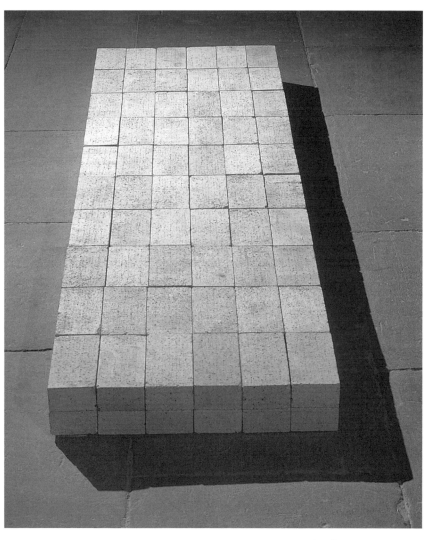

Minimal art

Carl Andre
Equivalent VIII 1966
Firebricks
12.7 × 68.6 × 229.2
Tate. Purchased 1972

is mostly three-dimensional but the painter Frank Stella is an important Minimalist. The other principal artists were Carl Andre, Dan Flavin, Donald Judd, Sol LeWitt, Robert Morris, and Richard Serra. There are strong links between Minimal and Conceptual art. Aesthetically, Minimal art offers a highly purified form of beauty. It can also be seen as representing such qualities as truth (because it does not pretend to be anything other than what it is), order, simplicity and harmony.

minjung art A socio-political art movement that emerged in 1980 in South Korea after the Gwangju Massacre in which some 200 peaceful demonstrators were killed by government troops. In the wake of the atrocities, artists sought to promote their desire for democracy through collective action, agitating for political change through mural paintings, banners and pamphlets. With their struggle, came a desire to create a truly Korean form of modern art that rejected the influences of the West and took inspiration instead from traditional Korean culture. Their struggle for democracy and human rights resulted in suppression, with artist Hong Sung-dam being imprisoned in 1987 on charges of collaboration with North Korea. The group disbanded in the early 1990s leaving a strong tradition of critical engagement for a new generation of artists. Artists associated with the group include Kim Bong-Chun, Lee Chul-Soo and O Jun.

Mir Iskutsstva see World of Art

mixed media Works composed of different media. The use of mixed media began around 1912 with the Cubist constructions and collages of Pablo Picasso and Georges Braque and has become widespread as artists developed increasingly open attitudes to the media of art. Essentially art can be made of anything or any combination of things. (See also assemblage; installation; Young British Artists)

mobile see kinetic art

Modern Art Week see Semana de Arte Moderna

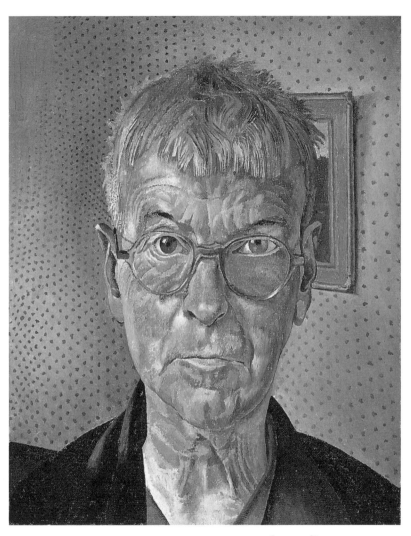

modern realism

Stanley Spencer
Self-Portrait 1959
Oil paint on canvas
50.8 × 40.6
Tate. Presented by the Friends
of the Tate Gallery 1982

modern realism In the nineteenth century Realism had a special meaning as an art term. Since the rise of modern art, realism, realist or realistic has come to be primarily a stylistic description, referring to painting or sculpture that continues to represent things in a way that more or less pre-dates Post-Impressionism and the succession of modern styles that followed. It is also true, however, that much of the best modern realist art has the edginess of subject matter that was the essential characteristic of nineteenth-century Realism. In the twentieth century, realism saw an upsurge in the 1920s when the shock of the First World War brought a reaction, known as the 'return to order', to the avant-garde experimentation of the pre-war period. In Germany this led to the Neue Sachlichkeit movement (Otto Dix, Christian Schad) and Magic Realism. In France, André Derain, previously a Fauve painter, became a central figure in what was called _traditionisme_. In the USA there was the phenomenon of Regionalism, and the great realist Edward Hopper. In Britain there was the Euston Road School and the painter Meredith Frampton. Among other major modern realist painters are Balthus, Lucian Freud, David Hockney (in his portraits), Gwen John, Giorgio Morandi and Stanley Spencer.

modernism In the field of art the broad movement in Western art, architecture and design which self-consciously rejected the past as a model for the art of the present. Hence the term modernist or modern art. Modernism gathered pace from about 1850 and proposed new forms of art on the grounds that they were more appropriate to the present time. It is thus characterised by constant innovation. But modern art has also been driven by various social and political agendas. These were often utopian, and modernism was in general associated with ideal visions of human life and society and a belief in progress. The terms modernism and modern art are generally used to describe the succession of art movements that critics and historians have identified since the Realism of Gustave Courbet, culminating in abstract art and its developments up to the 1960s. By that time modernism had become a dominant idea of art, and a particularly narrow theory of modernist painting had been formulated by the highly influential American critic Clement Greenberg. A reaction then took place that was quickly identified as Postmodernism.

Modernismo A profoundly influential cultural movement founded in São Paulo in the 1920s, Modernismo was an attempt to create a revolutionary new form of art that was modern and distinctly Brazilian. The artists, poets, writers and musicians associated with Modernismo were rebelling against European influence and the stuffy academic traditions that had dominated the arts in Brazil. Modernismo was inspired by native folklores and pre-Colombian art, and in 1922 a <u>Semana de Arte Moderna</u> (Modern Art Week) was held in São Paulo where this new vision of the future of art was presented to the public. By 1930 the movement had splintered on ideological grounds between those who saw it as nationalistic and agitated for social reform and those who were in sympathy only with its aesthetic principles. Yet it remains a culturally important moment in the development of Brazil's identity as a nation. Artists associated with Modernismo include Anita Malfatti, Emiliano Di Cavalcanti, Vicente do Rego Monteiro, Oswaldo Goeldi and Victor Brecheret.

modular A term used in relation to <u>Minimal art</u>, referring to a work of art with constituent parts that can be moved, separated and recombined. During the 1960s artists began creating simple <u>sculptures</u> made from industrial materials like sheet metal, plywood and bricks. In order to distance themselves from traditional sculpture, Minimalist artists would describe these artworks in very literal ways, calling them 'specific objects' or 'modules'. The term modular is closely associated with the artist Sol LeWitt, who, in 1965, began working on a series of open and closed cubes, like building blocks, which could be ordered and inter-locked in various different combinations in accordance with a pre-determined system.

monochrome Monochrome means one colour. For centuries artists used different shades (<u>tones</u>) of brown or black <u>ink</u> to create monochrome pictures on <u>paper</u>. The ink would simply be more or less diluted to achieve the required shades. Shades of grey oil paint were used to create monochrome <u>paintings</u>, a technique known as grisaille, from the French word *gris* (grey). In such work the play of light and dark (<u>chiaroscuro</u>) enabled the artist to define <u>form</u> and create a picture. In the twentieth century, with the rise of <u>abstract art</u>, many artists experimented with making monochrome painting. Among the first was Kasimir Malevich who about 1917–18 created

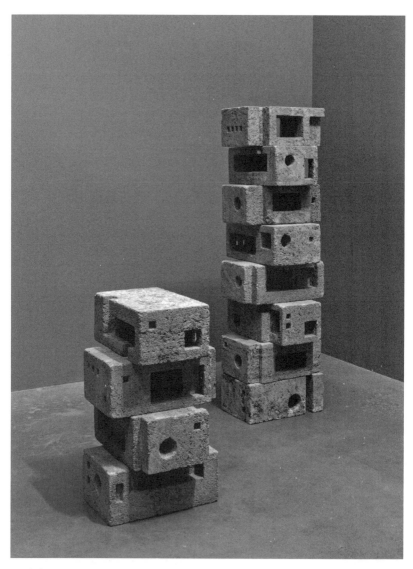

modular

Saloua Raouda Choucair
Infinite Structure 1963–5
Tufa stone
240 × 48 × 30
Tate. Purchased with funds provided
by the Middle East North Africa
Acquisitions Committee 2011

a series of white on white paintings (see Suprematism). In Britain, Ben Nicholson created a notable series of white reliefs in the mid-1930s. Monochrome painting became particularly widespread in the second half of the century with the appearance of Colour Field painting and Minimal art. The French artist Yves Klein became so famous for his all-blue paintings that he became known as Yves the monochrome.

Mono-ha A pioneering art movement that emerged in Tokyo in the mid-1960s led by the artists Lee Ufan and Nobuo Sekine in reaction to what they saw as the ruthless development and industrialisation of Japan. Mono-ha was one of a number of groups that was engaged in 'not making'. Founding member Lee observed that an artist's ability to make things had been nullified by technology. As a result he rejected traditional ideas of representation in favour of revealing the world as it is by engaging with materials and exploring their properties. In 1968 Sekine displayed a 2.7 metre-high tower of dirt next to an identically shaped hole in the ground as an illustration of this concept. The name Mono-ha (school of things), coined slightly derogatorily by a journalist, was initially resisted by the artists. As the movement gained international recognition, and through its association with Arte Povera, Mono-ha came to represent art that was critically engaged with the last days of modernism.

monoprint Essentially a unique variant of a conventional print. An impression is printed from a re-printable block, such as an etched plate or woodblock, but in such a way that only one of its kind exists, for example by incorporating unique hand-colouring or collage. The term can also refer to etchings which are inked and wiped in an expressive, not precisely repeatable manner; to prints made from a variety of printing elements that change from one impression to the next; or to prints that are painted or otherwise reworked by hand either before or after printing.

monotype A unique image printed from a polished plate, such as glass or metal, painted with ink but not a permanent printing matrix. A monotype impression is generally unique, though a second, lighter impression from the painted printing element can sometimes be made.

montage An assembly of images that relate to each other in some way to create a single work or part of a work of art. A montage is more formal than a collage and is usually based on a theme. It is also used to describe experimentation in photography and film, in particular the works of Man Ray and László Moholy-Nagy who made a series of short movies and photographic montages in the 1930s. (See also photomontage)

mosaic A picture made up of small parts. Traditionally these parts were made out of terracotta, pieces of glass, ceramics or marble, inlayed into floors and walls. Mosaic has been used as a decorative medium for over five thousand years. It was the Islamic mosaics introduced to Spain by the Moors in the eighth century that inspired the twentieth-century Catalan architect Antoni Gaudí, who arranged pieces of broken glazed tiles with fragments of glass bottles and china plates over walls in the Park Güell and in parts of the cathedral of the Sagrada Família, in Barcelona. Mosaics also became popular in Mexico, particularly in the art of Diego Rivera and Juan O'Gorman, who used stone mosaics in their murals that were based on socialist ideas and exalted the indigenous and popular heritage in Mexican culture (see Mexican Muralism). This workaday ethic became popular again in the 1970s when artists began rediscovering craft-based techniques. The British artist Matt Collishaw made a ceramic tile mosaic of a woman's face taken from a grainy photograph of a woman found on the internet.

motif A recurring fragment, theme or pattern that appears in a work of art. In the past this was commonly associated with Islamic designs, but it also alludes to a theme or symbol that returns time and again, like the noose and the cigarette in the paintings of American figurative painter Philip Guston, or a pattern, like the abstract drawings of the mid-twentieth-century abstract painter Victor Pasmore. The video artist Bill Viola often uses the motif of water to represent birth and death, as exemplified in his multi-video installation *Five Angels for the Millennium*. Motif can also refer to the subject of the artwork. The phrase 'to paint from the motif' arose in the context of Impressionism, meaning to paint on the spot.

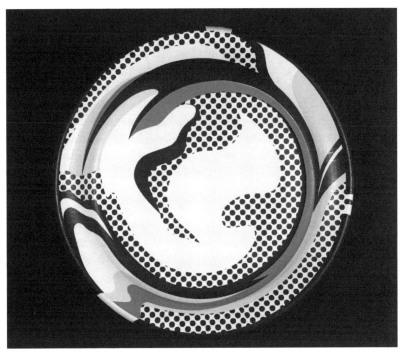

multiple

Roy Lichtenstein
Untitled (Paper Plate) 1969
Screenprint on paper
26.4 × 26.4
Tate. Presented by Simon Wilson
and the Lisson Gallery 1978

moving image The representation of filmed material when shown on a screen or some form of visual display unit. Unlike a painting or a photographic still, a moving image is in a constant state of kinetic motion which can add to the drama of the image, both psychologically and aesthetically. Usually moving image only refers to the visual element of the filmed material, rather than the aural component. Over the past fifty years, artists have been experimenting with the moving image, shifting it from the black box of the cinema to the white cube of the art gallery. A critical discourse has emerged around the use of the moving image, as a mechanically reproducible medium tied to low art, in the domain of fine art, which historically sought to separate itself from mass popular culture. Artists associated with moving image are Douglas Gordon, Mark Lecky and Chantal Akerman. (See also expanded cinema; video art)

multi-media First used in the 1960s in relation to mixed media works that had an electronic element. Andy Warhol's events staged with the rock group the Velvet Underground, under the title of the *Exploding Plastic Inevitable*, which combined music, performance, film and lighting, were described as multi-media. Since the late 1970s multi-media has come to define an artwork that uses a combination of electronic media, which could include video, film, audio and computers.

multiple Casting sculpture in bronze, and the various techniques of printmaking, have for many centuries made it possible to make multiple examples of a work of art. Each example of an edition of a print or a bronze is an authentic work of the artist, although there may be technical variations that might affect the value. The number produced is usually strictly limited, mainly for commercial reasons but, in the case of etchings in particular, also for technical reasons – etching plates wear very rapidly, so later impressions are inferior. About 1955, the artists Jean Tinguely and Agam, wanting to make their work more widely available, put forward the idea of very large, effectively unlimited, editions of works that could be sold very cheaply. It is they who seem to have invented the term multiple for such works, which would be made by industrial processes. The first multiples were eventually produced by the Denise René Gallery in Paris in 1962, and since then large numbers of artists have created multiples.

mural A painting applied directly to a wall in a <u>public</u> space is described as a mural. The popularity of the mural in the Western world began in the nineteenth century, with a new, community-orientated sense of national identity. The advantage of a mural is its accessibility to a large audience, which has endeared it to many political ideologies. In the 1930s there was a worldwide trend towards making art more public in reaction to the introspective development of modern art. In Latin America, the USA and Britain, mural painting became popular thanks to governmental sponsorship in the form of organisations like the <u>Artists International Association</u>. In 1933 Mario Sironi published his *Manifesto of Mural Painting* and commissioned murals by Giorgio de Chirico and Carlo Carrà. In Germany, Italy and the USSR murals reflected the totalitarian propaganda of the State. By the 1970s murals in the Western world were engineered to local politics, often revealing a sense of national, racial or civic pride in the area. (See also <u>Mexican Muralism</u>)

n

Nabis Les Nabis (from the Hebrew word for prophet) was a group of Post-Impressionist French painters active from 1888 to 1900. Some of its key members met at the Académie Julian in Paris, which offered a liberal alternative to the official Ecole des beaux-arts. Founded in secret by Paul Sérusier, the group included Pierre Bonnard, Edouard Vuillard and Maurice Denis. Inspired by Paul Gauguin's synthetism, these artists adopted a style characterised by flat patches of colour, bold contours and simplified drawing. Their unconventional outlook led them to experiment with painting on different supports including cardboard and velvet, and to create set designs for symbolist theatre (see symbolism).

naïve The word naïve means simple, unaffected, unsophisticated. As an art term it specifically refers to artists who also have had no formal training in an art school or academy. Naïve art is characterised by childlike simplicity of execution and vision. As such it has been valued by modernists seeking to get away from what they see as the insincere sophistication of art created within the traditional system. The most famous naïve artist of modern times is Henri Rousseau, known as Le Douanier (customs man) from the full-time job he held. Others are André Bauchant and, in Britain, the St Ives seaman Alfred Wallis, whose work famously influenced Ben Nicholson. Naïve artists are sometimes referred to as modern primitives (see primitivism). The category also overlaps with what is called outsider art, or in France, Art Brut. This includes artists who are on the margins of society, such as criminals and mentally ill people.

narrative A narrative is simply a story. Narrative art is art that tells a story. Much of Western art has been narrative, depicting stories from religion, myth and legend, history and literature. Audiences were assumed to be familiar with the stories in question. From about the seventeenth century genre painting showed scenes and narratives of everyday life. In the Victorian age, narrative painting of everyday life subjects became hugely popular and is often considered as a category in itself (i.e. Victorian Narrative painting). In modern art, formalist ideas have resulted in narrative being frowned upon. However, coded references to political or social issues, or to events in the artist's life, are commonplace. Such works are effectively modern allegories, and generally require information from the artist to be fully understood. The most famous example of this is Pablo Picasso's *Guernica*.

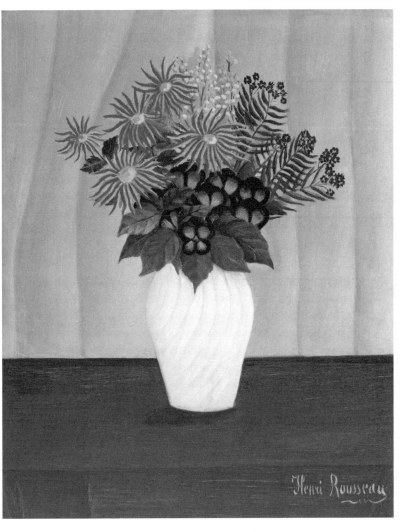

naïve

Henri Rousseau
Bouquet of Flowers c.1909–10
Oil paint on canvas
61 × 49.5
Tate. Bequeathed by C. Frank Stoop
1933

natural synthesis An ideology formulated in Nigeria in the late 1950s by the <u>Zaria Art Society</u>. Natural synthesis advocated a natural, unforced and unconscious merging of the best of indigenous art traditions, forms and ideas with the useful Western ones to create a truly modern Nigerian art. Members were encouraged to investigate indigenous <u>aesthetics</u> and then use them to develop individual styles of expression. A manifesto was published in 1960, the same year Nigeria gained independence from Britain, in which the artist and theorist Uche Okeke set out his desire to see an African art that embraced the rich variety of cultures from ethnic and religious groups living in Nigeria. Artists associated with natural synthesis include Jimoh Akolo, Yusuf Grillo, Demas Nwoko, Uche Okeke, Simon Okeke and Bruce Onobrakpeya.

naturalism Until the early nineteenth century both <u>landscape</u> and the human figure in art tended to be idealised or stylised according to conventions derived from the classical tradition. Naturalism was the broad movement to represent things closer to the way we see them. In Britain it was pioneered by John Constable who famously said 'there is room enough for a natural painture' (type of <u>painting</u>). Naturalism became one of the major trends of the century and combined with <u>realism</u> of subject led to <u>Impressionism</u> and modern art. Naturalism was often associated with <u>plein air</u> practice.

negative In photography, a negative is a unique image from which positive prints are produced. It is the total inversion of a positive image. The light areas appear dark and the dark areas appear light. Most negative images are generated in analogue cameras, where the plastic film, coated in light sensitive salts suspended in a binder or an emulsion, is exposed to light for a brief amount of time. This creates the negative, which is then used to produce a number of positive images through 1:1 contact process or enlargement. The resulting <u>print</u> then becomes known as the contact print, and is considered the unique master for its clarity and detail. Although digital photography has made the negative obsolete, artists and photographers continue to work with negatives, and there has been a renewed interest in old analogue techniques. The artist Thomas Ruff exhibited a series of Cyanotypes, a very early form of negative printing, at the Gagosian Gallery in 2015.

négritude A cultural and political movement founded by a group of African and Caribbean students in Paris in the 1930s. Lead by the Martinican poet Aimé Césaire, French Guianese poet Léon Damas and the future Senegalese President Léopold Sédar Senghor, négritude was anti-colonial and sought to reclaim the value of blackness and African culture. Both Surrealism and the Harlem Renaissance influenced the movement, which became widespread during the Second World War when its leaders left Paris for the Caribbean and Africa and new forms of négritude arose in these locations, including creolisation in the Caribbean and the natural synthesis movement in Nigeria. In this respect négritude can be seen as a forerunner of the Black Atlantic. (See also decolonisation)

Neo-Concrete The Neo-Concrete movement was a splinter group of the Concrete art movement, formed in Brazil in the 1950s. With the construction of the country's new utopian capital, Brasilia, and the formation of the São Paulo Biennial, young Brazilian artists were inspired to create art that drew on contemporary theories of cybernetics, gestalt psychology and the optical experiments of international artists like Bridget Riley and Victor Vasarely (see Op art). Lygia Clark, Lygia Pape, Am'lcar de Castro, Franz Weissmann, Reynaldo Jardim, Sergio de Camargo, Theon Spanudis and Ferreira Gullar were unhappy with the dogmatic approach of the Concrete group, so published the Neo-Concrete manifesto in 1959, which called for a greater sensuality, colour and poetic feeling in Concrete art. In 1960 Hélio Oiticica joined the group and his groundbreaking series of red and yellow painted hanging wood constructions effectively liberated colour into three-dimensional space.

Neo-Dada This term is sometimes applied to the work of Robert Rauschenberg and Jasper Johns in New York in the late 1950s because of their use of collage, assemblage and found objects, and their apparently anti-aesthetic agenda (see Dada). At the time there were also strong echoes of Dada in Installation art and happenings. The term has some justification due to the presence in New York of the great French Dada artist Marcel Duchamp whose ideas were becoming increasingly influential.

Neo-Expressionism This term came into use about 1980 to describe the international phenomenon of a major revival of painting in an expressionist manner. It was seen as a reaction to the Minimal and Conceptual art that had dominated the 1970s. In the USA leading figures were Philip Guston and Julian Schnabel, and in Britain Christopher Le Brun and Paula Rego. There was a major development of Neo-Expressionism in Germany, as might be expected with its Expressionist heritage, but also in Italy. In Germany the Neo-Expressionists became known as Neue Wilden (New Fauves). In Italy, Neo-Expressionist painting appeared under the banner of Transavanguardia (beyond the avant-garde). In France a group called Figuration Libre was formed in 1981 by Robert Combas, Remi Blanchard, François Boisrond and Hervé de Rosa.

Neo-Geo Short for Neo-Geometric Conceptualism. This term came into use in the early 1980s in America to describe the work of Peter Halley, Ashley Bickerton, Jeff Koons and others. Halley in particular was strongly influenced by the French thinker Jean Baudrillard. Their work aimed at being a critique of the mechanisation and commercialisation of the modern world. Seeing geometry as a metaphor for society, Halley made brilliantly coloured geometrically abstract paintings, which, however, have a figurative basis. They are derived from things such as circuit boards, which Halley uses to represent the individual organisms and networks of contemporary urban existence. The paintings are depictions of the social landscape, of isolation and connectivity. The work of Bickerton and Koons was mainly three-dimensional. Koons parodied consumer culture by presenting real consumer goods as works of timeless beauty. Bickerton, in works such as his *Biofragment* series, created a vision of apocalypse.

Neo-Impressionism The name given specifically to the Post-Impressionist work of Georges Seurat and Paul Signac and their followers. Both Camille Pissarro and Lucien Pissarro had a Neo-Impressionist phase and their work continued to bear strong traces of the style. Neo-Impressionism is characterised by the use of the divisionist technique (often popularly but incorrectly called pointillism, a term Signac repudiated). Divisionism attempted to put Impressionist painting of light and colour on a scientific basis

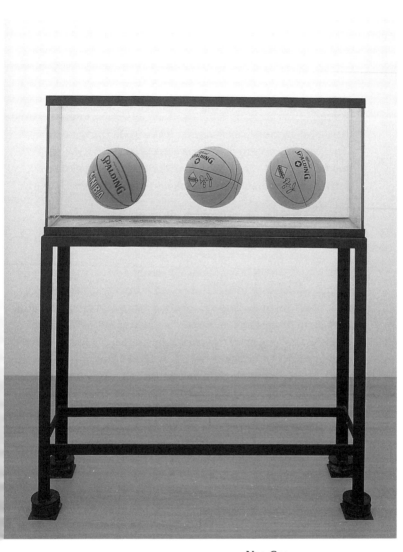

Neo-Geo

Jeff Koons
*Three Ball Total Equilibrium Tank
(Two Dr J Silver Series, Spalding NBA
Tip-Off)* 1985
Glass, steel, pneumatic feet, 3
rubber basketballs and water
153.6 × 123.8 × 33.6
Tate. Purchased 1995

by using optical mixture of colours. Instead of mixing colours on the palette, which reduces intensity, the primary-colour components of each colour were placed separately on the canvas in tiny dabs so they would mix in the spectator's eye. Optically mixed colours move towards white so this method gave greater luminosity. This technique was based on the colour theories of M-E. Chevreul, whose *De la loi du contraste simultanée des couleurs* (On the law of the simultaneous contrast of colours) was published in Paris in 1839 and had an increasing impact on French painters from then on, particularly the Impressionists and Post-Impressionists, as well as the Neo-Impressionists.

Neo-Plasticism A term adopted by the Dutch pioneer of abstract art, Piet Mondrian, for his own type of abstract painting. From the Dutch *de nieuwe beelding*, it basically means new art (painting and sculpture are plastic arts). Also applied to the work of the De Stijl circle of artists, at least up to Mondrian's secession from the group in 1923. In the first eleven issues of the journal *De Stijl* Mondrian published his long essay 'Neo-Plasticism in Pictorial Art' in which, among much else, he wrote: 'As a pure representation of the human mind, art will express itself in an aesthetically purified, that is to say, abstract form ... The new plastic idea cannot, therefore, take the form of a natural or concrete representation ... this new plastic idea will ignore the particulars of appearance, that is to say, natural form and colour. On the contrary it should find its expression in the abstraction of form and colour, that is to say, in the straight line and the clearly defined primary colour.' Neo-Plasticism was in fact an ideal art in which the basic elements of painting – colour, line, form – were used only in their purest, most fundamental state: only primary colours and non-colours, only squares and rectangles, only straight, horizontal or vertical lines. Mondrian had a profound influence on subsequent art.

Neo-Romanticism Term applied to the imaginative and often quite abstract landscape-based painting of Paul Nash, Graham Sutherland and others in the late 1930s and 1940s. Their work often included figures, was generally sombre, reflecting the Second World War and its approach and aftermath, but rich, poetic and capable of a visionary intensity. It was partly inspired by the landscapes of Samuel Palmer and the Ancients and partly by a more general emotional response to the British landscape and its history. Other major Neo-Romantics were Michael Ayrton, John Craxton, Ivon Hitchens, John Minton, John Piper and Keith Vaughan. The term sometimes embraces Robert Colquhoun and Robert MacBryde, and the early work of Lucian Freud; also the graphic work of Henry Moore of the period, especially his <u>drawings</u> of wartime air raid shelters. In the early 1920s in Paris a group of <u>figurative</u> painters emerged whose brooding, often nostalgic work quickly became labelled Neo-Romantic. Chief among them were the Russian-born trio of Eugène Berman and his brother Leonid, and Pavel Tchelitchew.

net art Art made on and for the internet is called net art. This is a term used to describe a process of making art using a computer in some form or other, whether to download imagery that is then exhibited online or build programs that create the artwork. Net art emerged in the 1990s when artists found that the internet was a useful tool to promote their art uninhibited by political, social or cultural constraints. For this reason it has been heralded as subversive, deftly transcending geographical and cultural boundaries and defiantly targeting nepotism, materialism and aesthetic conformity. Sites like Facebook and YouTube have become forums for art, enabling artists to exhibit their work without the endorsement of an institution. Pioneers of net art include Tilman Baumgarten, Jodi and Vuc Cosik. (See also <u>browser art</u>; <u>software art</u>)

Neue Künstlervereinigung München (NKV) The 'New Artists' Association of Munich' was founded as an <u>avant-garde</u> exhibiting society in Munich in 1909. With Wassily Kandinsky as president and members including Alexei Jawlensky and Gabriele Münter, the association mounted controversial exhibitions of <u>Fauvist</u>-influenced work in 1909, 1910 and 1911. Kandinsky resigned in 1911 and with Franz Marc, who had defended the NKV against widespread criticism the previous year, founded <u>Der Blaue Reiter</u>.

Neue Sachlichkeit Usually translated as New Objectivity this was a German <u>modern realist</u> movement of the 1920s, taking its name from the exhibition *Neue Sachlichkeit* held in Mannheim in 1923.

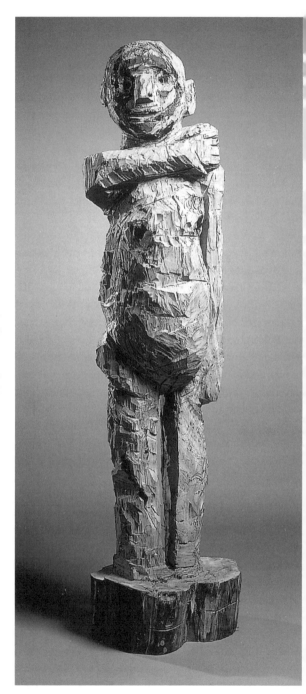

Neue Wilden

Georg Baselitz
Untitled 1982–3
Limewood
250 × 73 × 59
Tate. Acquired by
purchase and gift
from Hartmut and
Silvia Ackermeier,
Berlin 1993

It was part of the phenomenon of the 'return to order' following the First World War. The two key artists associated with Neue Sachlichkeit are Otto Dix and George Grosz, two of the greatest realist painters of the twentieth century. In their paintings and drawings they vividly depicted and excoriated the corruption, frantic pleasure-seeking and general demoralisation of Germany following its defeat in the war and the ineffectual Weimar Republic which governed until the arrival in power of the Nazi Party in 1933. But their work also constitutes a more universal, savage satire on the human condition. Other artists include Christian Schad and Georg Schrimpf.

Neue Slowenische Kunst (NSK) A pioneering artist collective formed in the 1980s in Slovenia during a period of great upheaval as the country was undergoing separation from former Yugoslavia. NSK (the name is the German translation of New Slovenian Art) consisted of four main groups, the painting collective Irwin, an artist-musician group called Laibach, a theatre collective known as Scipion Nasice Sisters and the design group New Collectivism. Together they addressed the social and political history of Slovenia, and in particular the complicated relationship between culture and a national identity that had been repeatedly compromised by successive occupations. The work of NSK has informed many successive generations of artists in Eastern Europe, particularly with those working in the fields of activism and collectivism.

Neue Wilden A term used in Germany for Neo-Expressionism. The Neue Wilden (i.e. New Fauves) included two artists who became major international figures, Georg Baselitz and Anselm Kiefer.

New British Sculpture Around 1980 there can be seen to have been a general reaction in Western art to the predominance of Minimal and Conceptual art in the previous decade. In painting this reaction took the form of Neo-Expressionism and related phenomena. In sculpture there was a notable return to the use of a wide range of techniques of fabrication and even the use of traditional materials and methods such as carving in stone and marble. Figurative and metaphoric imagery reappeared together with poetic or evocative titles. In Britain a strong group of young sculptors emerged whose work, although quite disparate, quickly became known as New British Sculpture. The principal artists associated with New British Sculpture were Stephen Cox, Tony Cragg, Barry Flanagan, Antony Gormley, Richard Deacon, Shirazeh Houshiary, Anish Kapoor, Alison Wilding and Bill Woodrow.

New English Art Club Founded in London in 1886 as an exhibiting society by artists influenced by Impressionism and whose work was rejected by the conservative Royal Academy. Key early members were J.A.M. Whistler (although he soon resigned), Walter Sickert and Philip Steer. Others in the first show included George Clausen, Stanhope Forbes and John Singer Sargent. Initially avant-garde, the NEAC quickly became increasingly conservative and Sickert and Steer formed an 'Impressionist nucleus' within it, staging their own show London Impressionists in 1889. NEAC remained important as a showcase for advanced art, until 1911 when challenged by the Camden Town Group and London Group, and continued to be influential into the 1920s with artists such as Augustus John and Stanley Spencer exhibiting. It still exists, now preserving the Impressionist tradition.

new figuration A blanket term referring to the revival of figurative art in Europe and America the 1960s following a period dominated by abstraction. The term, first used by the French critic Michel Ragon, sometimes argued that the move back to figuration occurred during an era of political and social turbulence in Europe and America. Artists David Hockney and Leon Golub can be seen as examples of new figuration.

New Generation sculpture The title used for a series of exhibitions of painting and sculpture by young British artists held at the Whitechapel Gallery in London in the early 1960s. The 1965 show was devoted to sculpture and brought to wide public attention the work of Phillip King, together with David Annesley, Michael Bolus, Tim Scott, William Tucker and Isaac Witkin. All these artists had been taught by Anthony Caro at St Martin's School of Art in London and are sometimes referred to as School of Caro as well as the New Generation sculptors. In 1960 Caro had developed a completely new form of abstract sculpture using steel beams, sheets and tubes, welded and bolted together and painted in bright industrial colours. King and the others soon developed their own work, exploring a basic vocabulary of sculptural form and using in addition materials such as plastic sheeting and fibreglass. New Generation sculpture became a major phenomenon of British art in the 1960s.

new genre public art A term coined by the American artist, writer and educator Suzanne Lacy in 1991, to define a type of American public art that was not a sculpture situated in a park or a square. The definition was first used in a public performance at the San Francisco Museum of Modern Art and later in Lacy's book *Mapping the Terrain: New Genre Public Art*. Lacy defined new genre public art as being activist, often created outside the institutional structure, which brought the artist into direct engagement with the audience, while addressing social and political issues. In 1993 an exhibition called *Culture in Action* presented a series of works that could be defined as new genre public art. It featured Mark Dion and his Chicago Urban Ecology Action Group, an installation about the ecology of their neighbourhood.

new media A term used to describe the sophisticated technologies that have become available to artists since the late 1980s. New media defines the mass influx of media, from the CD-ROM, to the mobile phone and the internet, that can enable the production and distribution of art digitally. Websites like DeviantArt and YouTube are key aspects of new media, being places that can distribute art to millions of people at the click of a button. (See also browser art; medium; net art; software art)

New Objectivity see Neue Sachlichkeit

New Spirit painting Virtually synonymous with Neo-Expressionism and its sub groups of Neue Wilden and Transavanguardia. *A New Spirit in Painting* was the title of a major exhibition at the Royal Academy, London in 1981. It attempted to sum up the state of painting at that point. It was an early response to the new currents that appeared in both painting and sculpture around 1980, and acted as a launchpad that brought these developments to public attention. The term New Spirit painting became used particularly

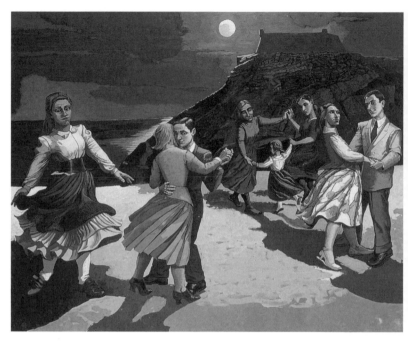

New Spirit painting

Paula Rego
The Dance 1988
Acrylic paint on
paper laid on canvas
212.6 × 274
Tate. Purchased 1989

in Britain, and is useful in that it also embraces aspects of new painting at that time that do not fit quite comfortably into the category of Neo-Expressionism, such as the American painters David Salle and Eric Fischl and in Britain Paula Rego, Stephen McKenna, Stephen Campbell or the <u>abstract</u> painter Sean Scully. In Britain particularly, the renewal of interest in painting in the early 1980s, especially <u>figurative</u> painting, brought into fresh focus the work of older artists such as Howard Hodgkin as well as those often called the <u>School of London</u>.

New Topographics A term coined by William Jenkins in 1975 to describe a group of American <u>photographers</u> whose pictures had a similar banal aesthetic, in that they were formal, mostly black and white prints of the urban landscape. Many, like Robert Adams, Lewis Baltz, Nicholas Nixon and Bernd and Hiller Becher were inspired by the man-made, selecting subject matter that was matter-of-fact – parking lots, suburban housing, warehouses – and depicting them with a beautiful stark austerity, almost in the way early photographers documented the natural landscape. An exhibition at the International Museum of Photography in Rochester, New York, featuring these photographers also revealed the growing unease about how the natural landscape was being eroded by industrial development. The New Topographics were to have a decisive influence on later photographers including those artists who became known as The Düsseldorf School of Photography.

New York Graphic Workshop Founded in New York in 1965 by the Latin American artists Luis Camnitzer, José Guillermo Castilo and Liliana Porter, the New York Graphic Workshop was an experimental group of printmakers whose aim was to redefine what printmaking could be. In their first manifesto, published the same year, they rejected the traditional techniques and aesthetics of printmaking in favour of industrial processes. They embraced the mechanical and the repetitive nature of printing, employing radical practices, like printing on the side of a ream of paper, and questioning the idea of what constitutes a print. From their workshop they encouraged artists to join the debate, staging exhibitions by mail and creating ephemeral editions.

New York School This term seems to have come into use in the 1940s to describe the artists of the intensely creative and innovative New York art scene that was giving birth to the radical and world-conquering new style of painting that in the early 1950s became known as Abstract Expressionism. The two terms are effectively interchangeable, that is the artists of the New York School are the Abstract Expressionists. New York School has echoes of School of Paris and may also be seen to reflect the notion that after the Second World War, New York took over from Paris as the world centre for innovation in modern art.

Newlyn School Following the extension of the Great Western Railway to West Cornwall in 1877 the Cornish fishing towns of St Ives and Newlyn both began to attract artists, drawn by the beauty of the scenery, quality of light, simplicity of life and drama of the sea. The artists known as the Newlyn School were led by Stanhope Forbes and

Nouveau Réalisme

Arman (Armand Fernandez)
Condition of Woman I 1960
Glass, wood, fabric, plastic, cork and metal
192 × 46.2 × 32
Tate. Purchased 1982

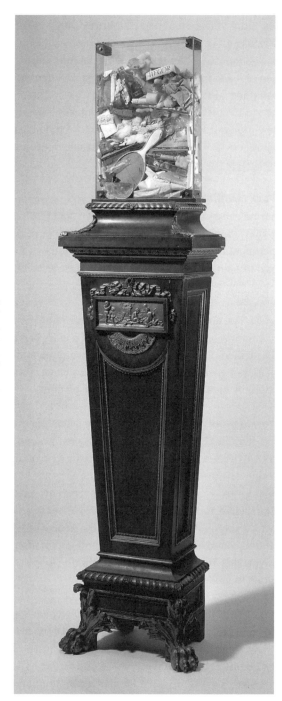

Frank Bramley who settled there in the early 1880s. Newlyn painting combined the Impressionist-derived doctrine of working directly from the subject and, where appropriate, in the open air (see plein air), with subject matter drawn from rural life, particularly the life of the fishermen. Forbes's *The Health of the Bride* and Bramley's *A Hopeless Dawn* are quintessential Newlyn masterpieces. (See also St Ives School)

non-objective art The Russian Constructivist painters Wassily Kandinsky and Kasimir Malevich and the sculptor Naum Gabo were pioneers of non-objective art. It defines a type of abstract art that is usually, but not always, geometric and was inspired by the Greek philosopher Plato who believed that geometry was the highest form of beauty. Non-objective art may attempt to visualise the spiritual, and can be seen as carrying a moral dimension, standing for virtues like purity and simplicity. In the 1960s a group of American artists, including Sol LeWitt and Donald Judd, embraced the philosophy of non-objective art. By creating highly simplified geometric art out of industrial materials they elevated these to an aesthetic level. Their work became known as Minimal art.

Nouveau Réalisme French movement (meaning New Realism) founded in 1960 by the critic Pierre Restany. It was the focus for developments that can be seen as the European counterpart to Pop art. As well as painting, Nouveau Réalistes made extensive use of collage and assemblage, using real objects incorporated directly into the work and acknowledging a debt to the readymades of Marcel Duchamp. The leading exponents of this aspect were Arman, César, Christo, Jean Tinguely and Daniel Spoerri. Raymond Hains, Mimmo Rotella, Jacques Mahé de la Villeglé and Wolf Vostell developed the décollage technique, making striking works from accumulated layers of posters they removed from advertising hoardings. Among the painters were Valerio Adami, Alain Jacquet, Martial Raysse (who also made notable installations) and the German, Gerhard Richter, who named his work Capitalist Realism. One of the most significant artists associated with Nouveau Réalisme was Yves Klein who died prematurely in 1962. He was enormously inventive in his short career, staging happenings and carrying out early examples of Performance art using his own body, and anticipating Conceptual art as well as making remarkable paintings.

Novecento Italiano Italian group formed in 1922 by Achille Funi, Mario Sironi, Carlo Carrà and others. It was officially launched in 1923 at a meeting in Milan, with Mussolini, the founder of the Italian Fascist Party who, in 1922, seized power to become dictator of Italy, as one of the speakers. After being represented at the Venice Biennale of 1924 the group split and was re-formed. The new Novecento Italiano staged its first group exhibition in Milan in 1926. The group's aim was to revive the tradition of large-format history painting in the classical manner. The group supported fascism and its work became associated with the state propaganda department.

Nsukka Group A revivalist movement that began at the University of Nigeria in 1970 following the appointment of the artist Uche Okeke as head of the Fine Art Department. Okeke had been a proponent of natural synthesis and, after the Nigerian Civil War, sought to raise questions about ethnic identity through the promotion of the traditional uli painting. Uli is a flat, decorative style of art, usually drawn onto the body that features specific motifs and symbols. Okeke took the aesthetics of uli and applied it to contemporary Nigerian art, inspiring his students to follow suit. As a result the Nsukka Group was formed and has been influential in the development of modern Nigerian art. Artists associated with the Nsukka Group include Tayo Adenaike, El Anatsui, Chike Aniakor, Olu Oguibe, Uche Okeke, Ada Udechukwu and Obiora Udechukwu.

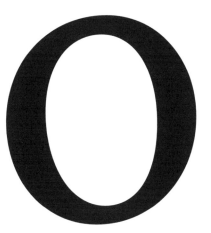

Objective Abstraction Name of a style of <u>abstract art</u> developed by a group of British artists in 1933. An exhibition titled *Objective Abstraction* was held in 1934 at the Zwemmer Gallery in London. The artists involved included Graham Bell, William Coldstream, Rodrigo Moynihan and Geoffrey Tibble, and the exhibition was organised by Moynihan. Not included in this show but an important practitioner was Edgar Hubert. On the other hand, works by non-Objective Abstraction artists Ivon Hitchens, Victor Pasmore and Ceri Richards were added to the show by the gallery's director. Objective Abstraction was a non-geometric form of abstract art in which the <u>painting</u> evolved in an improvisatory way from freely applied brushstrokes. Moynihan was inspired by the <u>brushwork</u> in the late paintings of J.M.W. Turner and Claude Monet. Objective Abstraction was part of the general ferment of exploration of abstraction in Britain in the early 1930s and was short-lived. A few years later many of these artists became members of the <u>realist</u> <u>Euston Road School</u>.

offset lithography see <u>lithography</u>

oil paint A dispersion of pigments in a drying oil that forms a tough, coloured film on exposure to air. The drying oil is a vegetable oil, often made by crushing nuts or seeds. For paints, linseed oil is most commonly used, but poppy, sunflower, safflower, soya bean and walnut oils have also been used. Drying oils initially cure through oxidation, leading to cross-linking of the molecular chains; this is a slow process affected by film thickness and paint components. Artists have used turpentine or mineral spirits to dilute oil paint. A heavily diluted layer dries relatively quickly, being tack-free in a few days. Thicker layers, containing more oil, take longer. Oil paint continues to dry, getting harder with age over many decades. Pigments and extenders will also affect the rate of drying, so different colours may dry at different speeds.

One-Dimension group In 1971 the artist Shakir Hassan Al-Said founded the pioneering One-Dimension group (Al Bu'd al Wahad) in Baghdad, Iraq, which promoted the modern calligraphic school in Arab art. Inspired by the mystic philosopher al-Hallaj, and in the principles of Islamic Sufism, Al-Said sought to create a more spiritual

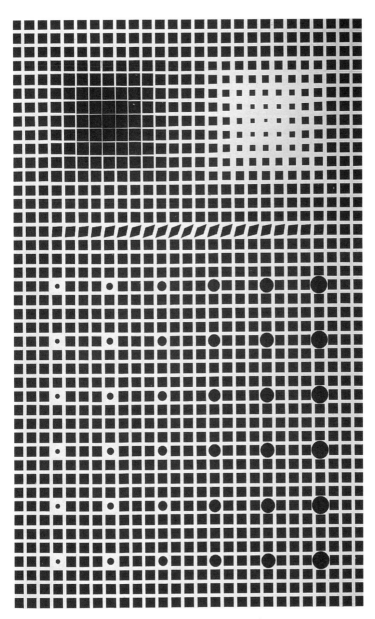

Op art

Victor Vasarely
Supernovae 1959–61
Oil paint on canvas
241.9 × 152.4
Tate. Purchased 1964

form of art that embraced universal truths. In order to achieve this, he gave up figurative depiction in his paintings and adopted the Arabic letter in its place, the metaphysical and physical qualities of the letters becoming the central subject of his compositions. Arabic calligraphy had historically been considered the highest form of religious craft in the Arab world, adhering to strict rules. By using it in his paintings, Al-Said subverted these principles. For Al-Said, One-Dimension represented the spiritual point of convergence between man and the divine. The incorporation by artists of Arabic letters into their artworks has become known as huruffiyya, and is now a widely adopted practice in Arabic art.

Op art A major development in the 1960s of painting that created optical effects for the spectator. These effects ranged from the subtle to the disturbing and disorienting. Op painting used a framework of purely geometric forms as the basis for its effects and also drew on colour theory and the physiology and psychology of perception. Leading figures were Bridget Riley, Jesus Raphael Soto and Victor Vasarely. Vasarely was one of the originators of Op art. Soto's work often involves mobile elements and points up the close connection between kinetic and Op art.

Orientalism First used by the philosopher Edward Said, Orientalism describes the way the West has created a mythological identity about the East. Over the centuries in art, literature and politics, Westerners have portrayed the East as exotic and strange. Many Western artists used oriental themes such as the harem or a Turkish bath as a pretext for portraying the nude in a sexual context. The West also saw the East as fundamentally inferior to the West's so-called enlightened values. Said argued that this historical construction dated back to the Crusades and their desire to impose Christianity on the East. While the West has a self-image of order and control, the East is presented as dangerous, exciting and indolent. Said's book *Orientalism*, published in 1978, had a huge impact on the way artists, both in the West and the East, thought about cultural identity

Orphism Sometimes called Orphic Cubism. The term was coined about 1912–13 by the French poet and art critic Guillaume

Apollinaire. He used it to describe the Cubist-influenced work of
Robert and Sonia Delaunay, and to distinguish their very <u>abstract</u>
and colourful work from Cubism generally. The name comes from
the legendary ancient Greek poet and musician Orpheus. Its use by
Apollinaire relates to the idea that <u>painting</u> should be like music,
which was an important element in the development of abstract
art. In the Delaunays's work patches of subtle and beautiful colour
are brought together to create harmonious <u>compositions</u>. Delaunay
himself used the term <u>simultanism</u> to describe his work.

otherness From the idea of other: meaning that which is different
from you, but also defines you. The philosopher Georg Hegel was the
first to use the term other, which he argued was a constituent part
of self-consciousness. As a result psychoanalysts like Sigmund Freud
and Jacques Lacan embraced it, and used it to formulate theories
about self-consciousness. Today, otherness is used by theorists to
signify ways in which members of dominant groups derive a sense
of self through defining smaller groups as different or other to them.
An example would be the taking of whiteness for granted, so that
blackness was considered to be other. The concept of otherness is
used in <u>identity politics</u>, <u>feminist art</u> and post-colonial discourse.
(See also <u>Orientalism</u>)

outsider art Sometimes called <u>Art Brut</u>, outsider art is used to
describe art that has a <u>naïve</u> quality, often produced by people who
have not trained as artists or are not commonly associated with the
production of art. Children, psychiatric patients and prisoners fall
into this category. In 1946 the French artist Jean Dubuffet started to
collect artworks he considered to be free from societal constraints.
This was termed Art Brut (raw art) and in 1948 he founded
the Compagnie de L'Art Brut with André Breton. The artist Ben
Nicholson discovered the naïve painter Alfred Wallis in St Ives in the
1920s. A retired fisherman, Wallis painted pictures of ships and the
town harbour on pieces of driftwood and cardboard.

p

painterly see <u>impasto</u>

painting What we call art in all its forms – painting, <u>sculpture</u>, <u>drawing</u> and <u>engraving</u> – appeared in human groups all over the world in the period known as the Upper Paleolithic, which is roughly from 40,000 to 10,000 years ago. Since then painting has changed in essence very little. Supports evolved from rock faces, through the walls of buildings, to portable ones of <u>paper</u>, wood, and finally cloth, particularly <u>canvas</u>. The range of pigments expanded through a wide range of earths and minerals, to plant extracts and modern synthetic colours. Pigments have been mixed with water and gum to make paint, but in the fifteenth century in Europe the innovation of using <u>oil</u> (linseed) produced a newly flexible and durable <u>medium</u> that played a major part in the explosion of creativity in Western painting at the Renaissance and after. At the same time subject matter expanded to embrace almost every aspect of life (<u>genres</u>).

palette A smooth, flat surface on which artists set out and mix their colours before <u>painting</u>, which is often designed to be held in the hand. The term also refers to the range of colours habitually used by and characteristic of an artist. A palette in computer graphics is a chosen set of colours that are each assigned a number, and it is this number that determines the colour of the pixel.

pan-Africanism An ideology of racial solidarity with Africa and its <u>diaspora</u> formed in the mid-nineteenth century. There are three thinkers associated with the evolution of the movement: the African-American priest Alexander Crummell, the politician and educator Edward Wilmot Blyden and, later, the writer and lawyer Henry Sylvester-Williams who formed the Pan-African Association. Pan-Africanism was the idea that in order to achieve their potential, all Africans on the continent and its diaspora needed to unify under the banner of race. This would lead to the establishment of political awareness and a cultural consciousness of racial pride through which they would be able to solve the problems of slavery, discrimination and attacks on the African race. Pan-Africanism informed many later ideological movements including <u>négritude</u> in the 1930s and the historically significant Pan-African Arts and Cultural Festival in Algiers in 1969.

pan-Arabism A political and cultural movement devoted to the unification and modernisation of the Arab-speaking world that gained currency in the late nineteenth century as Arab nations sought independence from the Ottoman Empire. In the 1950s there were several attempts at Arab unity, particularly in Egypt, Jordan and Syria, and an agreement was reached to accept the modernised version of the Quranic Arabic language as the universal written language of the Arab world. State financing of the arts by President Nasser in Egypt led to a cultural boom in the country. Pan-Arabism was socialist in outlook and strongly opposed to interference from Western powers, seeking to empower Arab nations by the formation of alliances and economic co-operation. Support for pan-Arabism began to decline in the 1960s after the Arab defeat by Israel in the 1967 Six-Day War.

panel A rigid support for <u>painting</u> onto, traditionally made of joined planks of wood, but more recently boards and composites.

paper Matted plant fibres made into sheet form either by hand (traditional) or machine (modern). Handmade paper was produced by drying pulp, produced from beating cotton or linen rags in water, on wire trays. The lines of thinner paper produced by these wires are visible in 'laid' paper. 'Wove' paper, developed in the mid-eighteenth century, is made from trays with a tightly woven wire mesh, which leave a smoother surface and no visible lines. Artists use both handmade and machine-made paper, although handmade is often used for printmaking. Paper is traditionally said to have been invented in China in the second century AD, but was not made in Europe until the twelfth century.

papier collé A specific form of collage that is closer to drawing than painting. The Cubist painter Georges Braque first used it when he drew on imitation woodgrain paper that had been pasted onto white paper. Both Braque and Pablo Picasso made a number of papiers collés in the last three months of 1912 and in early 1913, with Picasso substituting the wood-grain paper favoured by Braque with pages from the newspaper *Le Journal* in an attempt to introduce the reality of everyday life into the pictures. Picasso also developed the idea of the papier collé (pasted paper) into a three-dimensional assemblage when he made *Guitar* in 1912.

Papunya Tula An Aboriginal artist <u>collective</u> formed in 1972 in Papunya, Australia. In the late 1950s and early 1960s many Aboriginal communities were forcibly moved from the Western Desert to a place called Papunya in the Northern Territories. Here they were encouraged to assimilate into white Australian society. In response to this repressive order, the communities began to find other ways of representing their identity. Inspired by their teacher Geoffrey Bardon, who was working in Papunya, members of the aboriginal community began to paint <u>murals</u> depicting symbols inspired by traditional body and sand ceremonial art. Because many of the symbols have spiritual significance, the Papunya Tula artists use dots to camouflage the images. The Papunya Tula artists are widely credited with bringing Aboriginal art to Western attention. There are around 120 artists in the collective including Anatjari Tjakamarra, the first Aboriginal artist to have his work bought for a major museum collection.

parallel cinema A movement that began in the 1960s in India with a group of socially conscious film directors who began to produce low-budget films in parallel to the country's highly successful commercial Bollywood film industry. These films did not offer singing and dancing and instead focused on social and political issues affecting the country. The rise of parallel cinema happened for two reasons. In 1971 the Indian government did not renew their contract to import Hollywood films, a move that proved decisive in dislodging the dominance of American films in India and allowed home-grown directors to flourish. Early parallel cinema films were also state financed thanks to the establishment of the Film Finance Corporation in 1969. This funding was cut in the mid-1970s due to the leftish nature of many of the films being produced, yet the movement continued to grow and was financed by independent production companies. Filmmakers associated with parallel cinema include Shyam Benegal, Mani Kaul, Satyajit Ray and Kumar Shahani.

parchment see <u>vellum</u>

participatory art A term that describes a form of art that directly engages the audience in the creative process so that they become co-producers or participants in the event. In this respect, the artist

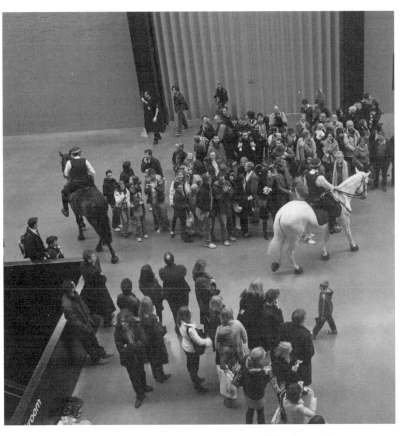

participatory art

Tania Bruguera
Tatlin's Whisper #5 2008
Performance, 2 people and 2 horses
Tate. Purchased with funds
provided by Alin Ryan von Buch
2009

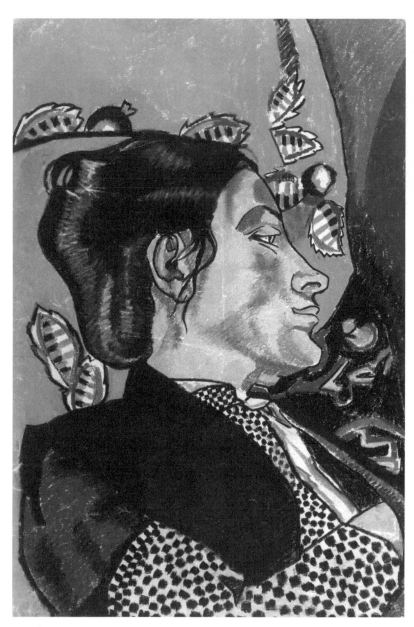

pastel

Henri Gaudier-Brzeska
Sophie Brzeska 1913
Pastel on paper
55.9 × 38.4
Tate. Purchased 1957

216

is seen as a collaborator and a producer of the situation, and these situations can often have an unclear beginning or end. Participatory art has its origins in the Futurist and Dada performances of the early twentieth century, which were designed to provoke, scandalise and agitate the public. In the late 1950s the artist Allan Kaprow devised performances called happenings, in which he would coerce the audience into participating in the experience. The French filmmaker and writer Guy Debord, founder of situationism (see Situationist International), also promoted a form of participatory art in that he wished to eliminate the spectator's position by devising industrial paintings; paintings created en masse. The contemporary artist Marvin Gaye Chetwynd relies entirely on willing participants to create her performances, as does the activist artist Tania Bruguera. In her work *Surplus Value,* participants were asked to wait in line and then randomly divided into those who could enter the work and others who were submitted to lie detector tests, in order to highlight the problems of immigration.

pastel Powdered pigments mixed with a small amount of binding medium to produce dry coloured sticks. Chalk can be added to soften intense pigments and to obtain a range of hues.

patina Usually refers to a distinct green or brown surface-layer on bronze sculpture. Patina can be created naturally by the oxidising effect of the atmosphere or weather, or artificially by the application of chemicals. Almost all bronze sculpture has been patinated one way or the other but Constantin Brancusi polished his bronzes to reveal the beautiful natural gold colour of the metal.

pen and ink Historically, drawings have been made by applying ink with a quill pen made by cutting the hollow stem of a large feather, from a bird such as a goose or a swan, to create a nib. Hollow reeds were also cut in the same way and used for writing and drawing. Metal pens succeeded the quill during the nineteenth century. Pen and ink is often used in conjunction with other techniques such as washes.

pencil see graphite

Penwith Society of Arts Artists society formed in 1948 at St Ives, Cornwall, Britain. It is part of the history of the development of modern and abstract art within the artists' colony of St Ives. The Penwith Society was formed by abstract artists breaking away from the St Ives Society of Artists, which was too conservative for them. They had already formed the splinter Crypt Group within the St Ives Society, but by 1988 felt the need for complete separation. The founders of the Penwith Society were Barbara Hepworth and Ben Nicholson together with the rest of the Crypt Group, including Peter Lanyon, who played a prominent role. They invited the eminent critic and supporter of modern art, Herbert Read, to be their president. (See also Newlyn School)

Perceptismo Founded in Argentina by the painter Raúl Lozza in 1947 after he split from the concrete movement Asociación Arte Concreto-Invencion. Perceptismo (Perceptism) evolved out of the artist's desire for truth when he became disenchanted with the Asociación's inability to prevent illusionism in art. He argued that art could not be viewed in isolation and so the artist should take into consideration the colour of the wall on which the artwork hung. As a result he developed the concept of 'open structure', a series of mathematical calculations that charted the relationships between the angles of the geometric figure and the saturation of colours used. In 1949 he published the magazine *Perceptismo* featuring his writings and paintings.

Performance art Art in which the medium is the artist's own body and the artwork takes the form of actions performed by the artist. Performance art has origins in Futurism and Dada, but became a major phenomenon in the 1960s and 1970s and can be seen as a branch of Conceptual art. In Germany and Austria it was known as Actionism. An important influence on the emergence of Performance art was the photographs of the Abstract Expressionist painter Jackson Pollock making his so-called action paintings, taken in 1950 by the photographer Hans Namuth. Performance art had its immediate origins in the more overtly theatrical happenings organised by Allan Kaprow and others in New York in the late 1950s. By the mid-1960s this theatrical element was being stripped out by early Performance artists such as Vito Acconci and Bruce Nauman.

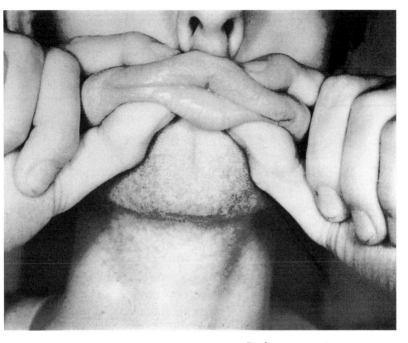

Performance art

Bruce Nauman
a
from *Studies for Holograms (a-e)*
1970
Screenprint on paper
51.7 × 66.2
Tate. Purchased 1994

In Europe, the German artist Joseph Beuys was a hugely influential pioneer of Performance art, making a wide impact with his 'actions' from 1963 on. These were powerful expressions of the pain of human existence, and complex <u>allegories</u> of social and political issues and man's relationship to nature. In Britain the artist duo Gilbert & George made highly original performance works from 1969. A major problem for early Performance artists was the <u>ephemeral</u> nature of the medium. Right from the start Performance pieces were recorded in <u>photography</u>, film and <u>video</u>, and these eventually became the primary means by which Performance reached a wide public.

performativity A term first introduced by the theorist J.L. Austin in his 1955 book *How to Do Things with Words*. Austin used the word performative to describe a sentence that was also an action; like uttering the words 'I name this ship the Queen Elizabeth' while smashing a bottle against the boat. This symbiotic relationship between words and actions that the performative encompassed became a key aspect of <u>Performance art</u>, with theorists and philosophers examining the role of actions, gestures and artistic decision-making through the idea of performativity. A work like Tania Bruguera's *Tatlin's Whisper #5* 2008, in which two mounted policemen perform crowd control with the audience submitting to their commands, is an example of performativity. Since Austin's first use of the word, there have been many philosophers who have elaborated on performativity including John Searle, Jacques Derrida and Judith Butler.

perspective A system for representing objects in three-dimensional space (i.e. for representing the visible world) on the two-dimensional surface of a picture. Basic or linear perspective was invented in Italy in the early fifteenth century and first developed by the painter Paolo Uccello. Perspective rests on the fact that although parallel lines never meet, they appear to do so as they get further away from the viewer towards the horizon, where they disappear. The sides of a road, or later, railway lines, are obvious examples. In <u>painting</u> all parallel lines, such as the roof line and base line of a building, are drawn so as to meet at the horizon if they were extended. This creates the illusion of distance, and the point at which the lines meet is called the vanishing point. Things look smaller the further away they are, and perspective enabled painters accurately and consistently to calculate the size things should be in relation to their supposed distance from the viewpoint. Early perspective systems used a single fixed viewpoint with a single vanishing point. Later, multiple vanishing points were introduced which enabled a much more naturalistic representation of a scene to be made, because it was closer to the way we actually see, that is, from two eyes which are in constant motion. Atmospheric or aerial perspective creates the sense of distance in a painting by utilising the fact that the atmosphere appears more blue in the distance.

PESTS An anonymous protest and pressure group of artists operating in New York in the 1980s. Their aim was to expose the discrimination, exclusion and tokenism directed towards artists from racial minorities by commercial galleries and public museums. Much of their art was in the form of ephemera – flyers, posters and brochures – in which they would highlight examples of racial discrimination. In one flyer they wrote: "THERE ARE AT LEAST 11,009* ARTISTS OF COLOR IN NEW YORK. WHY DON'T YOU SEE US?" Their logo was a wasp with an elongated jaw and they printed this image on all their publications. None of the members have ever identified themselves, although it is thought a member of the Guerrilla Girls founded the group. (See also activist art)

the photobook A book of photographs by a photographer that has an overarching theme or follows a storyline. It is a convenient and reasonably cheap way of disseminating the work of a photographer to a mass audience and early photobooks were used to illustrate the work of individual photographers or a new type of photographic process. William Henry Fox Talbot published a photobook in 1844 called *The Pencil of Nature* in order to promote his Calotype photographic process. Over the years, photobooks have helped to establish the idea that a sequence of images represents a narrative in its own right. The German photographer August Sander published *Face of Our Time* in 1929, part of his life-long project to create a comprehensive photographic index of the German population. Today photobooks are crucial for financing and circulating modern photography enabling enthusiasts to access the work of a wide range of photographers from across the world.

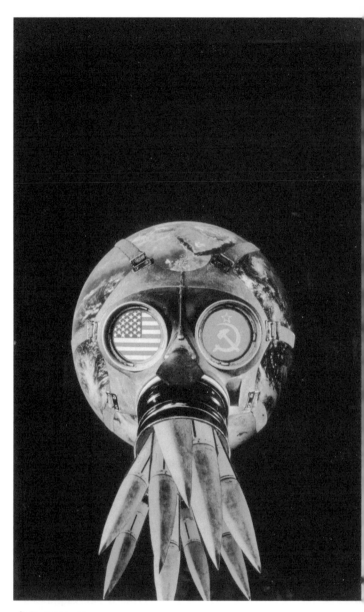

photomontage

Peter Kennard
Defended to Death 1983
Photographs on paper and gouache
on card
47 × 31.5
Tate. Purchased from the artist 2007

photogram see <u>rayograph</u>

photograph An image created by the action of light on a light-sensitive material at some stage during its making. It can be either a positive or <u>negative</u> image and made using one of many processes.

photomontage A <u>collage</u> constructed from photographs that has often been used as a means of expressing political dissent. First used by the <u>Dadaists</u> in 1915 in their protests against the First World War, it was later adopted by the <u>Surrealists</u> who exploited the possibilities photomontage offered by using free association to bring together widely disparate images, to reflect the workings of the unconscious mind. In 1923 the Russian <u>Constructivist</u> Aleksander Rodchenko began experimenting with photomontage as a way of creating striking socially engaged imagery concerned with the placement and movement of objects in space. Other key exponents of the medium are John Heartfield, the German artist who reconstructed images from the media to protest against Germany's Fascist regime, and Peter Kennard, whose photomontages explored issues such as economic inequality, police brutality and the nuclear arms race between the 1970s and the 1990s.

photorealism A style of painting that emerged in Europe and the USA in the late 1960s, photorealism was characterised by its painstaking detail and precision. It rejected the painterly qualities by which individual artists could be recognised, and instead strove to create pictures that looked photographic. Visual complexity, heightened clarity and a desire to be emotionally neutral led to banal subject matter that likened the movement to <u>Pop art</u>. Artists associated with photorealism include the painter Chuck Close and Richard Estes. The early 1990s saw a renewed interest in photorealism, thanks to new technology in the form of cameras and digital equipment, which offered more precision. Younger artists practising this technique today include Raphaella Spence, Clive Head and Bertrand Meniel. (See also <u>Hyper-Realism</u>)

The Photo-Secession Founded by Alfred Stieglitz in New York in 1902, The Photo-Secession was a group of American photographers who believed that photography was a fine art. The name was invented by Stieglitz as a way of affiliating the photographers with the <u>modernist</u> <u>Secession</u> movements in Europe. The other members were Alvin Langdon Coburn, Gertrude Käsebier, Edward Steichen and Clarence H. White, who all placed great influence on fine photographic printing and used techniques to emulate paint and pastel. The results were printed in their magazine *Camera Work* that Stieglitz edited from 1903 to 1907, and exhibited in their gallery, The Little Galleries of the Photo-Secession, later known simply as 291.

Pictorialism An experimental photographic movement that sought to elevate the <u>photograph</u> to the status of <u>painting</u> or <u>drawing</u>. By 1845 cameras were so easy to operate that a debate began as to whether photography could be considered art, arguing that in reality it was simply a mechanical copying device. As a result a number of photographers began using highly technical processes to create images that looked more like paintings. These photographers played with light and shade, creating pictures that were atmospheric and mysterious. As many of the photographers who promoted Pictorialism had originally trained as artists, like Alvin Langdon Coburn, Alfred Stieglitz and Oscar Gustave Rejlander, they understood the lexicon of painting and strove to reproduce these ideas in photographic form.

picture plane In traditional <u>illusionistic</u> <u>painting</u> using <u>perspective</u>, the picture plane can be thought of as the glass of the notional window through which the viewer looks into the representation of reality that lies beyond. In practice the picture plane is the same as the actual physical surface of the painting. In modern art the picture plane became a major issue. <u>Formalist</u> theory asserts that a painting is a flat object and that in the interests of truth it should not pretend to be other than flat. In other words, there should be no illusion of three dimensions and so all the elements of the painting should be located on the picture plane.

Pictures Generation Name given to a group of American artists who came of age in the early 1970s and were known for their critical analysis of media culture. Inspired by philosophers such as Roland Barthes, who had questioned the very idea of originality and authenticity in his manifesto *The Death of the Author*, this loose-knit group of artists set out to make art that analysed their relationship with popular culture and the mass media. They worked in photography, film, video and performance, creating art that used the same mechanisms of seduction and desire that played upon them. Cindy Sherman took photographs of herself dressed as B-movie heroines; Richard Prince deconstructed mass consumerism with his pictures of cowboys taken from adverts. In 1977 an exhibition called *Pictures Generation* featuring many of these artists was held at the Artist's Space in New York.

Pittura Metafisica Italian art movement meaning Metaphysical Art. Created by Giorgio de Chirico and the former Futurist, Carlo Carrà, in the north Italian city of Ferrara. Using a realist style, they painted dream-like views of the arcaded squares typical of such Italian cities. The squares are unnaturally empty, and in them objects and statues are brought together in strange juxtapositions. The artists thus created a visionary world of the mind, beyond physical reality, hence the name. Strictly speaking the movement only lasted around six months in 1917 while de Chirico and Carrà worked together, de Chirico changing his style the following year. However, the term is generally applied to all de Chirico's work from about 1911 when he first developed what became known as Pittura Metafisica. His *The Uncertainty of the Poet* of 1913 is a quintessential example of the style. Pittura Metafisica was also highly influential, most importantly on the development of the dream-like, or oneiric, kind of Surrealist painting, particularly that of Max Ernst.

plane A plane is a flat surface, and any discrete flat surface within a painting or sculpture can be referred to as a plane. The flat patches seen in Cubist paintings are often referred to as planes, and geometric abstract artists refer frequently to planes in discussing their work.

Plaster of Paris A fine white powder (calcium sulphate hemihydrate) which, when mixed with water, forms fully hydrated calcium sulphate, a white solid. Widely used by sculptors for moulds and preliminary casts.

plein air French term meaning 'out of doors', this refers to the practice of painting an entire finished picture out of doors as opposed to simply making preparatory studies or sketches. It was pioneered by John Constable in Britain c.1813–17, then from c.1860 became fundamental to Impressionism. An important technical approach in the development of naturalism, it subsequently became extremely widespread and part of the practice of rural naturalists, for example. It was sometimes taken to extremes: there exists a photograph of Stanhope Forbes painting on a beach in high wind, with his canvas and easel secured by guy ropes.

plinth A heavy base for supporting sculpture.

pluralism Refers to a social structure in which many small groups maintain their unique cultural identity within a broader culture. In an art context, pluralism refers to the late 1960s and 1970s when art, politics and culture merged as artists began to believe in a more socially and politically responsive form of art. The art historian Rosalind Krauss characterised this period as 'diversified, split and factionalized. Unlike the art of the last several decades, its energy does not seem to flow through a single channel for which a synthetic term, like Abstract Expressionism, or Minimalism, might be found.'

Polaroid print A Polaroid print is a positive print that is produced shortly after exposure by a Polaroid camera. The film contains chemicals needed for developing and fixing the photograph. A negative sheet is exposed inside the camera, then lined up with a positive sheet and squeezed through a set of rollers between which a coating of reagent is spread. This activates the developing process in which unexposed silver halide grains are solubilised by the reagent and transferred by diffusion from negative to positive. This process takes roughly a minute, after which time the negative is peeled away to reveal the image, which has been transferred to the positive receiving sheet. The first Polaroid cameras, invented by Edwin H. Land, were marketed in 1947 and produced black and white images. Polaroid instant colour prints and slides were launched in 1963.

Political Pop An art movement that emerged in China the 1980s, partly in response to the rampant modernisation of the country, but also as a way of coming to terms with the <u>Cultural Revolution</u>. Political Pop combined Western <u>Pop art</u> with <u>Socialist Realism</u> to create art that questioned the political and social climate of a rapidly changing China. With Pop's banality and semi-ironic approach to capitalism, combined with propaganda images from the era of Chairman Mao, artists challenged the prevailing attitudes to art in China. A work like *Blue Mao* by Li Shan referenced Andy Warhol's <u>screenprint</u> <u>portraits</u> of the Chinese leader, while Wang Guangyi's *Great Criticism: Coca Cola* depicted Chinese workers in a socialist realist style painting a sign for Coca Cola. Critics of Political Pop have argued that the movement does not fully engage because of its strategy of imitating propaganda and consumerist discourse. The artists have also been accused of using stereotypes to meet the demands of the Western market.

polyptych A <u>painting</u> made up of more than three <u>panels</u>. Paintings of three panels are <u>triptychs</u> and of two, <u>diptychs</u>.

Pont-Aven The coastal town in north-west France which Paul Gauguin frequented between 1886 and 1894. With a group that included Emile Bernard and Paul Sérusier he developed a Synthetic style of painting that emphasised, through bold outline and simplified structure, a symbolic and emotional response to the Breton people and landscape. (See also <u>synthetism</u>)

Pop art Name given to British and American versions of art that drew inspiration from sources in popular and commercial culture. These sources included Hollywood movies, advertising, packaging, pop music and comic books. In Europe a similar movement was called <u>Nouveau Réalisme</u> (New Realism). Pop began in the mid-1950s and reached its peak in the 1960s. It was a revolt against prevailing orthodoxies in art and life and can be seen as one of the first manifestations of <u>Postmodernism</u>. <u>Modernist</u> critics were horrified by the Pop artists' use of such low subject matter and by their apparently uncritical treatment of it. In fact, Pop took art into new areas of subject matter and developed new ways of presenting it in art. Chief artists in America were Roy Lichtenstein, Claes Oldenburg and Andy Warhol; in Britain, Peter Blake, Patrick Caulfield, Richard Hamilton, David Hockney, Allen Jones and Colin Self.

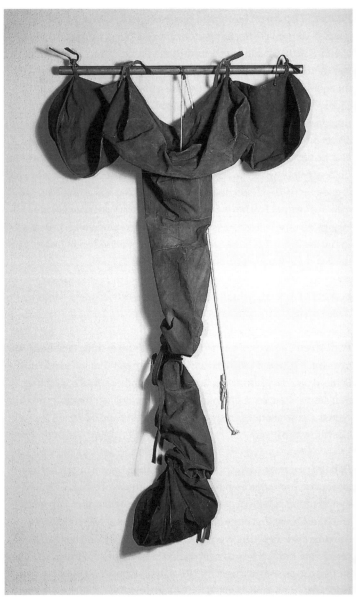

Pop art

Claes Oldenburg
Soft Drainpipe – Blue (Cool) Version 1967
Acrylic on canvas and steel
259.1 × 187.6 × 35.6
Tate. Purchased 1970

portfolio A group of <u>prints</u>, often – though not necessarily – by the same artist and presented as a group, usually based on a related theme. Sometimes they will be considered as a set or series of images. The term also applies to the physical folder in which such series may be held.

portrait A <u>representation</u> of a particular person. Portraiture is a very old art form going back at least to ancient Egypt, where it flourished from about 5,000 years ago. Before the invention of <u>photography</u>, a painted, <u>sculpted</u> or drawn portrait was the only way to record the appearance of someone. But portraits have always been more than just a record. They have been used to show the power, importance, virtue, beauty, wealth, taste, learning or other qualities of the sitter. Portraits have almost always been flattering, and painters who refused to flatter, such as William Hogarth, tended to find their work rejected. A notable exception was Francisco Goya in his apparently bluntly truthful portraits of the Spanish royal family. Among leading modern artists, portrait <u>painting</u> on commission became increasingly rare. Instead artists painted their friends and lovers in whatever way they pleased. Most of Pablo Picasso's pictures of women, for example, however bizarre, can be identified as portraits of his lovers. At the same time, photography became the most important <u>medium</u> of traditional portraiture, bringing what was formerly an expensive luxury product within the purse of almost everyone. Since the 1990s artists have also used video to create living portraits, but portrait painting continues to flourish. (See also <u>conversation piece</u>; <u>genres</u>)

postcolonial art Art produced in response to the aftermath of colonial rule, frequently addressing issues of national and cultural identity, race and ethnicity. Frantz Fanon provided a theoretical framework for interpreting the oppression of the individual under imperialism – a significant element of much postcolonial art – and initiated the investigation of diversity and hierarchy in postcolonial cultures undertaken by writers such as Edward Said, Stuart Hall and Homi Bhabha.

Post-Impressionism Umbrella term to describe changes in Impressionism from about 1886, the date of the last Impressionist group show in Paris. There were four major figures who developed and extended Impressionism in distinctly different directions. Paul Cézanne retained the fundamental doctrine of painting from nature but with added rigour, reportedly saying 'I want to re-do Poussin from nature' (Nicolas Poussin was a notoriously intellectual pioneer of French landscape). Georges Seurat put Impressionist painting of light and colour on a scientific basis (Neo-Impressionism, divisionism). Paul Gauguin retained intense light and colour but rejected painting from nature and reintroduced imaginative subject matter. Vincent van Gogh painted from nature but developed a highly personal use of colour and brushwork, directly expressing an emotional response to the subject and his inner world.

Post-internet art A term which emerged in the mid-2000s, it describes a form of art that reflects the influence of the internet on contemporary culture. Post-internet art is not necessarily made on the internet (like net art), rather it is a Conceptual movement that tries to reflect this fragmentary and fractured new world, where humans and technologies exist in unison, questioning the disjunctions between our bodily lives and our experience of ourselves as ghosts in a digital machine. An example of Post-internet art is Laure Provoust's Turner Prize winning film *Wantee* 2013 which weaves together fact, fiction, art history and modern technology, while making reference to the streaming of images online.

Post-Minimalism A term used to describe the developments in art that succeeded Minimalism in the USA. By the late 1960s, there was a reaction to the impersonal nature of Minimalism. Its strict adherence to simple geometric shapes and industrial materials had become limiting. Artists began experimenting with softer, more malleable materials that were harder to control and brought in an element of chance to the work. In 1971 the art critic Robert Pincus-Witten described the sculptures of Eva Hesse, who was pioneering the use of rope and latex, as Post-Minimalist. Other aspects of Post-Minimalism included theoretical exercises in the means of production. Wall drawings by Sol LeWitt existed as descriptions that needed to be realised by a second party. Other Post-Minimalist

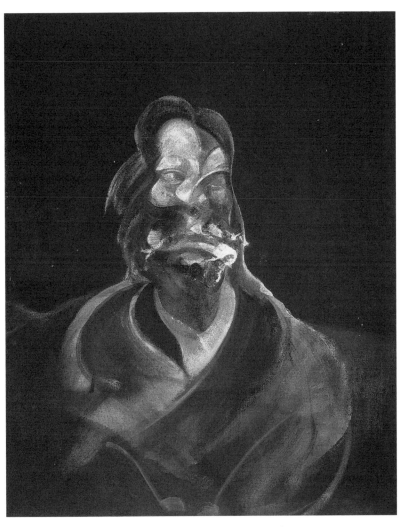

portrait

Francis Bacon
Portrait of Isabel Rawsthorne 1966
Oil paint on canvas
81.3 × 68.6
Tate. Purchased 1966

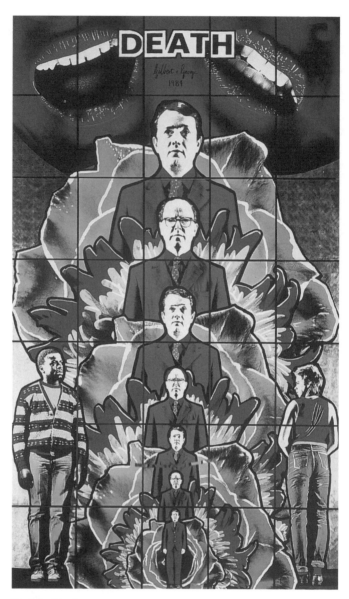

Postmodernism

Gilbert & George
Death Hope Life Fear 1984
First panel of a quadripartite picture
252 photographs, black and white, on
paper with dye mounted onto panels
422 × 250
Tate. Purchased 1990

artists did away with materials altogether, using their bodies as the medium. Vito Acconci's *Seedbed* 1972 consisted of the artist lying under a wooden ramp masturbating. He used the sound of visitors' footsteps on the ramp above to fuel his sexual fantasies, which he recounted into a microphone.

Postmodernism A term used from about 1970 to describe changes seen to take place in Western society and culture from the 1960s onwards. These changes arose from anti-authoritarian challenges to the prevailing orthodoxies across the board. In art, Postmodernism was specifically a reaction against modernism. It may be said to begin with Pop art and to embrace much of what followed including Conceptual art, Neo-Expressionism, feminist art, and the Young British Artists of the 1990s. Some outstanding characteristics of Postmodernism are that it collapses the distinction between high culture and mass or popular culture; that it tends to efface the boundary between art and everyday life; and that it refuses to recognise the authority of any single style or definition of what art should be.

Post-Painterly Abstraction A blanket term covering a range of new developments in abstract painting in the late 1950s and early 1960s. In 1964 an exhibition of thirty-one artists associated with these developments was organised by the critic Clement Greenberg at the Los Angeles County Museum of Art. He titled it *Post-Painterly Abstraction*. Leading figures were Helen Frankenthaler, Morris Louis and Kenneth Noland. Post-Painterly Abstraction set abstract painting on a more rigorous, i.e. more purely abstract, basis than before. It grew very directly out of the existing traditions of abstract art, synthesising elements from Jackson Pollock, Mark Rothko and Barnett Newman as well as looking to Ad Reinhardt and Ellsworth Kelly, to the late work of Henri Matisse and to the targets and flags of Jasper Johns. However, the Post-Painterly Abstractionists were ruthless in their rejection of the inwardness and mysticism of Abstract Expressionism and of any residual references to the external world, and they also explored new ways of composing. What they created was a purely factual kind of art which, more than ever before, functioned in terms of the basic elements of the medium itself; form, colour, texture, scale, composition and so on.

primitivism A term used to describe the fascination of early modern European artists with what was then called primitive art. This included tribal art from Africa, the South Pacific and Indonesia, as well as prehistoric and very early European art, and European folk art. Such work has had a profound impact on modern Western art. The discovery of African tribal art by Pablo Picasso around 1906 was an important influence on his painting in general, and was a major factor in leading him to Cubism. Primitivism also means the search for a simpler more basic way of life away from Western urban sophistication and social restrictions. The classic example of this is Paul Gauguin's move from Paris to Tahiti in the South Pacific in 1891. Primitivism was also important for Expressionism, including Brücke. As a result of these artists' interest and appreciation, what was once called primitive art is now seen as having equal value to Western forms and the term primitive is avoided or used in quotation marks.

print An impression made by any method involving transfer from one surface to another.

process art Art in which the process of its making is not hidden but remains a prominent aspect of the completed work, so that a part or even the whole of its subject is the making of the work. Process became a widespread preoccupation of artists in the late 1960s and the 1970s, but like so much else can be tracked back to the Abstract Expressionist paintings of Jackson Pollock. In these, the successive layers of dripped and poured paint can be identified and the actions of the artist in making the work can be to some extent reconstructed. The later Colour Field paintings of Morris Louis clearly reveal his process of pouring the paint onto the canvas. In process art too there is an emphasis on the results on particular materials of carrying out the process determined by the artist. In Louis again, the forms are the result of the interaction of the artist's action, the type and viscosity of the paint, and the type and absorbency of the canvas. Richard Serra made work by throwing molten lead into the corners of a room, and Robert Morris by making long cuts into lengths of felt and then hanging them on a nail or placing them on the floor and allowing them to take on whatever configurations were dictated by the interaction of the innate properties of the felt, the artist's action and gravity. The British painter Bernard Cohen made paintings by establishing a set process for the work and then carrying it through until the canvas was full. John Hilliard's photographic work *Camera Recording its Own Condition* of 1971 is a particularly pure example of process art, as is Michael Craig-Martin's *4 Complete Clipboard Sets*.

proof A printing term applied to all individual impressions made before work on a printing plate or block is completed, in order to check progress of the image. Also referred to as 'trial proof' or 'colour trial proof'. This should not be confused with the terms Artist's Proof ('AP') and Printer's Proof ('PP'), which are impressions of the finished print made in addition to the published edition for the artist or printer.

proportion The relationship of one part of a whole to other parts. In art it has usually meant a preoccupation with finding a mathematical formula for the perfect human body. At the time of the Renaissance, Leonardo da Vinci and Albrecht Dürer attempted to find a formula that would enable the body to be exactly inscribed in a square or a circle. Their system seems to have been to first make the height the same as the full width of the outstretched arms, and then to add to the height so that the total height was equal to eight heads. Renaissance researches into proportion were inspired by the ancient Roman writer of a treatise on architecture, Vitruvius. A more general formula for perfect proportion is the golden section or golden ratio. This is defined as a line divided so that the smaller part is to the larger part as the larger part is to the whole. It works out at roughly 8:13 or a bit over one third to two thirds. In one way or another the golden section can be detected in most works of art. It so named because it was considered to have some special aesthetic virtue in itself.

provenance A history of ownership of a work of art. The word comes from the French verb *provenir* (to come from). Provenance is essential in identifying, with certainty, the authorship of a work of art. When the chips are down, no amount of connoisseurship can beat a good provenance. The ideal provenance would consist of a history of ownership traceable right back to the artist's studio. Another important aspect of the history of an artwork is the exhibitions it has been in. The importance of provenance has not escaped the attention of forgers (see fake). In the 1990s a forger inserted fake references to forged paintings into material such as exhibition catalogues in museum archives. This convinced buyers even when the quality of the forgery was not especially good.

psychedelic art Generally associated with the 1960s and the mind-expanding drug LSD. There are many earlier examples of artists taking drugs in order to heighten their awareness and enlarge their mental vision, but it was the hallucinatory effects of LSD that had such a powerful effect on artists. Day-glo and anti-naturalistic in colour, psychedelic art often contained swirling patterns, erotic imagery and hidden messages, all aiming to refer to the changing states of consciousness while under the influence of the drug. Much of the art grew out of the hippy community in San Francisco, in particular the artists Stanley Mouse, Rick Griffin and Alton Kelley who were commissioned by the rock promoter Bill Graham to produce posters for the bands The Grateful Dead, Jimi Hendrix and Big Brother and the Holding Company.

psychogeography A term coined by the Marxist theorist Guy Debord in 1955 in order to describe the effect of a geographical location on the emotions and behaviour of individuals. Inspired by Charles Baudelaire's concept of the flâneur – an urban wanderer – Debord suggested playful and inventive ways of navigating the urban environment in order to closely examine the architecture around us. As a founding member of the avant-garde movement Situationist International, Debord wanted a revolutionary new approach to architecture, one that was less functional and more open to exploration. Psychogeography has its roots in Surrealism and Dada, and a painting like *La Route des Alpes* by Tristram Hillier could be described as an early example of the concept. Psychogeography gained popularity in the 1990s when artists, writers and filmmakers like Iain Sinclair and Patrick Keiller began using the idea to create work based on pedestrian exploration.

public art Artwork that is in the public realm, regardless of whether it is situated on public or private property or whether it has been purchased with public or private money. Usually, but not always, the art has been commissioned specifically for the site in which it is situated (site-specific). Monuments, memorials and civic statues and sculptures are the most established forms of public art, but public art can also be transitory, in the form of performances, dance, theatre, poetry, graffiti, posters, street art and installations. Public art can often be used as a political tool, like the propaganda posters and statues of the Soviet Union (Agit-prop) or the murals painted by the Ulster Unionists in Northern Ireland. Public art can also be a form of civic protest, as in the graffiti sprayed on the sides of New York Subway trains in the 1980s. (See also Mexican Muralism)

Purism Movement founded by Edouard Jeanneret (better known as the modern architect Le Corbusier) and Amédée Ozenfant. They set out the theory of Purism in their book *Après le Cubisme* (After Cubism) published in 1918. They criticised the fragmentation of the object in Cubism and the way in which Cubism had become, in their view, decorative by that time. Instead they proposed a kind of painting in which objects were represented as powerful basic forms stripped of detail. A crucial element of Purism was its embrace of technology and the machine, and it aimed to give mechanical and industrial subject matter a timeless, classical quality. References to ancient Greek architecture can be seen in the fluting (like a Greek column) on the bottles in Ozenfant's still life compositions. The most important other artist associated with Purism was Fernand Léger. Purism reached a climax in Le Corbusier's Pavillon de l'Esprit Nouveau (Pavilion of the New Spirit), built in 1925 for the International Exposition of Decorative and Industrial Arts in Paris. This was hung with work by the three principals and also included the Cubists, Juan Gris and Jacques Lipschitz. After this the key relationship between Ozenfant and Le Corbusier broke up.

q

queer aesthetics Art of homosexual, lesbian or transgender
imagery that is based around the issues that evolved out of the
gender and identity politics of the 1980s. Although there have been
many representations of homosexuality and lesbianism in the history
of art, it was in the 1980s, in the wake of the feminist movement
and the AIDS crisis, that the queer aesthetic was born. Artists began
to document a cultural landscape that was rapidly disappearing,
as well as the backlash that had taken place against sexual
freedom. Much of the art resonates with themes of life and death, in
particular the photographs of Nan Goldin and Wolfgang Tillmans
and the installations of Felix Gonzalez-Torres. There is also a critical
exploration of representation, as in the photographs of lesbians by
Catherine Opie and in the studies of the gay S&M scene in New York
by Robert Mapplethorpe. (See also feminist art)

r

rational painting A style of painting that emerged in the mid-1980s in the Northern provinces of China and was part of a utopian idea of a new spiritual culture, one detached from history and tradition, and based on rationality. The concept of rational painting was formulated by the Northern Art Group a collection of artists, writers and scientists who lived in the Northern provinces of China. The aesthetic, inspired by the inhospitable wilderness of China's northern landscape, was cool, mystical and detached, focusing on the reduction of the image. The paintings depicted strange symbols in subdued colours and subject matter alluded to the alienation of the individual. The rational painting trend inspired many later Chinese artists. Artists associated with rational painting are Wang Guangyi, Shu Qun, Ren Jian, Liu Yan, Zhang Peili, Geng Jianyi and Wang Qiang.

Rayograph Photograms are photographic prints that do not require the use of a camera and are made by laying objects directly onto photosensitive paper and exposing it to light. The process is as old as photography itself, but emerged again in various avant-garde contexts in the early 1920s. Man Ray refined and personalised the technique to such an extent that the new prints eventually carried his name – rayographs.

Rayonism One of the Russian avant-garde movements that proliferated in Moscow and St Petersburg in the from about 1910 to 1920. Rayonism, or Rayism, was the invention of Mikhail Larionov and his partner Natalia Goncharova in 1912. It was an early form of abstract art, based on landscape and consisting of dynamically interacting linear forms ultimately derived from rays of light. Of his Rayonist painting *Nocturne* Larionov later wrote: 'This painting was inspired by the dusk at Odessa. It is a problem of the combination of staircases, interiors and exteriors of houses and represents the pressure of the body of dark colours on the semi-light tones. The problem of this painting is to organise these tones in a certain order. It is the conflict of the semi-light rays with the dark rays.'

readymade The term used by the French artist Marcel Duchamp to describe works of art he made from manufactured objects. His earliest readymades included *Bicycle Wheel* of 1913, a wheel

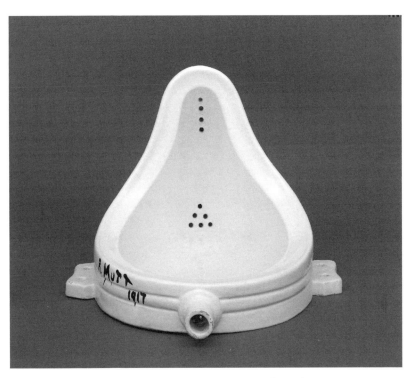

readymade

Marcel Duchamp
Fountain 1917, replica 1964
Porcelain
36 × 48 × 61
Tate. Purchased with assistance
from the Friends of the Tate Gallery
1999

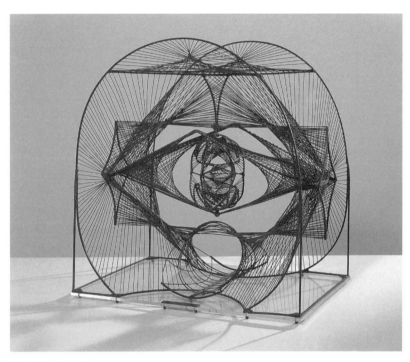

Réalités Nouvelles

Antoine Pevsner
*Maquette of a Monument Symbolising
the Liberation of the Spirit* 1952
Bronze
47.2 × 46.5 × 31
Tate. Purchased 1953

mounted on a wooden stool, and *In Advance of the Broken Arm* of 1915, a snow shovel inscribed with that title. In 1917 in New York, Duchamp made his most notorious readymade, *Fountain*, a men's urinal signed by the artist with a false name and exhibited laid flat on its back. Later readymades could be more elaborate and were referred to by Duchamp as assisted readymades. The theory behind the readymade was explained in an article, anonymous but almost certainly by Duchamp himself, in the May 1917 issue of the avant-garde magazine *The Blind Man* run by Duchamp and two friends: 'Whether Mr Mutt with his own hands made the fountain or not has no importance. He CHOSE it. He took an ordinary article of life, and placed it so that its useful significance disappeared under the new title and point of view – created a new thought for that object.' There are three important points here: first, that the choice of object is itself a creative act. Secondly, that by cancelling the 'useful' function of an object it becomes art. Thirdly, that the presentation and addition of a title to the object have given it 'a new thought', a new meaning. Duchamp's readymades also asserted the principle that what is art is defined by the artist. Duchamp was an influential figure in Dada and Surrealism, an important influence on Pop art, environments, assemblage, installation, Conceptual art and much art of the 1990s such as the Young British Artists. (See also Postmodernism)

Realism Until the nineteenth century Western art was dominated by the academic theory of history painting and high art. Then, the development of naturalism began to go hand in hand with increasing emphasis on realism of subject, meaning subjects outside the high art tradition. The term Realism was coined by the French novelist Champfleury in the 1840s and in art was exemplified in the work of his friend, the painter Gustave Courbet. In practice, Realist subject matter meant scenes of peasant and working-class life, the life of the city streets, cafés and popular entertainments, and an increasing frankness in the treatment of the body and sexual subjects. Such subject matter combined with the new naturalism of treatment caused shock among the predominantly upper- and middle-class audiences for art. (See also Fantastic Realism; Hyper-Realism; Magic Realism; Social Realism; Socialist Realism)

realism Since the rise of modern art, realism, realist or realistic, with a lower case 'r', has come to be primarily a stylistic description, referring to painting or sculpture that continues to represent things in a way that more or less pre-dates Post-Impressionism. The term generally implies a certain grittiness of choice of subject. (See also modern realism; photorealism; ugly realism)

Réalités Nouvelles The Salon des Réalités Nouvelles (New Realities) was an exhibiting society devoted to pure abstract art, founded in Paris in 1939 by Sonia Delaunay and others. After the interruption of the Second World War it was re-established in 1946 with the help of Delaunay, and continues today. In the postwar era it provided the same focus for the purest tendencies in abstract art that Abstraction-Création had before the war. The name reflects the fundamental idea that abstract art is a new reality because it does not refer to or imitate any existing reality.

reception theory A key concept of Postmodernism, reception theory emerged in the early 1970s and had an enormous impact on the interpretation of literature and art. First alluded to by the German theorist Hans Robert Jauss in an essay in 1969 entitled 'The change in the paradigm of literary scholarship', reception theory, in relation to art, is based on the idea that meaning is located somewhere between the viewer and the artwork; each person will decode the artwork slightly differently depending on the knowledge and access to the frameworks of power that the person has. Since Jauss introduced the concept, other theorists have used it to study the cultural world. In Britain, Stuart Hall notably used reception theory as a way of discussing cultural representation in relation to the way the British establishment misrepresented black communities in the media. The concept of reader-response criticism – in which the focus is on the audience's experience of the artwork, rather than the creator and the content and form of the work – is often also associated with reception theory, although Robert C. Holub in his critical introduction to reception theory argues that these ideas are mutually exclusive.

recto/verso The recto is the front or face of a single sheet of paper, or the right-hand page of an open book. The back or underside of a single sheet of paper, or the left-hand page of an open book, is known as the verso.

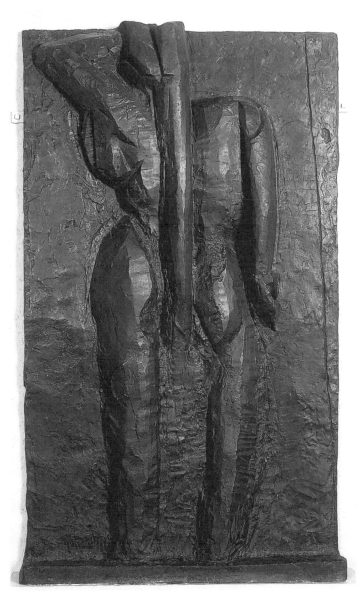

relief

Henri Matisse
Back III c.1916–17, cast 1955–6
Bronze
188 × 113 × 17.1
Tate. Purchased with assistance
from the Matisse Appeal Fund 1957

relational aesthetics The French <u>curator</u> Nicolas Bourriaud published a book called *Relational Aesthetics* in 1998 in which he described the term as meaning 'a set of artistic practices which take as their theoretical and practical point of departure the whole of human relations and their social context, rather than an independent and private space.' He saw artists as facilitators rather than makers and regarded art as information exchanged between the artist and the viewers. The artist, in this sense, gives audiences access to power and the means to change the world. Bourriaud cited the art of Gillian Wearing, Philippe Parreno, Douglas Gordon and Liam Gillick as artists who work to this agenda.

relief A wall-mounted <u>sculpture</u> in which the three-dimensional elements are raised from a flat base. Any three-dimensional element attached to a basically flat wall-mounted work of art is said to be in relief or a relief element.

replica A copy of a work of art that is virtually indistinguishable from the original. Unlike a <u>fake</u>, a replica is not trying to pass for the original and is often made by the artist and used for historical and educational purposes. The vogue for collecting replicas reached the height of popularity in the mid- to late nineteenth century when few people could afford to travel on the Continent, so museums acquired reproductions of important monuments and works of art to complement their collections. Replicas in modern art are made as a result of original works of art decaying or being lost. Marcel Duchamp's *Fountain*, the most famous of the artist's <u>readymade</u> sculptures, was replicated in collaboration with Duchamp from a photograph of the lost original. Tate holds the largest collection of plastic <u>sculptures</u> by Naum Gabo, but despite controlled storage conditions, many of these works are cracking and warping. Computer software will be used to help virtually restore the sculpture models, so that replicas can be made of the originals. (See also <u>simulacrum</u>)

reportage photography A form of photography that records the news and is a powerful means of communication. Reportage photographers bear witness to the world, whether it is by documenting the exploits of day-to-day life or the front line of a war zone. Sometimes there is a subjective intention behind the pictures; to move hearts, change minds and influence politics, while other reportage photographers try to be purely objective. In either case, the photographer and the viewer of the pictures are presented with a moral dilemma, that of voyeur. This is explored in Susan Sontag's book *Regarding the Pain of Others*. In 1980 the art critic Michel Nuridsany asserted that all photography, with the exception of reportage photography, belonged to the realm of art. This has been challenged in recent years, through large scale exhibitions of reportage photographers at Tate Modern and the V&A, and by artists like Jeff Wall and Roy Arden who have used a reportage-style in their art.

representational A blanket term for art that represents some aspect of reality in a more or less straightforward way. The term seems to have come into use after the rise of modern art and particularly abstract art as a means of referring to art not substantially touched by modern developments. It is not quite the same as figurative art, which seems to apply to modern art in which the elements of reality, while recognisable, are nevertheless treated in modern ways, as in expressionism for example. The term figurative also implies a particular focus on the human figure. The term non-representational is frequently used as a synonym for abstract.

resin An organic solid, usually transparent. 'Natural' resins derive from either plants or insects, whereas 'synthetic' resins (for example alkyd and acrylic) are manufactured industrially. They can usually be dissolved in organic solvents to produce a clear solution, although many synthetic resins are produced as dispersions.

resistance art A form of art that emerged in South Africa in the mid-1970s after the Soweto uprising, which marked the beginning of social change in the country. Resistance art focused on resisting apartheid and celebrating African strength and unity. It grew out of the Black Consciousness Movement, a grass-roots, anti-apartheid movement that emerged in the 1960s lead by the charismatic activist Steve Biko. Much of the art was public, taking the form of murals, banners, posters, t-shirts and graffiti with political messages that were confrontational and focused on the realities of life in a segregated South Africa. One of the leading artists of resistance art was Thamsanga Mnyele who was killed by South African commandos in 1985. Other artists associated with resistance art include Dikobe Martins and Norman Catherine.

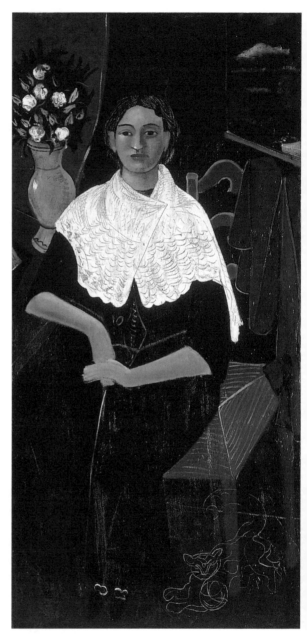

'return to order'

André Derain
*Madame Derain
in a White Shawl*
c.1919–20
Oil paint on canvas
195.5 × 97.5
Tate. Purchased 1982

'return to order' From the French *retour à l'ordre*, this was a phenomenon of European art in the years following the First World War. The term is said to derive from the book of essays by the artist and poet Jean Cocteau, *Le rappel a l'ordre*, published in 1926. The First World War administered a huge shock to European society. One of the artistic responses to it was to reject the extreme <u>avant-garde</u> forms of art that had proliferated before the war. Instead, more reassuring and traditional approaches were adopted. The term 'return to order' is used to describe this phenomenon. <u>Cubism</u>, with its fragmentation of reality, was rejected, even by its inventors Georges Braque and Pablo Picasso. <u>Futurism</u>, with its worship of the machine and its enthusiasm for war, was particularly discredited. Classicism was an important thread in the 'return to order', and in the early 1920s Picasso entered a Neoclassical phase. Braque painted calm <u>still life</u> and figure pictures that, while still having some Cubist characteristics, were simple and readable. The former <u>Fauve</u> painter André Derain and many other artists turned to various forms of <u>realism</u>. In Germany <u>Neue Sachlichkeit</u> can be seen as part of the 'return to order'.

rural naturalism Paintings of rural life in a naturalist manner, but the subjects tend to be sentimentalised, distinguishing them from more gritty <u>realist</u> work. In Britain the style was exemplified by the <u>Newlyn School</u> and the work of artists such as George Clausen, Henry Herbert La Thangue and Edward Stott.

Ruralists Group of British artists founded in 1975 around the <u>Pop artist</u> Peter Blake, after his move from London to the countryside near Bath. The full name was The Brotherhood of Ruralists and this, combined with the original number of seven members, gives a conscious echo of the nineteenth-century Pre-Raphaelite Brotherhood, which the Ruralists deeply admired. The members of the group were, in addition to Blake, Ann Arnold, Graham Arnold, Jann Haworth (Blake's then wife), David Inshaw, Annie Ovenden and Graham Ovenden. The Ruralists aimed to revive and update the vein of imaginative <u>painting</u> of romantic figure subjects in idyllic rural settings, in a style of high-precision <u>realism</u>, found in the early work of the Pre-Raphaelites. The painting *Ophelia* by John Everett Millais was a talismanic example. They also looked to the earlier visionary landscapes of Samuel Palmer and the Ancients. The children's book *Alice's Adventures In Wonderland* and its illustrations by John Tenniel and Arthur Rackham were another source of inspiration. Blake, Haworth and Inshaw left the group in the early 1980s but it continues with the Arnolds and Ovendens.

S

St Ives School Term referring to the artists associated with the fishing town of St Ives in West Cornwall, Britain. The town became a particular magnet for artists following the extension to West Cornwall of the Great Western Railway in 1877. In 1928 the artists Ben Nicholson and Christopher Wood visited St Ives where they were struck by the work of the naïve artist Alfred Wallis, whose painting confirmed Nicholson in the modern direction of his work. In 1939 at the outbreak of the Second World War, Nicholson and his then wife the sculptor Barbara Hepworth, both by then fully fledged abstract artists, settled near St Ives, where they were soon joined by the Russian Constructivist sculptor Naum Gabo. After the war St Ives became a centre for modern and abstract developments in British art led by Hepworth and Nicholson (Gabo departed in 1946). From about 1950 there gathered in St Ives a group of younger artists and it is with this group, together with Hepworth and Nicholson (until his departure in 1958), that the term St Ives School is particularly associated. The principal figures of the St Ives School include Wilhelmina Barns-Graham, Paul Feiler, Terry Frost, Patrick Heron, Roger Hilton, Peter Lanyon, Karl Weschke and Bryan Wynter, together with the pioneer modern potter, Bernard Leach. The heyday of the St Ives School was in the 1950s and 1960s but in 1993 Tate St Ives, a striking purpose-built new gallery in a remarkable situation on Porthmeor Beach in St Ives, was opened. It exhibits the Tate collection of St Ives School art and related types of art and has given the town a whole new lease of artistic life.

salon Originally the name of the official art exhibitions organised by the French Académie Royale de Peinture et de Sculpture (Royal Academy of Painting and Sculpture) and its successor the Académie des Beaux Arts (Academy of Fine Arts). From 1725 the exhibitions were held in the room called the Salon carré in the Louvre and became known simply as the Salon. This later gave rise to the generic French term of 'salon' for any large mixed art exhibition. By the mid-nineteenth century the academies had become highly conservative, and by their monopoly of major exhibitions resisted the rising tide of innovation in naturalism, Realism, Impressionism and their successors. By about 1860 the number of artists being excluded from the official Salon became so great and such a scandal that in 1863 the government was forced to set up an alternative, to accommodate the refused artists. This became known as the Salon des refusés. Three further Salons des refusés were held in 1874, 1875 and 1886. In 1884 the Salon des Indépendents was established by the Neo-Impressionists Georges Seurat and Paul Signac, together with Odilon Redon, as an alternative exhibition for innovatory or anti-academic art. It held annual exhibitions until the start of the First World War. In 1903 the Salon d'automne was founded, also as an alternative exhibition for innovatory artists. It was there that Fauvism came to public attention in 1905. The Salon d'automne continues to be held in Paris every year.

sampling In its most basic form sampling simply re-processes existing culture, usually technologically, in much the same way a collage does. In the early 1980s artists began cannibalising fragments of sound, image, music, dance and performance to create new works of art. These hybrid projects used sampling to generate live or time-based events that subverted our notions of time, space, artist and audience, virtual and actual. In the past two decades this DIY punk aesthetic has come to represent a radical challenge to the notions of authorship, originality and intellectual property, while creating new narratives and refreshing the cultural archive. Artists like Christian Marclay and Candice Breitz manipulate film and music, remixing familiar footage into epic narratives.

São Paulo Biennial see biennial

School of Altamira Avant-garde art school (Academia Altamira) in Buenos Aires, Argentina, founded in 1946 by the Argentinian-born Italian artist Lucio Fontana and others. Its aim was to promote the idea that a new art was necessary to reflect the modern world as revealed by science. In practice this art was abstract. Also in 1946 Fontana and a group of his students published the *Manifiesto Blanco* (White Manifesto) setting out their ideas. Strongly influenced by Futurism, it called for an art that was a synthesis of colour, sound, movement, time and space. Among Fontana's pupils at the Altamira Academy was the Brazilian artist Sergio de Camargo. In 1947 Fontana returned to Italy.

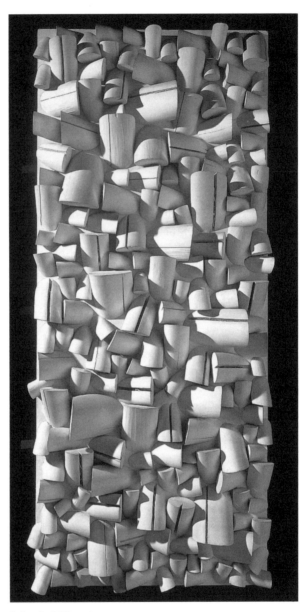

School of Altamira

Sergio de Camargo
Large Split Relief No.34/4/74 1964–5
Polyvinyl acetate paint on limewood on
plywood support
215.3 × 92.1 × 27.3
Tate. Purchased 1965

School of London In 1976, at the height of <u>Minimal art</u> and <u>Conceptual art</u>, the American painter R.B. Kitaj, then based in Britain, organised an exhibition titled *The Human Clay* at the Hayward Gallery, London. It exclusively consisted of <u>figurative drawing</u> and <u>painting</u> and proved highly controversial. In his catalogue text, Kitaj used the term School of London to loosely describe the artists he had brought together. The name has stuck to refer to painters at that time who were doggedly pursuing forms of figurative painting in the face of the prevailing <u>avant-garde</u> forms. The chief artists associated with the idea of the School of London, in addition to Kitaj himself, were Michael Andrews, Frank Auerbach, Francis Bacon, Lucian Freud, David Hockney (although living in the USA), Howard Hodgkin and Leon Kossoff. The work of these artists was brought into fresh focus and given renewed impetus by the revival of interest in figurative painting by a younger generation that took place in the late 1970s and the 1980s. (See also <u>Neo-Expressionism</u>; <u>New Spirit painting</u>)

School of Paris During the nineteenth century Paris, France, became the centre of a powerful national school of <u>painting</u> and <u>sculpture</u>, culminating in the dazzling innovations of <u>Impressionism</u> and <u>Post-Impressionism</u>. As a result, in the early years of the twentieth century Paris became a magnet for artists from all over the world and the focus of the principal innovations of modern art, notably <u>Fauvism</u>, <u>Cubism</u>, <u>abstract art</u> and <u>Surrealism</u>. The term School of Paris grew up to describe this phenomenon. The twin chiefs (*chefs d'école*) were Pablo Picasso who settled in Paris from his native Spain in 1904, and the Frenchman Henri Matisse. Also in 1904, the pioneer modern sculptor Constantin Brancusi arrived in Paris from Romania, and in 1906 the painter and sculptor Amedeo Modigliani from Italy. Chaïm Soutine arrived from Russia in 1911. The Russian painter Marc Chagall lived in Paris from 1910 to 1914 and then again from 1923 to 1939 and 1947 to 1949, after which he moved to the South of France. The Dutch pioneer of pure abstract painting, Piet Mondrian, settled in Paris in 1920 and Wassily Kandinsky in 1933. The heyday of the School of Paris was ended by the Second World War, although the term continued to be used to describe the artists of Paris. However, from about 1950 its dominance ceded to the rise of the <u>New York School</u>.

School of Rome see <u>Scuola Romana</u>

screenprint A variety of stencil printing using a screen made from fabric (silk or synthetic) stretched tightly over a frame. The non-printing areas on the fabric are blocked out by a stencil, which can be created by <u>painting</u> on glue or lacquer, by applying adhesive film or <u>paper</u>, or painting a light-sensitive resist onto the screen that is then developed as a <u>photograph</u> (photo-screenprint). <u>Ink</u> or paint is forced through the open fabric with a rubber blade, known as a squeegee, onto the paper. Screenprinting has been used commercially since the 1920s and by artists since the 1950s. When it was taken up by artists in 1930s America the term 'serigraph' was used to denote an artist's <u>print</u>, as opposed to commercial work. The term 'silkscreen' (silk was originally used for the mesh) was and still is used, particularly in America.

sculpture A three-dimensional artwork made by one of four basic processes. These are carving (in stone, wood, ivory or bone); modelling in clay; modelling (in clay or wax) and then <u>casting</u> the model in bronze; constructing (a twentieth-century development). The earliest known human artefacts recognisable as what we would call sculpture date from the period known as the Upper Paleolithic, which is roughly from 40,000 to 10,000 years ago. These objects are small female figures with bulbous breasts and buttocks carved from stone or ivory, and are assumed to be fertility figures. The most famous of them is known as the Venus of Willendorf (the place in Austria where it was found in 1908). Sculpture flourished in ancient Egypt from about 5,000 years ago and in ancient Greece from some 2,000 years later. In Greece it reached what is considered to be a peak of perfection in the period from about 500 to 400 BC. At that time, as well as making carved sculpture, the Greeks brought the technique of casting sculpture in bronze to a high degree of sophistication. Following the fall of the Roman Empire the technique of bronze casting was almost lost but, together with carved sculpture, underwent a major revival at the Renaissance. In the twentieth century a new way of making sculpture emerged with the <u>Cubist</u> constructions of Pablo Picasso. These were <u>still life</u> subjects made from scrap (found) materials glued together. Constructed sculpture in various forms became a major stream in modern art

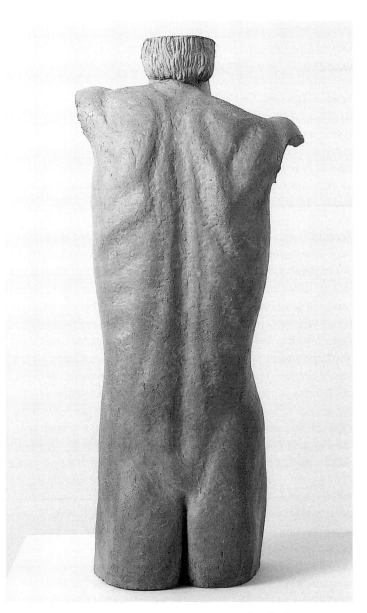

Scuola Romana

Arturo Martini
Torso of a Young Man
1928, cast 1928 or 1929
Terracotta
86 × 47 × 19
Tate. Purchased 1994

(see assemblage; Constructivism; installation; Minimal art; New Generation sculpture). Techniques used included welding metal, introduced by Julio González, who also taught it to Picasso.

Scuola Romana Umbrella term for artists based in Rome, or having close links with it, in the 1920s and 1930s. Like the School of Paris, the Scuola Romana (School of Rome) embraces a wide variety of types of art. However, a return to classicism was a dominant current (see 'return to order'). Major artists include Giorgio de Chirico, Giacomo Balla, Renato Guttuso, Arturo Martini, Fausto Pirandello and Gino Severini.

Secession As a general term this is used to describe the breaking away of younger and more radical artists from an existing academy or art group, to form a new grouping. The word is originally German and its earliest appearance seems to be in the name of the Munich Secession group formed in 1892. In the same year this was followed by the Berliner Secession, led by Max Liebermann and later Lovis Corinth, and in 1913 by the Freie Secession in which Max Beckmann and Ernst Barlach were involved. The most famous secession group is the Vereinigung bildener Künstler Oesterreichs (Secession) founded in 1897 and generally known simply as the Vienna Secession. It was led by one of the greatest of all symbolist painters, Gustav Klimt. In 1898 the Secession commissioned the architect Joseph Olbrich to build an exhibition hall. The result is a masterpiece of Art Nouveau architecture that remains one of the gems of Vienna. It also contains Klimt's great mural the *Beethoven Frieze*. Over following years the Vienna Secession held a series of exhibitions (several a year) that brought together a roll call of the international avant-garde. There was a particular emphasis on architecture and design, and the Vienna Secession played a major part in the broader Art Nouveau movement and the beginnings of modern design. In 1903 a design company was founded called the Wiener Werkstätte (Vienna Workshops), inspired by the English Arts and Crafts Movement. Its products are now museum pieces. Later major artists associated with the Vienna Secession include Egon Schiele and Oskar Kokoschka, two of the great pioneers of Expressionism.

Second Festival of Black Arts and Culture see Festac

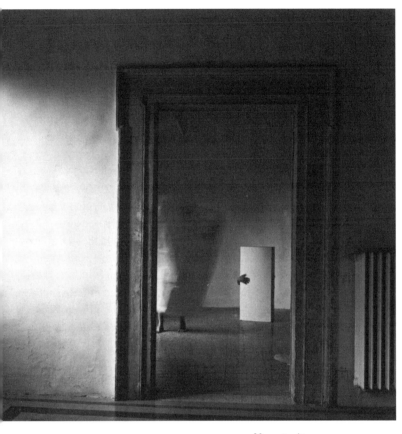

self-portrait

Francesca Woodman
From Angel Series, Roma, September 1977 1977
Photograph, gelatine silver print on paper
9.3 × 9.3
Tate / National Galleries of Scotland. ARTIST ROOMS. Acquired jointly with the National Galleries of Scotland through The d'Offay Donation with assistance from the National Heritage Memorial Fund and the Art Fund 2008

self-portrait A <u>portrait</u> of the artist by the artist. Self-portraits are an interesting subgroup of portraiture and can often be highly self-revelatory.

Semana de Arte Moderna An arts festival held in São Paulo at the Municipal Theatre in February 1922, which was to be the first manifestation of Brazilian <u>modernism</u>. Organised by an avant-garde group of intellectuals, Semana de Arte Moderna (Modern Art Week) consisted of exhibitions of plastic arts, concerts, poetry and prose readings and lectures on contemporary <u>aesthetic</u> theory. Its artistic ideology is best summarised by the poet and writer Oswald de Andrade who declared that Brazil's cultural mission was to devour Europeans, just as the indigenous people had reputedly dispatched their colonisers. Although the event was beset with controversy with audience members heckling the artists, it brought into focus a cultural explosion in the arts in Brazil and made São Paulo the radical centre of this new wave of creativity. It was anarchical and <u>avant-garde</u> and its purpose was to shock modern art in Brazil into existence. Artists who participated in the Semana de Arte Moderna include Emiliano Di Cavalcanti, Anita Malfatti, Tarsila do Amaral and Lasar Segall, the sculptor Victor Brecheret and the composer Heitor Villa-Lobos. (See also <u>decolonisation</u>; <u>Modernismo</u>)

sensorial Used to describe art that seeks to engage the audience by activating the senses. A good example of this would be Derek Jarman's last film *Blue*, an immersive <u>installation</u> in which a blue screen echoes the artist's fading eyesight. Jarman sought to evoke for the viewer the mental, physical and emotional strain caused by a terminal illness. Another exponent of sensorial art is the New York-based Brazilian artist duo, assume vivid astro focus. The installation *Make it With You: A Slow Dance Club* 2004, features a room in which people can slow dance to romantic music.

serial art Art that adheres to a strict set of rules to determine its <u>composition</u> or series of compositions. Serial art has its roots in <u>Conceptual art</u> and <u>Minimal art</u> and gained popularity in America and Europe in the 1960s as a way for artists to create art without recourse to personal expression. There are three basic operating assumptions that define serial art: that it follows a systematically predetermined <u>process</u>, the order takes precedence over the execution and the completed work is self-exhausting. Some works are modular and are based on the repetition of a standard unit, like Andy Warhol's soup cans or Joseph Albers's coloured squares, while others offer variations on a theme, like Sol LeWitt's *Serial Project No.1* which showed all the different combinations of an open and closed cube.

Seven and Five Society The Seven and Five Society was formed in London in 1919 and held its first exhibition the following year. Initially it was a conservative group and can be seen as a British manifestation of the <u>'return to order'</u> that followed the First World War. The first exhibition catalogue explained that the society was not formed 'to advertise a new "ism" … [we] feel that there has of late been too much pioneering along too many lines in altogether too much of a hurry'. This perfectly encapsulates the 'return to order' attitude. However, in 1924 Ben Nicholson, one of the pioneers of <u>abstract art</u> in Britain, joined the Seven and Five Society. He was followed by other <u>modernists</u> including Barbara Hepworth, Henry Moore and, later, John Piper. They effectively hijacked the group, expelling the non-modernists. In 1935 they renamed it the Seven and Five Abstract Group and held the first all-abstract exhibition in Britain at the Zwemmer Gallery in London.

shaped canvas A term that gained currency in the 1960s to describe a <u>canvas</u> that was not rectangular in shape. Although there have been many examples of irregular shaped canvases throughout the history of art, the term shaped canvas tends to be associated with a type of geometric <u>abstract</u> painting that came to prominence in the late 1950s early 1960s. Artists like Frank Stella used the edges of irregular shaped canvases to define the form of the <u>painting</u>. Shaped canvases also raised questions about the painting as an object in its own right, not as something representative or illustrative of something else. In this sense shaped canvas paintings are sometimes described as <u>sculptures</u>. (See also <u>format</u>; <u>tondo</u>).

significant form see <u>formalism</u>

simulacrum A term from Greek Platonic philosophy that meant a copy of a copy of an ideal form. In postmodernist thought, particularly through the writings of Gilles Deleuze and Jean Baudrillard, the term has been revived in the context of arguments about the relationship between an original work of art and its replication. For Baudrillard the simulacrum takes precedence over the original, with the effect that the original is no longer relevant.

simultanism The term invented by French painter Robert Delaunay to describe the abstract painting developed by him and his wife Sonia Delaunay from about 1910. Their work was also named Orphism by the poet and critic Guillaume Apollinaire. The term is derived from the theories of M-E. Chevreul whose book of colour theory *De la loi du contraste simultanée des couleurs* (On the law of the simultaneous contrast of colours) was published in Paris in 1839. It had an increasing impact on French painters, particularly the Impressionists and Post-Impressionists, and even more so on the Neo-Impressionists. The Delaunays' paintings consisted of interlocking or overlapping patches, or planes, of contrasting (or complementary) colours. In Chevreul's theory, and in reality, contrasting colours brought together (i.e. simultaneous) enhance each other, giving the painting greater intensity and vibrancy of colour. The compositions were initially derived from architecture but by 1912 Delaunay had begun to make paintings in totally abstract circular formats. These compositions were still ultimately based on nature, however.

site-specific Refers to a work of art designed specifically for a particular location and that has an interrelationship with the location. If removed from the location it would lose all or a substantial part of its meaning. Site-specific is often used to describe installation works, and Land art is site-specific almost by definition.

Situationist International Revolutionary alliance of European avant-garde artists, writers and poets formed at a conference in Italy in 1957 (as Internationale Situationiste or IS). It combined two existing groupings, the Lettrist International and the International Union for a Pictorial Bauhaus. The leading figure was the writer and film maker Guy Debord and the group also prominently included

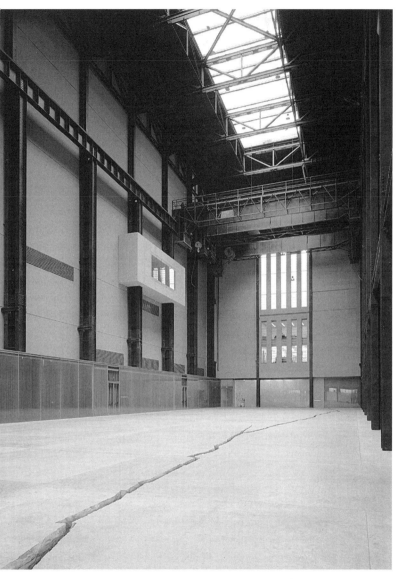

site-specific

Doris Salcedo
Shibboleth I
from *Shibboleth* 2007
Digital print on paper
64 × 46.6
Tate. Presented by the artist, White Cube, London and Alexander and Bonin, New York 2008

the former CoBrA painter Asger Jorn. The former CoBrA artist
Constant was also a member, and the British artist Ralph Rumney
was a co-founder of the movement. The IS developed a critique of
capitalism based on a mixture of Marxism and Surrealism, and
Debord identified consumer society as the Society of the Spectacle
in his influential 1967 book of that title. In the field of culture
Situationists wanted to break down the division between artists and
consumers and make cultural production a part of everyday life.
Situationist ideas played an important role in the revolutionary Paris
events of 1968. The IS was dissolved in 1972.

slide A small, square, specially mounted transparency that has been
generated from reversal film. Reversal film is a type of photographic
film that produces a positive image on a transparent base, rather
than a negative image. The slide is used to project an enlargement
of the image onto a screen, through the use of a slide projector or a
light box. Slides became popular in the 1960s, when artists wanted
their images to be seen collectively so projected them onto gallery
walls. The artist Nan Goldin used slides in the early 1980s, staging
slide performances in night clubs, that enabled her to show her
photographs to a large number of people in a confined space. Since
the advent of digital technology, slides are not as common as they
once were.

Social Realism Refers to any realist painting or other work that
depicts everyday life and also carries a discernible social comment
or message. Common in Western art from at least the eighteenth
century onwards. Not to be confused with Socialist Realism.

social sculpture A theory developed by the artist Joseph Beuys
in the 1970s, which united his idealistic ideas of a utopian society
together with his aesthetic practice. It was based on the concept that
everything was art and every aspect of life could be approached
creatively, and as a result, everyone had the potential to be an
artist. Beuys believed that life is a social sculpture that everyone
helps to shape. Many of Beuys social sculptures had political and
environmental concerns. *7000 Oaks* began in 1982 as a five-year
project to plant 7,000 trees in Kassel in Germany. It raised many
questions about city planning, the future of the environment and

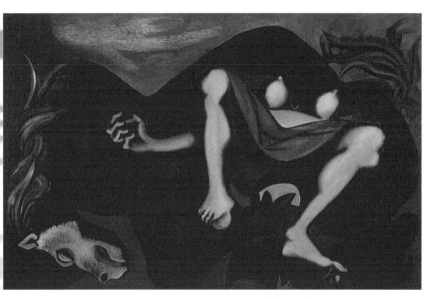

Socialist Realism

André Fougeron
Martyred Spain 1937
Oil paint on canvas
98.2 × 153.9
Tate. Presented by the Friends of
the Tate Gallery 2001

social structures. The concept of social sculpture continues today with artists like Pedro Reyes who collected 1,527 weapons from residents of Cuiliacán in Western Mexico, which were exchanged for electronics. The artist then melted the weapons down into shovels, which were used to plant 1,527 trees.

social turn A term coined by the art historian Claire Bishop in 2006 to describe a return to socially engaged art that is collaborative, often participatory and involves people as the medium or material of the work. Art that operates under the umbrella of social turn tends to happen outside museums or galleries, although this is not always the case. Because much of the art is collaborative and focuses on constructive social change, it is rarely commercial or object-based – two things that are seen as elitist and consumerist. An example of social turn would be *Tennantspin* 1999, an artwork by Superflex in which they devised an internet TV station for the elderly residents of a Liverpool housing project. Often when discussing social turn, the filmmaker, writer and founder of situationism, Guy Debord, is alluded to for his promotion of a participatory art in which he wished to eliminate the spectator's position (see Situationist International).

Socialist Realism A form of modern realism imposed in Russia by Stalin following his rise to power after the death of Lenin in 1924. The doctrine was formally proclaimed by Maxim Gorky at the Soviet Writers Congress of 1934, although not precisely defined. In practice, it meant painting using realist styles to create rigorously optimistic pictures of Soviet life. Any pessimistic or critical element was banned and it was therefore quite simply propaganda art. It has an ironic resemblance to the Fascist realism imposed by Hitler in Germany (see degenerate art). Outside the Soviet Union, socialist artists produced much freer interpretations of the genre.

socially engaged practice see social turn

software art In the 1960s, software programs were the digital tool with which artists could create art on computers. Since then, these programs have become so sophisticated that they can now be considered the work of art rather than just a facilitator. Software art is closely related to net art because of its reliance on the internet as a tool for dissemination. Often software art parodies or reconfigures existing computer programs. *Web Stalker*, created by the art collective I/O/D, was a radical reinterpretation of an internet browser and Adrian Shaw's *Signwave* parodied the computer program Adobe Photoshop. The rise of software art has led to several international new media festivals, namely FILE (Electronic Language International Festival) held in São Paulo in Brazil and transmediale in Berlin. The rise of software art has provoked questions about the de-materialisation of art and culture and how this has had an effect on the world of Conceptual art. (See also browser art; net art)

solarisation Discovered accidentally by Man Ray and Lee Miller, solarisation is created by briefly exposing a partially developed photograph to light, before continuing processing. Man Ray quickly adopted solarisation as a means to 'escape from banality' and often applied the technique to photographs of female nudes, using the halo-like outlines around forms and areas of partially reversed tonality to emphasise the contours of the body.

Sots art A descriptive term since 1972 that takes its name from 'Sots'ialisticheskiy Realism (Socialist Realism) and Pop 'art'. It describes a kind of art that appeared in the USSR in the 1970s and 1980s which adapts the techniques of Socialist Realism to critique its ideological basis and question its cultural implications.

sound art Art about sound, using sound both as its medium and as its subject. It dates back to the early inventions of Futurist Luigi Russolo who, between 1913 and 1930, built noise machines that replicated the clatter of the industrial age and the boom of warfare, and subsequent experiments in the Dada and Surrealist movements. Marcel Duchamp's composition *Erratum Musical* featured three voices singing notes pulled from a hat, a seemingly arbitrary act that had an impact on the compositions of John Cage, who in 1952 composed *4' 33"*, a musical score of four minutes and thirty-three seconds of silence (four minutes thirty-three seconds is 273 seconds. The temperature minus 273 Celsius is absolute zero). By the 1950s and 1960s visual artists and composers like Bill Fontana were using kinetic sculptures and electronic media, overlapping live and pre-recorded sound, in order to explore the space around them. Since the introduction of digital technology sound art has undergone a radical transformation. Artists can now create visual images in response to sounds, allow the audience to control the art through pressure pads, sensors and voice activation, and in examples like Jem Finer's *Longplayer*, extend a sound so that it resonates for a thousand years.

Spazialismo Italian movement *Movimento Spaziale* (spacialist movement or spacialism) started by the Argentine-born Italian artist Lucio Fontana after his return to Italy from Argentina in 1947. The movement was launched in 1947 with the first *Manifiesto Spaziale* (Spatialist Manifesto – several more followed) in which Fontana developed the ideas of the *Manifiesto Blanco* issued at the <u>School of Altamira</u> in Buenos Aires the year before. There he had called for an art that embraced science and technology and made use of such things as neon light, radio and television. In 1949 Fontana installed his *Ambiente Spaziale* at the Galleria del Naviglio in Milan. It consisted of an <u>abstract</u> object painted with phosphorescent paint and lit by a neon light and was a pioneering example of what became known as <u>installation</u>. He subsequently went on to make the works on <u>canvas</u> to which he gave the generic title of *Concetto Spaziale* (spatial concept) although continuing to make installations using light. The basis of the Concetto Spaziale works was the piercing or slashing with a razor of the canvas to create an actual dimension of space. Fontana made a long series of these and extended the idea into <u>sculpture</u> in his *Concetto Spaziale, Natura* series. Other Spazialismo artists included Giovanni Dova and Roberto Crippa.

Spiral A New York based African-American <u>collective</u> formed in 1963 by Richard Mayhew, Romare Bearden and Hale Woodruff in direct response to the March on Washington for Jobs and Freedom, a political rally for human rights which drew nearly a quarter of a million advocates for racial equality. Spiral was created in order to discuss how African-American artists should respond to America's changing political and cultural landscape and how they, through social unity, could respond to racism and represent their black communities. Many of the artists associated with the group were <u>Abstract Expressionists</u>, but their work was ignored by many of the proponents of Abstract Expressionism, like the critic

Clement Greenberg who said their art was too autobiographical to be considered. Other's like Romare Bearden used paint and collage in order to symbolise the merging of different communities and traditions. The group continued to operate throughout the 1960s and into the early 1970s. Artists associated with Spiral are Charles Alston, Emma Amos, Romare Bearden, Calvin Douglas, Perry Ferguson, Reginald Gammon, Felrath Hines, Alvin Hollingsworth, Norman Lewis, William Majors, Richard Mayhew, Earle Miller, William Pritchard, Merton Simpson, James Yeargans and Hale Woodruff.

Stars Group A short-lived avant-garde group of self-taught artists operating in Beijing between 1979 and 1983. The members of Stars Group staged outdoor exhibitions, street demonstrations and public readings. In September 1979 they displayed their artworks without permission on railings adjoining the China Art Gallery. When they were forced to remove the works they organised a protest march and as a result were given permission to exhibit their art in an event that was attended by more than 80,000 people. While this marked a watershed for artistic freedom in China, it was short-lived. The group faced harsh official criticism and in 1983, due to political pressure, it disbanded with many of the members leaving China. Artists associated with Stars group include Ai Weiwei, Huang Rui, Li Shuang, Ma Desheng and Wang Keping.

De Stijl Name of journal founded in 1917 in Holland by pioneers of abstract art Piet Mondrian and Theo van Doesburg. This Dutch term means 'style'. The name De Stijl also came to refer to the circle of artists that gathered around the publication. *De Stijl* became a vehicle for Mondrian's ideas on art, and in a series of articles in the first year's issues he defined his aims and used, perhaps for the first time, the term Neo-Plasticism. This became the name for the type of abstract art he and the De Stijl circle practised. It was based on a strict geometry of horizontals and verticals. Other members of the group included Bart van der Leck, Georges Vantongerloo and Friedrich Vordemberge-Gildewart, as well as the architects Gerrit Rietveld and J.J.P. Oud. Mondrian withdrew from De Stijl in 1923 following Van Doesburg's adoption of diagonal elements in his work. Van Doesburg continued the publication until 1931. De Stijl had a profound influence on the development both of abstract art and modern architecture and design.

still life One of the principal genres (subject types) of Western art. Essentially, the subject matter of a still life painting or sculpture is anything that does not move or is dead. So still life includes all kinds of man-made or natural objects: cut flowers, fruit, vegetables, fish, game, wine and so on. Still life can be a celebration of material pleasures such as food and wine, but it is often a warning of the ephemerality of these pleasures and of the brevity of human life (see memento mori). In modern art simple still life arrangements have often been used as a relatively neutral basis for formal experiment, for example by Paul Cézanne and the Cubist painters. Note the plural of still life is still lifes, and the term is not hyphenated.

street art A genre related to graffiti writing, but separate and with different rules and traditions. Where as modern-day graffiti revolves around 'tagging' and text-based subject matter, street art is far more open and is often related to graphic design. There are no rules in street art, so anything goes. However, some common materials and techniques include fly-posting (also known as wheat-pasting), stencilling, stickers, freehand drawing and projecting videos. Street artists will often work in studios, hold gallery exhibitions or work in other creative areas: they are not anti-art, they simply enjoy the freedom of working in public without having to worry about what other people think. Many well-known artists started their careers working in a way that we would now consider to be street art, for example, Gordon Matta-Clark, Jenny Holzer and Barbara Kruger.

Stridentism see Estridentismo

Stuckism Founded by Billy Childish and Charles Thomson in 1999, Stuckism is an art movement that is anti-conceptual and champions figurative painting. Thomson derived the name from an insult by the Young British Artist Tracey Emin, who told her ex-lover Childish that his art was 'stuck, stuck, stuck'. Since its modest beginnings Stuckism is now an international art movement with over a hundred members worldwide. Childish left in 2001, but the group continues its confrontational agenda, demonstrating against events like the Turner Prize or Beck's Futures which the movement argues are among a number of art world events controlled by a small number of art world insiders.

Subjective Photography An international movement founded in Germany by the photographer Otto Steinert in 1951. The movement evolved out of the Fotoform group started by Steinart and Peter Keetman in the late 1940s, which aimed to use photography to explore the inner psyche of the human condition rather than reflecting the world outside. The group held three exhibitions entitled *Subjektive Fotografie* in 1951, 1954 and 1958, and Steinart published a manifesto in which he wrote that Subjective photography 'means humanised, individualised photography'. This was partly an attempt to distance the Subjective photographers from the rise of commercial, documentary and reportage photography. The group retained many of the experimental techniques used at the Bauhaus before the Second World War, but their subject matter was more complex, reflecting the darker aspects of the human condition through their expressionistic and hallucinatory images. The movement was international, and included photographers from Brazil, Germany, Japan, Sweden and the USA. Photographers associated with Subjective photography are Harry Callahan, Thomaz Farkas, Gaspar Gasparian, Marcel Giró, Peter Keetman, Takashi Kijima, Siegfried Lauterwasser, Kiyoshi Niiyama, Toni Schneiders, Aaron Siskind, Otto Steinert, Christer Strömholm and Ludwig Windstosser.

the sublime A theory of art put forward by Edmund Burke in *A Philosophical Enquiry into the Origin of our Ideas of the Sublime and Beautiful* published in 1757. He defined the sublime as an artistic effect productive of the strongest emotion the mind is capable of feeling and wrote 'whatever is in any sort terrible or is conversant about terrible objects or operates in a manner analogous to terror, is a source of the Sublime.' The notion that a legitimate function of art can be to produce upsetting or disturbing effects was an important element in Romantic art and remains fundamental to art today.

superflat A concept devised by the Japanese artist Takashi Murakami, superflat is about things existing simultaneously in the present. He argued that all creative works on a flat surface are two-dimensional and as a result should be given equal weight be they fine art, pop videos, animation, graphic design or new media. For Murakami, it was a way of levelling the playing field between high and low culture, or for that matter between ancient and modern history or between Eastern and Western cultures. With superflat, Murakami set out to translate the postwar popular culture of Japan and in so doing created a foundation for Japanese contemporary art to be understood in the West.

supra-sensorial A term devised by the Brazilian artist Hélio Oiticica to describe the experience of being in one of his installations. Oiticica created environments that were designed to encourage the viewer's emotional and intellectual participation. He would invite the audience to walk barefoot on sand and straw or listen to Jimi Hendrix records while relaxing in a hammock. The brutal military dictatorship in Brazil during the 1960s and 1970s had caused Oiticica to advocate the radical potential of hanging out, rather than complying with society's demands. Supra-sensorial was about activating all the senses, in order to promote the idea of individual freedom.

Suprematism The name given by the Russian artist Kasimir Malevich to the abstract art he developed from 1913. The first actual exhibition of Suprematist paintings was in December 1915 in St Petersburg, at an exhibition called *O.10*. The exhibition included thirty-five abstract paintings by Malevich, among them the famous black square on a white ground (Russian Museum, St Petersburg) which headed the list of his works in the catalogue. In 1927 Malevich published his book *The Non-Objective World*, one of the most important theoretical documents of abstract art. In it he wrote: 'In the year 1913, trying desperately to free art from the dead weight of the real world, I took refuge in the form of the square.' Out of the 'Suprematist square', as he called it, Malevich developed a whole range of forms including rectangles, triangles and circles often in intense and beautiful colours. These forms are floated against a usually white ground, and the feeling of colour in space in Suprematist painting is a crucial aspect of it. Suprematism was one of the key movements of modern art in Russia and was particularly closely associated with the Revolution. After the rise of Stalin from 1924 and the imposition of Socialist Realism, Malevich's career languished. In his last years before his death in 1935 he painted realist pictures. In 1919 the Russian artist El Lissitsky met Malevich and was strongly influenced by Suprematism, as was the Hungarian-born László Moholy-Nagy.

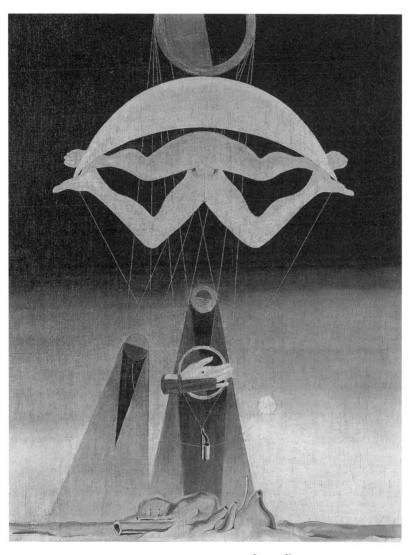

Surrealism

Max Ernst
Men Shall Know Nothing of This
1923
Oil paint on canvas
80.3 × 63.8
Tate. Purchased 1960

Surrealism Movement launched in Paris in 1924 by French poet André Breton with publication of his *Manifesto of Surrealism*. Breton was strongly influenced by the theories of Sigmund Freud, the founder of psychoanalysis. Freud identified a deep layer of the human mind where memories and our most basic instincts are stored. He called this the unconscious, since most of the time we are not aware of it. The aim of Surrealism was to reveal the unconscious and reconcile it with rational life. The Surrealists did this in literature as well as art. Surrealism also aimed at social and political revolution and for a time was affiliated to the Communist party. There was no single style of Surrealist art but two broad types can be seen. These are the oneiric (dream-like) work of Salvador Dalí, early Max Ernst and René Magritte, and the <u>Automatism</u> of later Ernst and Joan Miró. Freud believed that dreams revealed the workings of the unconscious, and his famous book *The Interpretation of Dreams* was central to Surrealism. Automatism was the Surrealist term for Freud's technique of free association, which he also used to reveal the unconscious mind of his patients. Surrealism had a huge influence on art, literature and the cinema as well as on social attitudes and behaviour.

symbolism A term coined in 1886 by the French critic Jean Moréas to describe the poetry of Mallarmé and Verlaine. It was soon applied to art where it describes the continuation, in the face of <u>Impressionism</u>, <u>realism</u> and <u>naturalism</u>, of traditional mythological, religious and literary subject matter, but fuelled by new psychological content, particularly erotic and mystical. Symbolism was a complex international phenomenon but is seen as especially French (Gustave Moreau, Odilon Redon, Paul Gauguin), Belgian (Fernand Khnopff, Jean Delville) and British (Dante Gabriel Rossetti, Edward Burne-Jones, George Frederic Watts, Aubrey Beardsley).

synaesthesia A neurological condition in which the stimulation of a sense (like touch or hearing) leads involuntarily to the triggering of another sense (like sight or taste). For example, a person with synaesthesia might see the colour blue when they hear the word 'fish' or, as in mirror-touch synaesthesia, they would feel a physical sense of touch on their own bodies when they witness touch to other people or objects. This intersensory mixing is caused when the brain uses the resources usually used for seeing for other senses.

People with synaesthesia tend to be drawn towards the creative arts and some artists have explored the concept in their works, like the Russian abstract artist Wassily Kandinsky, who had an interest in visualising music in his paintings. In the film *Sensorium Tests*, which explores mirror-touch synaesthesia, the contemporary artist Daria Martin challenges the idea that the act of looking is a passive experience.

Synthetic Cubism The later phase of Cubism, generally considered to run from about 1912 to 1914, characterised by simpler shapes and brighter colours. In an attempt to classify the revolutionary experiments made in Cubism by Georges Braque, Pablo Picasso and Juan Gris, historians tend to divide Cubism into two stages, Analytical and Synthetic. Synthetic Cubism began when the artists started adding textures and patterns to their paintings, experimenting with collage using newspaper print and patterned paper. Analytical Cubism was about breaking down an object (like a bottle), viewpoint-by-viewpoint, into a fragmentary image, whereas Synthetic Cubism was about flattening out the image and sweeping away the last vestiges of illusion of three-dimensional space. Picasso's papiers collés are a good example of Synthetic Cubism.

synthetism A term associated with the style of symbolic representation of observed reality favoured by Paul Gauguin and his followers at Pont-Aven in the 1880s, whereby the artwork, rather than offering naturalistic representation, synthesises the subject-matter with the emotions of the artist and aesthetic concerns. An exhibition of 'Synthétisme' was mounted by the Pont-Aven artists in 1889 and the 'Groupe Synthétiste', including Gauguin and Emile Bernard, was founded in 1891. Another follower of the movement, Paul Sérusier, founded the Nabis group.

systems art Loosely describes a group of artists who radically rethought the object of art in the late 1960s early 1970s. They sought to connect with the political developments of the decade and make their art more responsive to the world around them. Building on the structures of Minimal art and Conceptual art, they reacted against art's traditional focus on the object by adopting experimental aesthetic systems across a variety of media including photography, dance, <u>performance</u>, <u>painting</u>, <u>installation</u>, <u>video</u> and film. Examples of systems art include Richard Long, who imposed rigid structures to his walks across the landscape.

t

tableau First used by the eighteenth-century French philosopher Denis Diderot to describe an anti-theatrical style of painting. Diderot described a tableau as a <u>painting</u> in which an arrangement of characters appeared absorbed and completely unaware of the existence of the beholder. The paintings were natural and true to life, and had the effect of walling off the observer from the drama taking place, transfixing the viewer like never before. In the 1860s, the concept of the tableau reached a crisis with Édouard Manet, who, in his desire to make paintings that were realistic rather than idealised, decisively rejected the concept of the tableau as suggested by Diderot and painted his characters facing the viewer with a new vehemence that challenged the beholder. In the 1970s, a group of ambitious young artists like Jeff Wall and Andreas Gursky began to make large format <u>photographs</u> that, like paintings, were designed to hang on a wall. As a result these photographers were compelled to engage with the very same issues revealing the continued relevance of the tableau in contemporary art.

Tachisme French term for the improvisatory non-geometric <u>abstract art</u> that developed in Europe in the 1940s and 1950s and was the European equivalent to <u>Abstract Expressionism</u> in America. Tachisme is virtually synonymous with <u>Art Informel</u>. The name derives from the French word *tache*, meaning a stain or splash (e.g. of paint). The introduction of the term to describe these postwar developments is usually credited to the critic Pierre Guéguen in 1951. However, it was used in 1889 by the critic Félix Fénéon to describe the <u>Impressionist</u> technique, and again in 1909 by the artist Maurice Denis referring to the <u>Fauve</u> painters.

tactical media Refers to a reawakening of social, political and media activism brought on by access to cheap forms of communication, in particular the internet (see <u>net art</u>). The phrase is thought to have come from the French philosopher Michel de Certeau, who suggested in his 1974 essay 'The Practice of Everyday Life' that as consumers were arguably the producers within our society, it was up to us to infiltrate the structures of power in a creative manner which would ultimately undermine them. Actions have included Flash-mob events, in which hundreds of people descend on a designated place at a particular time, clever manipulation of funding applications and rogue websites that purport to be official domains. Groups like Critical Art Ensemble print manuals on how to hack into classified websites, and the annual self-publishing event Publish and be Damned promotes fanzines, novels and comics, bypassing the usual official channels.

Taller Gráfica Popular An artist's print collective founded in Mexico in 1937 by artists Leopoldo Méndez, Pablo O'Higgins and Luis Arenal. Taller Gráfica Popular (The People's Print Workshop) shared the post-revolutionary idealism of the Mexican Muralists, fighting for their own culture against the hegemony of the European avant-garde in art. Like the Mexican Muralists, they were socio-political and wanted to reach as large an audience as possible, printing their works as cheaply as possible in order to disseminate them widely. To show their solidarity with the people, their subject matter reflected the social realities of the time, predominantly workers and their struggles and the exploitation of the poor.

telematic art Alain Minc and Simon Nora first used the term 'telematic' in the late 1970s to describe the way computers transmit information. In the early 1990s, the British artist and theorist Roy Ascott coined the term telematic art to describe art that uses the internet and other digital means of communication, like email and mobile phones, in order to make a more interactive form of art. Much of the writing surrounding telematic art focuses on the human aspect of the medium; the desire to communicate with another, even in the virtual world, and how this is central to the creation of the medium. (See also browser art; digital art; net art; software art)

tempera The technique of painting with pigments bound in a water-soluble emulsion, such as water and egg yolk, or an oil-in-water emulsion such as oil and a whole egg. Some tempera paints are made with an artificial emulsion using gum or glue. Traditionally applied to a rigid support such as a wood panel, the paint dries to a hard film.

Ten Concrete Painters see Diez Pintores Concretos

time-based media Refers to art that is dependent on technology and has a durational dimension. Usually time-based media are video, slide, film, audio or computer based and part of what it means to experience the art is to watch it unfold over time according to the temporal logic of the medium as it is played back. Early examples of time-based media date back to the 1960s, in particular the art of Bruce Nauman, who would record happenings to be played back in the gallery. His *Performance Corridor*, made in 1968, was a recording of a performance in which people edged their way down a dark narrow tunnel. Since Nauman's early explorations, artists have also experimented with the elasticity of the medium in order to stretch time and space. In 1993 Douglas Gordon slowed down Alfred Hitchcock's film *Psycho* to twenty-four hours.

tondo A circular painting or relief sculpture. (See also format)

tone In painting, tone refers to the relative lightness or darkness of a colour (see also chiaroscuro). One colour can have an almost infinite number of different tones. Tone can also mean the colour itself. For example, when Vincent van Gogh wrote in a letter 'I exaggerate the fairness of the hair, I even get to orange tones, chromes and pale citron-yellow', he is referring to those colours at a particular tonal value. The term seems to have come into widespread use with the rise of painting directly from nature in the nineteenth century, when artists became interested in identifying and reproducing the full range of tones to be found in a particular subject. This in turn led to an interest in colour for its own sake and in colour theory. However, tone is also a musical term and its use in relation to painting reflects the theory that became increasingly important from about 1870, that painting can be like music. From about that time the painter J.A.M. Whistler, for example, made paintings using a very limited range of closely related tones of just one or two colours, and gave them musical titles. This kind of painting is known as tonal painting. In 1908, in his *A Painter's Notes*, Henri Matisse wrote: 'When I have found the relationship of all the tones the result must be a living harmony of all the tones, a harmony not unlike that of a musical composition.'

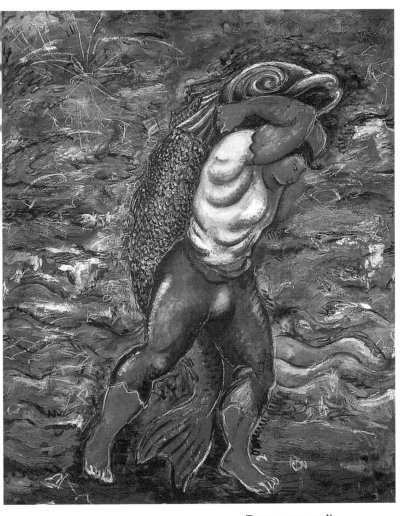

Transavanguardia

Sandro Chia
Water Bearer 1981
Oil paint and pastel on canvas
206.5 × 170
Tate. Purchased 1982

Transavanguardia Italian <u>Neo-Expressionist</u> group. The term was coined by the critic Achille Oliva in his texts for an exhibition he organised in 1979 in Genanzzano titled *Le Stanze*. The leading Italian Transavanguardia artists were Sandro Chia, Francesco Clemente, Enzo Cucchi, Nicolo de Maria and Mimmo Paladino.

triennial A large-scale contemporary art exhibition that occurs every three years. Like a <u>biennial</u> it is often attached to a particular place and is typified by its national or international outlook. The Tate Triennial showcases new developments in British art and the Asia Pacific Triennial of Contemporary Art, which was established in 1993, is the only major international exhibition to focus on art from Asia, the Pacific and Australia.

triptych A <u>painting</u> made up by three <u>panels</u>.

trompe l'oeil see <u>illusionism</u>

Tropicália The name used for an explosion of cultural creativity in Rio de Janerio and São Paulo in 1968 as Brazil's military regime tightened its grip on power. The word Tropicália comes from an <u>installation</u> by the artist Hélio Oiticica, who created <u>environments</u> that were designed to encourage the viewer's emotional and intellectual participation. Many of the artists, writers and musicians associated with Tropicália came of age during the 1950s during a time of intense optimism when the cultural world had been encouraged to play a central role in the creation of a democratic, socially just and modern Brazil. But a military coup in 1964 had brought to power a right-wing regime at odds with the concerns of left-wing artists. Tropicália became a way of exposing the contradictions of modernisation under such an authoritarian rule. From its beginning, Tropicália was seen as a re-articulation of <u>anthropophagia</u> (cannibalism), an artistic ideology promoted by Oswald de Andrade.

Tucuman Arde A politically charged exhibition held in Buenos Aires and Rosario in 1968 by the Vanguard Artists' Group that sought to highlight the terrible working and living conditions in Tucuman, in north-west Argentina, home to sugar mills and farms that had been forcibly closed by the government. Artists outraged by Juan Carlos Onganía's dictatorship's treatment of the people living there, together with their frustration of the stringent censorship rules, staged an exhibition of photographs that documented the plight of the Tucuman workers. Tucuman Arde (Tucuman is Burning) was attended by 3,000 people and is considered today to be an important moment in the history of Argentinean art. Among the artists who participated in the exhibition was Roberto Jacoby of the Arte de los Medios de comunicación de masas group.

u

ugly realism A style of <u>painting</u> developed in the 1970s that combined fine draughtsmanship with images that were considered ugly. These were rendered with a chilling photographic clarity designed to highlight the shallow and alienating brutality of the modern world. Many of the artists associated with the movement were originally members of the cooperative gallery Grossgörschen 35, founded in Berlin in 1964. Arguments between the group led to a split in 1966, and Ulrich Baehr, Charles Diehl, Wolfgang Petrick and Peter Sorge went on to start the Galerie Eva Poll, which became home to this new brand of <u>realism</u>.

the uncanny A Freudian concept, first identified by Ernst Jentsch in his essay 'On the Psychology of the Uncanny', 1906. Jentsch describes the uncanny (in German 'unheimlich' or unhomely) as something new and unknown that can often be seen as negative at first. Sigmund Freud wrote about the uncanny in 1925, describing it as a strange and anxious feeling that individuals experience with familiar objects. The artists of the <u>Surrealist</u> movement used this description of the uncanny to make artworks that combined familiar things in odd ways, like Salvador Dalí's *Lobster Telephone* 1936. Freud held that the uncanny is what should have remained hidden but has been brought into the light; in the uncanny he saw evidence of past experience that had been repressed.

underground art First used in relation to the cultural phenomenon of the 1960s and early 1970s, exemplified in what was called the underground press, magazines like *Oz magazine*, *International Times*, *East Village Other* and *The San Francisco Oracle*, and in the comix of West Coast America. Its precursors were the Beat Generation and the Paris Existentialists, groups that were perceived to exist outside or on the fringes of popular culture. These days the term underground art is used to describe a subculture of art, like <u>graffiti art</u> or <u>comic strip art</u>. Since the late 1990s the internet has become a forum for underground art thanks to its ability to communicate with a wide audience for free and without the support of an art establishment (see <u>net art</u>).

Unit One British group formed by Paul Nash in 1933 to promote modern art, architecture and design. At this point, the two major currents in modern art were seen as being <u>abstract art</u> on the one hand and <u>Surrealism</u> on the other. Unit One embraced the full spectrum, Nash himself made both abstract and Surrealist work in the mid-1930s and played a major part in organising the *International Surrealist Exhibition* in London in 1936. The launch of the group was announced in a letter from Nash to the *Times* newspaper, in which he wrote that Unit One was 'to stand for the expression of a truly <u>contemporary</u> spirit, for that thing which is recognised as peculiarly of today in painting, sculpture and architecture'. The first and only group exhibition was held in 1934 accompanied by a book Unit One, subtitled The Modern Movement in English Architecture, Painting and Sculpture. It consisted of statements by all the artists in the group, <u>photographs</u> of their work, and an introduction by the critic and poet Herbert Read, who was an important champion of <u>modernism</u> in Britain. The other artists involved were John Armstrong, John Bigge, Edward Burra, Barbara Hepworth, Henry Moore, Ben Nicholson, Edward Wadsworth and the architects Welles Coates and Colin Lucas.

The Useful Art Association An association started in New York by the Cuban artist Tania Bruguera through her project *Immigrant Movement International*. The movement promotes the idea of art as a <u>process</u> that should have real effect in society, as part of everyday life, rather than a rarefied spectator experience. Viewers are transformed into activated users, shifting the role of art from the passive realm of aesthetics to one of action and activism (see <u>participatory art</u>). An example is *Tatlin's Whisper #5*, staged at Tate Modern 2008, in which mounted police enacted crowd control, corralling visitors and controlling their movements. The name comes from the *Manifesto de Arte Util* written by the Argentine artist Eduardo Costa in 1969. The Useful Art Association has worked alongside a number of artists and institutions to create work that has a purposeful practicality. At the Van Abbemuseum in Eindhoven the association set up an exhibition where they asked questions such as how can the museum be a civic institution for production? And how can art change the way we act?

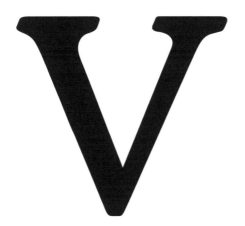

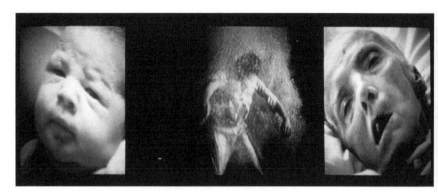

video art
Bill Viola
Nantes Triptych 1992
Video, 3 projections,
colour and sound
(stereo)
Duration: 29 min.,
46 sec.
Tate. Purchased with
assistance from the
Patrons of New Art
through the Tate
Gallery Foundation
and from The Art
Fund 1994

vanishing point see perspective

vanitas see memento mori

vellum Vellum and parchment are made from the skins of calves, goats and sheep. While there is no sharp distinction between the two, vellum is generally a finer quality than parchment, since it is made from younger hides and so is smoother and has fewer or finer hair follicles. Parchment, made from the skins of older animals, tends to be coarser.

Venice Biennale see biennial

verism From the Italian term *verismo*, meaning realism in its sense of gritty subject matter. It was originally applied around 1900 to the violent melodramatic operas of Puccini and Mascagni. In painting it has come to mean realism in its modern sense of representing objects with a high degree of truth to appearances. (See also modern realism; naturalism)

verso see recto

video art The introduction of video in the 1960s radically altered the progress of art. The most important aspect of video was that it was cheap and easy to make, enabling artists to record and document their performances easily. This put less pressure on where their art was situated, giving them freedom outside the gallery. One of the early pioneers of video art was Bruce Nauman, who used video to reveal the hidden creative processes of the artist by filming himself in his studio. As video technology became more sophisticated, the art evolved from real-time, grainy, black and white recordings to the present-day emphasis on large-scale installations in colour. Bill Viola's multi-screened works are theatrical and often have a narrative; and Gillian Wearing uses a documentary style to make art about the hidden aspects of society. (See also moving image; expanded cinema)

virtual reality The computer scientist Jaron Lanier popularised the term virtual reality in the early 1980s to describe a technology that enables a person to interact with a computer-simulated environment, be it based on a real or an imagined place. Virtual reality environments are usually visual experiences, displayed on computer screens or through special stereoscopic displays. Some simulations include additional sensory information such as sound through speakers or headphones. Explorations into virtual reality by artists began in a relatively modest way; in 2002 the duo Langlands and Bell created a virtual reality tour of Osama Bin Laden's hideout in Afghanistan and audiences were invited to navigate the building using a joystick. With the introduction of Second Life on the internet, artists are now installing galleries and staging virtual exhibitions in the alternative virtual world. The Dutch team Art Tower stage exhibitions and sell art in Second Life and Cao Fei, who represented China at the 2007 Venice Biennale, reproduced her exhibition in the Chinese Pavilion in Second Life.

visual ethnography Ethnography describes the study and interpretation of social organisations and cultures in everyday life. It is a research-based methodology and when this research is conducted using photography, video or film, it is called visual ethnography. Artists operating in this field arguably date back to the 1930s and 1940s with projects like Mass Observation, which documented everyday British life, or the Farm Security Administration in America, which portrayed the challenges of rural poverty. The theorist Hal Foster argued that visual ethnography emerged as a debate in art in the 1960s, thanks to the rise of Performance art and social movements like feminism. It was no longer possible to describe audiences as simply observers, just as it was no longer possible to describe the institutions in which the art was shown in terms of space. As a result art passed into the expanded field of culture that anthropology surveys. An artwork like *The Battle of Orgreave* by Jeremy Deller could be described as an example of visual ethnography in that the artist collaborated with a community to recover a suppressed history. (See also experimental ethnography)

vitrine A large, glazed cabinet used for displaying art objects. Often used in museums, the vitrine was appropriated by artists like Joseph Cornell in the 1950s and Joseph Beuys in the mid-1960s to display unusual materials they invested with spiritual or personal significance. Other artists who have used vitrines in their work include the American Neo-Geo artist Jeff Koons and the British sculptor Rebecca Warren.

vivencias A term coined by the Brazilian artist Hélio Oiticica to mean an interaction with life, or lived experiences. This was manifested in his visceral installations that were designed to stimulate the senses and encourage intellectual and emotional responses in the viewer.

vivo-dito Coined by the Argentinean artist Alberto Greco, vivo-dito means 'the act of pointing' and was devised by Greco to describe the contradictory position he found himself in with relation to life and the institution of art, or to put it another way, the oppositional forces of living and representation. To illustrate this paradox he devised a number of enigmatic performances in which he drew lines in chalk around passers-by in the street and signed them.

Vorticism A British avant-garde group formed in London in 1914 by the artist, writer and polemicist Wyndham Lewis. It started with the Rebel Art Centre, which was founded by Lewis as a meeting place for artists to discuss revolutionary ideas and teach non-representational art. Their only group exhibition was held in London the following year. Vorticism was launched with the first issue (of two) of the magazine *Blast* which contained among other material two aggressive manifestos by Lewis 'blasting' what he considered to be the effeteness of British art and culture and proclaiming the Vorticist aesthetic: 'The New Vortex plunges to the heart of the Present ... we produce a New Living Abstraction'. Vorticist painting combines Cubist fragmentation of reality with hard-edged imagery derived from the machine and the urban environment, to create a highly effective expression of the Vorticists' sense of the dynamism of the modern world. It was in effect a British equivalent to Futurism, although with doctrinal differences – and Lewis was deeply hostile to the Futurists. Other artists were Lawrence Atkinson, Jessica Dismorr, Cuthbert Hamilton, William Roberts, Helen Saunders, Edward Wadsworth, and the sculptors Jacob Epstein and Henri Gaudier-Brzeska. David Bomberg was not formally a member of the group but produced major work in a similar style. The First World War brought Vorticism to an end, although in 1920 Lewis made a brief attempt to revive it with Group X.

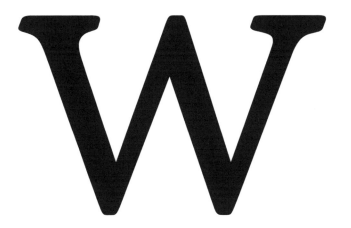

Washington Color School An art movement that emerged in the late 1950s in Washington DC and flourished in the 1960s. The artists associated with Washington Color School promoted a form of <u>abstract art</u> developed from <u>Colour Field painting</u>. Founded by Morris Louis and Kenneth Noland, the group were responding to the <u>Abstract Expressionism</u> of the <u>New York School</u>. An exhibition of their paintings in 1965 at the Washington Gallery of Modern Art cemented their reputation for creating paintings that disregarded structure for colour. Many of the artists used <u>acrylic paint</u> on raw <u>canvas</u>, which led to the description <u>Hard Edge painting</u>. Artists associated with Washington Color School include Sam Gilliam, Louis Morris, Kenneth Noland and Alma Thomas.

watercolour A <u>medium</u> or work of art made with paint consisting of fine pigment particles suspended in an aqueous binder that usually consists of gum, glucose, glycerine and wetting agents, applied to <u>paper</u>. As watercolour is semi-transparent, the white of the paper gives a natural luminosity to the washes of colour. White areas of the image are often left unpainted to expose the paper. Watercolour paints are sold as cakes of dry paint or as liquid in tubes, to which water is added. The paint can be applied in various techniques such as wet-on-wet and wet-on-dry to obtain different effects.

watermark An image or mark in a sheet of <u>paper</u> visible when viewed by transmitted light. It is created using a pattern of wire sewn into the mould on which the sheet of pulp is dried; the paper that settles above the wires is thinner, and so more translucent. The image usually represents the papermaker's trademark design or logo, sometimes with a name, initials or date. Although more common in historical papers (handmade), modern specialist printmaking papers often contain a watermark.

welding The process of joining two pieces of <u>metal</u> by softening or melting both surfaces to be joined by the application of heat.

white cube Refers to a certain gallery aesthetic that was introduced in the early twentieth century in response to the increasing abstraction of modern art. With an emphasis on colour and light,

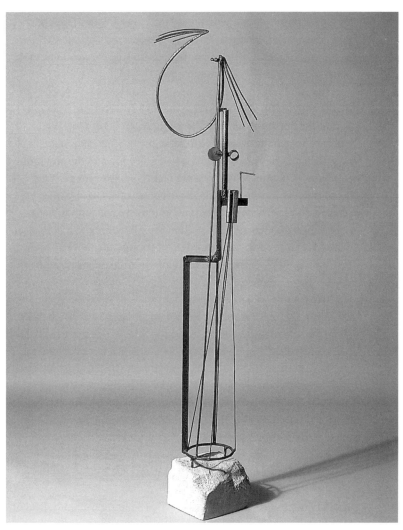

artists from groups like <u>De Stijl</u> and the <u>Bauhaus</u>
preferred to exhibit their works against white walls in
order to minimise distraction. The white walls were also
thought to act as a frame, rather like the borders of a
photograph. A parallel evolution in architecture and
design provided the right environment for the art. The
white cube was characterised by its square or oblong
shape, white walls and a light source usually from the
ceiling. In 1976 Brian O'Doherty wrote a series of essays

welding

Julio González
Maternity 1934
Steel and stone
130.5 × 40.6 × 23.5
Tate. Purchased 1970

for *Art Forum* magazine, later turned into a book called *Inside the White Cube*, in which he confronted the modernist obsession with the white cube arguing that every object became almost sacred inside it, making the reading of art problematic.

wood engraving A printmaking method distinct from woodcut in that the line is incised into the woodblock, rather than the background being cut away to leave a line in relief. So it is an intaglio method. Wood engraving is usually done on the end grain of a block of boxwood, which is very hard, and so extremely fine detail is possible. Wood engraving became widely used in the nineteenth century as a method of reproducing pictures in books, newspapers and journals before the invention of photo-mechanical methods of reproduction, but was also occasionally used by artists, such as Edward Calvert, as an original printmaking medium.

woodcut A method of relief printing from a block of wood cut along the grain. The block is carved so that an image stands out in relief. The relief image is then inked and paper placed against its surface and run through a press. It is possible to make a woodcut without a press (Japanese Ukiyo-e prints, for example) by placing the inked block against a sheet of paper and applying pressure by hand. Woodblock printing was used in Europe from the twelfth century, at first for printing textiles, though images were printed on paper by the late fourteenth century.

Works Progress Administration (WPA) see Federal Art Project

World Festival of Negro Arts The first state-sponsored festival of black arts was held in Dakar in April 1966. Organised by Senegal's first president Léopold Sédar Senghor, one of the founding members of the cultural and political movement négritude, the World Festival of Negro Arts provided the first occasion for many black artists, musicians, writers, poets and actors to participate in a global examination of African culture. It was Senghor's first opportunity to promote the concept of négritude, and he hoped that the festival would promote it as a viable philosophical model. The festival was also a chance for a complex re-evaluation of African tribal art, which had until then been viewed with a certain indifference by the African diaspora. For the first time in Africa, tribal art was to be examined as art. The event led to the beginnings of the international black arts movement. (See also Festac)

World of Art A Russian avant-garde artistic group promoted through the journal of the same name that ran from 1898 to 1905. Serge Diaghilev was instrumental in founding the group and organising its first exhibition in St Petersburg in January 1899. World of Art (Mir Iskutsstva) offered a focus for Post-Impressionist, symbolist and aesthetic developments in Russian art, with particular emphasis on the history and folklore of Russia. Artists included Leon Bakst and Ivan Bilibin; newcomers in the final exhibition of the original group in 1906 included Alexei Jawlenski and Mikhail Larionov. The group's series of exhibitions was revived in 1910 by Alexandre Benois and ran until 1924; new members included Chagall, Kandinsky, El Lissitzky and Tatlin.

Worpswede Group Worpswede is a village set in beautiful countryside in Lower Saxony, Germany, near the city of Bremen. In 1889 the painters Fritz Mackensen, Otto Modersohn and Hans am Ende moved there and founded an artists' colony. Worpswede painting was initially in the plein air tradition but later embraced more modern tendencies, particularly Expressionism. From the beginning they were closely connected with Carl Vinnen, who lived on his farm at Ostendorf, Bremerhaven. In 1892 they were joined by Fritz Overbeck, and in 1894 by Heinrich Vogeler. The most important early Worpswede artist is considered to be the pioneer Expressionist Paula Modersohn-Becker, who moved there in 1898 and remained until her death in 1907. The poet Rainer Maria Rilke was a major literary figure who lived there from 1900 to 1902. After the first phase, Worpswede continued to attract artists and today remains a focus for artistic and literary events.

X

Xiamen Dada A <u>Conceptual art</u> group from Xiamen in southern China that first came to prominence in 1983 with a controversial exhibition held at the Cultural Palace in Xiamen featuring <u>assemblage</u> and <u>paintings</u>. Their original desire was to resist the influence of <u>Socialist Realism</u> from the Soviet Union. The group were inspired by the relationship between European <u>Dada</u> and Chan Buddhism, and embraced absurdity. They were particularly interested in the concept of chance, using it to determine the making of the artworks. In 1986 the group took part in a public <u>action</u> known as the Burning Event in which they set fire to sixty artworks and painted slogans on the ground including the statement 'Dada is Dead!' This resulted in the group being banned from mounting any further public art exhibitions. Artists associated with Xiamen Dada include Huang Yong Ping, Lin Jiahua, Jia Yaoming, Yu Xiaogang and Xu Chengdou.

y

Young British Artists (YBAs) In the late 1980s British art entered what was quickly recognised as a new and excitingly distinctive phase, the era of what became known as the YBAs – the Young British Artists. Young British Art can be seen to have a convenient starting point in the exhibition *Freeze* organised, while he was still a student at Goldsmiths College in London in 1988, by Damien Hirst, who became the most celebrated, or notorious, of the YBAs. Goldsmiths, which was attended by many of the YBAs, and numbered Michael Craig-Martin among its most influential teachers, had been for some years fostering new forms of creativity through its courses that, for example, abolished the traditional separation of the <u>media</u> of art. The label YBA turned out to be a powerful brand and marketing tool, but of course it concealed huge diversity. Nevertheless certain broad trends, both in <u>form</u> and theme, can be discerned. Formally, the era is marked by a complete openness towards the materials and <u>processes</u> with which art can be made and the form that it can take. Leading artists have preserved dead animals (Damien Hirst), crushed <u>found objects</u> with a steamroller (Cornelia Parker), <u>appropriated</u> objects from medical history (Christine Borland), presented their own bed as art (Tracey Emin), made <u>sculpture</u> from fresh food, cigarettes or women's tights (Sarah Lucas), made extensive use of film, <u>video</u> and <u>photography</u>, used <u>drawing</u> and printmaking in every conceivable way, increasingly developed the concept of the <u>installation</u> (a multi-part work occupying a single space) and, not least, refreshed and revitalised the art of <u>painting</u>.

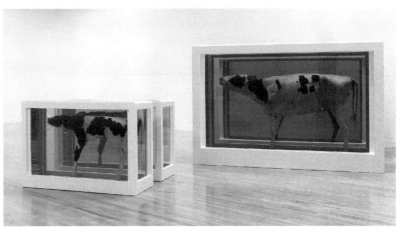

Young British Artists

Damien Hirst
Mother and Child (Divided)
Exhibition copy 2007
(original 1993)
Glass, stainless steel, Perspex,
acrylic paint, cow, calf and
formaldehyde solution
2 parts: 208.6 × 322.5 × 109.2,
208.6 × 322.5 × 109.2
Tate. Presented by the artist 2007